THE GREAT BLACK WAY

THE GREAT BLACK WAY

L.A. in the 1940s and the Lost
African-American Renaissance

RJ SMITH

PUBLICAFFAIRS
New York

Copyright © 2006 by RJ Smith

Published in the United States by PublicAffairs™, a member of the Perseus Books Group.

All rights reserved. Printed in the United States of America. No Part of this book may be reproduced in any manner whatsoever without written permission except in the case of brief quotations embodied in critical articles and reviews. For information, address PublicAffairs, 250 West 57th Street, Suite 1321, New York, NY 10107.

PublicAffairs books are available at special discounts for bulk purchases in the U.S. by corporations, institutions, and other organizations. For more information, please contact the Special Markets Department at the Perseus Books Group, 11 Cambridge Center, Cambridge, MA 02142, call (617) 252-5298, or email special.markets@perseusbooks.com.

DESIGNED BY JEFF WILLIAMS

Library of Congress Cataloging-in-Publication Data

Smith, RJ, 1959-
The Great Black Way : L.A. in the 1940s and the lost African-American renaissance / RJ Smith.
    p. cm.
Includes bibliographical references and index.

ISBN-13 978-1-58648-295-4 (hardcover : alk. paper)
ISBN-10 1-58648-295-5 (hardcover : alk. paper)

1. African Americans—California—Los Angeles—Intellectual life—20th century. 2. African American arts—California—Los Angeles—History—20th century. 3. Central Avenue (Los Angeles, Calif.)—History—20th century. 4. African American neighborhoods—California—Los Angeles—History—20th century. 5. Community life—California—Los Angeles—History—20th century. 6. Los Angeles (Calif.)—Intellectual life—20th century. 7. African Americans—California—Los Angeles—Interviews. 8. Los Angeles (Calif.)—Biography. 9. Interviews—California—Los Angeles. 10. Los Angeles (Calif.)—Race relations—History—20th century. I. Title.

F869.L89N4155 2006
305.896'073079494—dc22

2006011968

10 9 8 7 6 5 4 3 2 1

CONTENTS

swing, Buddy, swing

INTRODUCTION

Los Angeles is the capital of forgetting. It is a place so fixated on to-morrows or so set on seeming brand-new or so much a jumble of re-gions and races that agree on nothing or so *something* that it's all but impossible to gather a crowd to, say, preserve a building. We do the fu-ture: until recently we barely accepted we had a past. A past is what many of us came here to escape. So the idea of preserving a past has crawled forward from incomprehensible to merely incongruous. Do it on your own time. One person's memory palace is another person's hot dog stand—meaningless, waiting for a bulldozer. Los Angeles is the capital of bulldozers.

That's what I thought when I started working on this book in 1997. *The Great Black Way* began with me looking on the shelves of local li-braries and bookstores for something about the history of the African American community here. What was known, by and large, was pre-served in whispers and asides; trapped in newspaper morgues and am-ber, maybe, but not in books. Anecdote, liner note, lore: maybe in the end that's where history lives most, but for too much African American history the anecdote was all an interested party could find. I had wanted to read about the history of the place, and finding not much available, I decided to write the kind of book I wished to read.

It seemed natural to focus on the music scene thriving along Central Avenue, because one thing many people know about black Los Angeles is that Central Avenue was its business and entertainment mainline, and what most people knew about Central Avenue is that once it swung. That Duke Ellington and Charlie Parker and Charles Mingus and Lionel Hampton all at one time or another called it home. But as I began researching the musical life of the place, it became utterly transparent how that life was folded into something more interesting still. Walled off by segregation and custom, black L.A. built an infinitely rich world. Once upon a time, black L.A. was a stand-alone city within a city, and the more I understood that, the more artificial it seemed to separate music from the rest of people's lives. Once upon a time, everything was connected: the civil rights leader Clayton Russell was good friends with the R&B artists. He appears fictionalized in one of the early L.A. books of black novelist Chester Himes. On Central Avenue the jazz musicians were civil rights champions; the actors were tied to the gangsters; the gangsters courted the crusading newspaper editor, who was allied with the Communist Party; the renegade communist was a member of the gay subculture; the gay subculture's meeting place, Brother's after-hours club, was also the site of fabled jazz jam sessions. With the help of guides, an amazingly fertile and unexamined world opened up to me. I hope to throw it open to others.

A single decade—the 1940s—provided a useful frame for the stories I was hearing. World War II stirred the mood of African Americans everywhere. A new spirit of protest surfaced, one based on a faith that white consciences could be pricked at a time when blacks were fighting to defeat a doctrine of racial superiority overseas yet victimized by one at home. In Los Angeles, black leaders saw the war as a pivotal moment for advancing a civil rights agenda. Here, where aviation and shipbuilding were dominant industries, the appeal from black leadership had special force and special success. For if Southern California with its shipyards and aircraft makers was the arsenal of democracy, it became as well the engine for a new mode of protest. It all came together on Central Avenue.

The war years turned the Avenue upside down and made it glow like a neon dream. The clubs hummed while the after-hours spots purred. The defense plants were open around the clock, and thousands of poor newcomers found there was money, and something like freedom, to be had. A mass movement that set the pace for the civil rights struggles of the 1950s and 1960s was already in place in 1940s L.A. And a nascent upwelling of black popular culture was also flourishing—the black noir of Chester Himes's fiction, the thrum of the jam session scene and the proto R&B cracking the national charts, the first black standup comic and the last black comic to perform in blackface. All of it could be heard in the voice of John Kinloch, a young writer who'd turned his back on Harlem and come alive in L.A. His adopted home, he knew, was a daily uproar whose only constant was that it wasn't going to last forever. So much came out of this scene, and when it was over, with the grip of segregation starting to slip—if hardly let go—by the end of the decade, many moved away from the Avenue. I focused on the 1940s because the population exploded at the beginning, and by the end the chimera of integration broke it wide open.

Edward "Abie" Robinson was one of those who stayed. A newspaperman and keeper of stories, he was one of the first people I spoke to as I was beginning my research. A stranger passed his number on to me, and after a few insistent calls, Abie invited me over.

When I visited his house on E. 46th Street, not far from the old heart of the Avenue, he directed me to the place out back. After that, I had to change my thinking about Los Angeles and its thirst for forgetting. Out in the yard was a modest tin shack. He had a name for it, which I've forgotten; when I'd come over to talk we'd repair to this shelter and he'd dig into his story. I would sit on a folding chair and Abie would put the local jazz station on the radio, while a pit bull barked from over the fence. It was impossible not to gape at his shack—on every inch of its inner surface were pictures of African American figures he'd known or admired, some dating back many decades: Jackie Robinson, Dinah Washington, A. Philip Randolph, musicians, athletes, artists and, of course, the person he worked with for many decades and knew as few have, local civil rights attorney and newspaperman Loren Miller. From the outside it looked like a place where you might store garden tools, but with the rusting door open it was a refuge, a zone of freedom, and an architectural expression of how we remember heroes. I began to think of the structure as a collective memory, secret, beat up, and as complete as one man could make it. With *The Great Black Way*, I hope I have come within shouting distance of Abie's example: I want to build a model of remembrance, a representation of all the shrines people carry around with them that the pit bulls and neighbors never even see.

Abie was gruff—I learned to stay out of his way as he spoke and not ask questions he wasn't ready to field—and he was kind enough to point me to many more folks to interview. One led to another. "You know who you should really talk to . . ." became the sweetest words I've ever heard.

In the process of researching this book, more than one interview subject made reference to a lost novel by Carl Van Vechten, the white writer and financial patron of the 1920s Harlem Renaissance. They wanted to know if I'd heard of a certain work he'd written. Indeed, I had: *Nigger Heaven* was its title, and the book was a scandal upon publication. From the name clear on through its dismaying caricatures of Harlem life, the novel shaped many African Americans' feelings about a man who actually had done a lot of good in supporting black culture but will always be remembered by many as an opportunist, a visitor who misused the trust he'd been given. Asking if I knew of the book was people's way of warning me not to play their confidence cheap and a reminder that good intentions are meaningless unto themselves. As a white man I hit walls in plenty of interviews, asked questions folks didn't feel comfortable answering. As well, maybe, being white gave me license to ask some of the most sweeping open-ended questions possible. I didn't know; I wasn't there. What was it like? This book exists because of the kindnesses of the 100-plus people I spoke to, people who let a stranger sit in their kitchens and living rooms and tool sheds and ask them to go back over it again. All praise to them.

In talking with Avenue residents, one subject came up surprisingly little: Hollywood. To the world at large, Hollywood is the face of L.A. To Angelenos at large, it is the company. But Hollywood in the 1940s was a thorn in the side of black L.A. as much as it was an employer—the set of images it furnished did more damage than was offset by the unreliable, complicated opportunities it offered a handful, including Dorothy Dandridge, Calvin Jackson, Carlton Moss, Willie Best, Lena Horne, Canada Lee. This book describes how black L.A. seized control of culture-making opportunities on assorted fronts—onstage at the Lincoln, in the pages of the newspaper the *California Eagle*, in blues dives and wrestling rings. Hollywood dangled prize and promise before the Avenue's talent, but never anything that even rhymed with control. Thus Hollywood looms so small in a book about black power.

A word about a word: Upon occasion I used a noun with different connotations today—*Negro*—because to do otherwise would wrench the reader out of the era and into the present day. It was the collective noun of choice on the Avenue, used freely in the black press and even among some I have spoken to today. It was part of the sounds I was hearing.

This book is about the sounds and sensations of a fabulous street, about a din that knocked down walls, which today is all but forgotten. Everything was connected. You just had to look at the signs on the street to see what was going on. The writer Lionel Trilling urged those studying history to contemplate the "hum and buzz of implication," to ponder the cultural product that "never gets fully stated, coming in the tone of greetings and the tone of quarrels, in slang and humor and popular songs, in the way children play, in the gesture the waiter makes when he puts down the plate, in the very nature of the food we prefer."

To which Timmie Rogers, America's first black standup comic and a performer who got going on the Avenue in the 1940s, might add: "Oh *yeah*."

PROLOGUE

The Great Black Way

STEP OFF THE TRAIN AND SAY HEY TO SMILING MAN. WALK INTO THE depot and he walks a step behind you, carrying your luggage without you having to ask. Stop at the shoeshine stand, there again he waits: the man with the 1,000-watt grin, popping his work rag with an eloquent dexterity that begs for your patronage, your pocket change. On the corner, in the bank lobby, in the elevator, on his knees in the hallway, look out the window at the billboard and he's there, too, promoting pancake mix. Doing what smiling man does better than anybody else in the City of Angels: putting the white folks at ease.

All through the 1930s and all across the country, smiling man was the public face of black city life. As valet and shoeshine boy, chauffeur and doorman, busboy, garbage man, caddy, Red Cap, janitor and caretaker, smiling man was the picture of service, the figure of humility. In Los Angeles he became head waiter to Hollywood. Movies turned the black domestic worker into an eager buffoon, assigned him names like Birmingham Brown, Sambo, George, Algernon, Wellington, Snowflake, Uncle Billie. Smiling man was bigger than life: teeth never seemed as vast and white as they did in the mouth of a 1930s Hollywood Negro. But smiling man fit in your hand, too; he was a bottle opener who bit the cap right off; his mouth was fashioned into a dice cup, the cubes pouring out of his merry leer onto the bar top.

Los Angeles sure was one happy village in the 1930s. There were also smiling women—maids and mammies, Beulah, Petunia and Lollypop too. The *California Eagle* in 1938 reported on local employment agencies that hired black workers to clean apartments, withheld payment for weeks, and then fired workers who asked for their salary. "Here in Los Angeles," wrote *Eagle* editor Charlotta Bass, "the Negro domestic worker is becoming one of the most brazenly exploited group of laboring groups. The plight of those cooks, waitresses, and general housework employees who have been forced to accept starvation wages from individual employers has long been known and lamented."

The city was growing, workers arriving in droves to a place where the anti-union open shop system thrived. In factories blacks were hired, when they were hired at all, as union busters. For the most part they were locked out of manufacturing jobs and instead flocked to the service sector, where tourism and show business money were generating large demand. In 1930s L.A. the most important black union was the Dining Car Cooks and Waiters Union, and although it raised the standard of living for its workers, the union barely existed outside of Southern California.

Well into the decade, blacks in Los Angeles did better than those in many other parts of the country. The Depression had a smaller impact for a while. Factories mostly hired only whites, so when the crisis hit and factories shut down, it was whites who were laid off. The smile business greatly softened the blow of the Depression, at first; in 1930, 40 percent of all black male workers and 87 percent of women were employed in domestic service. But by 1940, the Depression had hit Southern California in full force, and then blacks suffered worse than they did in many other parts of the country.

A job smiling became precious and rare, and those who held one loomed large in the community. Those hired as Pullman porters were among the most respected. Pullman porters were the uniformed men who carried luggage, made the rooms and served food and beverages

on railroad cars, and since Los Angeles was an ever-booming rail desti-
nation, the porter became a local economic force. He embodied the
ironies of power in black Los Angeles: among the most revered and
successful members of the community, he was a homeowner and civic
leader who symbolized black success. Porters belonged to a powerful
all-black union with a national profile and won important victories for
black workers. They had fought for their very names: one of the
porters' most significant victories was the right to ignore travelers who
called them "George" (George Pullman owned the railroad cars; the
common practice suggested slaves taking the names of their masters).
On the job, porters traveled far and wide, signifying social mobility
and, in their spotless uniform—pressed slacks, shiny buttons, white
jacket and sable hat—they signified grace and pride. And yet they
smiled and toted bags. They achieved their status by putting themselves at the service of the white traveler. Their institutionalized sub-
servience was the source of the respect they enjoyed in the community,
and everyone within the community who noticed their success also felt
the incongruity of it. If the Pullman porter evoked pride, he was also
capable of summoning its opposite. That was the funny-unfunny thing
about the smiling man: he was an icon and also a stigma. Naturally, the
movies drew the porter as a simple figure, but on the streets of Los Angeles few men were more complicated. They turned on the smile, and
you never knew what they were really thinking. Their smile was a door
opening onto a brick wall.

Downtown held Union Station, where porters went to work. Racial
ironies flourished downtown, where a sprawl of residential and business districts were punctuated with exotic ethnic amusement quarters.
There was Olvera Street, a faux–Mexican village built by a society ma-
tron for tourists who wished to glimpse life in a pueblo. There was
Chinatown, decorated by a Paramount set designer and featuring
props used in Cecil B. DeMille's *The Good Earth*. Such Potemkin vil-
lages dotted the landscape, representing the city's ethnicities to white
visitors and natives alike.

Black Los Angeles enjoyed no such tribute from the city fathers, no
Smileville, no Portertown. Yet downtown was one of the few places in

which black political influence was clearly visible, able to be sized up for all that it mattered, for all that it didn't. This power rested on the hall benches just outside the city council chambers. There, the so-called black city council convened: In a place where black neighborhoods were gerrymandered to keep representation in the hands of whites, an informal group of unelected politicos would sit and banter, talking about what they'd do if it was their lot deliberating behind closed doors.

Meanwhile, perhaps demonstrating how to push a broom down the hallway of a downtown office building, you might find the most influential black man in town, L. G. Robinson. The head of the county janitorial services, Robinson hired black Angelenos to mop halls and operate elevators, and from this he built a formidable power base and fortune. He picked up after the white folks, and it made him an ambassador to the entire city. "Anything the power structure wanted to know about blacks in Los Angeles," said Gilbert Lindsay, "they would say 'Call L. G.' Now, this is a janitor. And he was the power for the whole Negro community of Los Angeles! . . . L. G. Robinson spoke for the Negroes." Lindsay would have known; back in those days he was a member of the black city council, riding the bench in the corridors of power.

Downtown was at the mouth of Central Avenue, which started at First Street in the picturesque Little Tokyo district. "Central was like a river," recalled musician Clifford Solomon. "A mighty river like the Amazon or the Nile, or in this case, the Congo. And all the streets were tributaries that branched off from this great river." Heading south from there was one route to black Los Angeles, and certainly the most direct. But to really apprehend Central Avenue, you had to do more than cross over First Street. To penetrate a place that had drawn in and grown jumbled upon itself, psychic lines and timelines had to be crossed as much as a line on a map. "There are many avenues of the Avenue," a wise man and band singer once said. The best route, however, started with a single footfall. You had to enter the maw, step through the Smile.

Imagine a prewar nightclub floorshow, some palatial dance emporium in which leggy chorus girls performed among preposterous stage sets. Imagine the set of one show: dancers paraded through vast lips, a great minstrel smile. Let us now step through just such a gateway, lunge across huge incisors and tumble through the happy-making lips—watch your step—and collect ourselves as we land at the other extreme. The lights flicker for a minute as if a large bird has passed overhead, and then the sun returns. You're on Central Avenue now. It's 1940.

Come, let's stroll. But friend-to-friend, you'd best tend to those kicks. Your scuffed Florsheims are gonna get a workout, and you want to walk in style. There's really only one place to go. The corner of 12th Street and Central is a key intersection, the place where the B and the U streetcar lines intersect. It's a commuter crossroads and a commercial dynamo. A spot where hot dog hawkers and newsboys, astrologists and shoe shines all vie for the wayfarer's attention.

For decades the Spikes Brothers Music Store has flourished at 12th and Central, selling instruments, records and sheet music to black, white, Mexican and Gypsy musicians. Reb, John and Richard Spikes all came from New Orleans, and along the way Reb and John played in minstrel shows and the mine camps of the West, polishing an act they called the Musical Meat Market. Various instruments were designed to look like cuts of meat and the brothers took the stage dressed as butchers, albeit butchers capable of extracting polyphony from the flesh arrayed before them. Reb and John arrived as accomplished jazz musicians and helped build Los Angeles's first jazz scene, bringing pianist Jelly Roll Morton to the coast in 1917, cutting the first jazz record in town, and running important clubs.

But the Spikes boys have learned other things, too. Richard is a barber, trained in the head-cutting arts by his father. Reb is a healer, a "drugless physician," as he puts it, able to melt tumors in female patients with the assistance of a glass tube inserted in their vaginas. Medicine flows through the tube and the tumor flows out in a vaporous form. Hemorrhoids and eczema are also a specialty. The brothers are additionally inventors, who boast of having devised a rotating barber chair, a railroad crossing light, guns for fighter planes, and a revolutionary milk bottle stopper. This morning, right out on the corner of

12th Street and Central, they are demonstrating their latest labor-saving device, a new manner of shoeshine stand. It is elaborately mechanical, with levers and valves concealed beneath a streamlined façade.

After you. Sit. The bootblack depresses a button and the chair elevates automatically to the proper height. Note the electric cigar lighter and ashtray; espy the curtain available to female patrons, hiding their legs from the passing gaze of strangers. A numerical counter logs the sum of shoes gleamed each day. Thus while the proprietor goes to the bank or visits his Chinese lottery man, his stable of twelve teenage bootblacks work away, and at day's end he will know if his crew is shorting him.

Good shoes are a must, because there is ever the possibility that one might need to pick them up and lay them down promptly here in the thicket of the upper Avenue. From 1st to 12th streets Central is a welter of gimlet-eyed railroad men and trusting newcomers. The thrum of deals going down and billfolds being fondled is constant. There is money to be made, a stash of hard-saved layers to be tendered. Look yonder, where the armless boy thrills the crowd by shooting marbles with his toes. Behind him there, through that open door, is the sanctum of Prince Pat, master of the supernatural, able to find lost family members, avenge cheating spouses, locate buried treasure. Across the street there's even a kid with a telescope who'll show you the mountains of the moon for a nickel.

These blocks at the north end of the Avenue have been home to blacks for decades, but as we move south of 12th, the neighborhood becomes more varied. Dominating both sides of Central is the gridiron long beloved of tract developers who devised whole neighborhoods at a single throw. Single-family houses are the standard, block after right-angled block from the early decades of the twentieth century. Guttering down the middle of this grid, from downtown to Watts, runs the Avenue. The street is scored by numbered roads rising from 1st up past 100th Street, where, about 10 miles from 1st Street, Central crosses into Watts. Different people call it different things: Swing Street, the Main Stem, Whoopee Highway, Sun Tan Avenue, Brown Broadway, Harlemwood Boulevard, *Avenida Centrale*, the Great Black Way. The area around Spikes Brothers Music Store by day seems solid, clean and safe. One- and two-story buildings flourish, many brown brick, some decorated in glazed tiles. There are shops and stores on the ground floor, apartments overhead. Particularly when the Santa Ana winds blow in from the east, there is a clarity and firmness to the scene. But there are alleys behind the buildings, and courtyards and cul-de-sacs. There are narrow passageways among the buildings and plenty of doors fronting the street that stay locked and unobtrusive until after the sun goes down. By day it is proportionate and tangible, but at night it is slippery and perfumed with possibility, even danger. There is a pool hall behind the barbershop, and a room full of gambling machines behind the pool hall. By day the buildings have two simple stories, awnings over the windows, but in the moonlight there are levels upon levels, and rooms opening onto private spaces.

A mezuzah here, a sign written in Russian there. Blacks aren't the only ones around, nor will they be the last group to arrive. But in a city in which geography is destiny and where destiny is beyond the control of black Angelenos, Central Avenue takes on layers of meaning. People, too, have layers. The Sugar Hill mansion owned by the respectable couple is the scene of all-night high-society orgies; the newspaper editor is a Republican activist and Communist Party recruit; the blues singer who has the women panting is secretly yearning for men. The Avenue is so lived-in it is as if blacks have been here for thousands of years, instead of a century or so. More than that, it is a place from which culture flows. Most of all, it is a place where you could live.

Or so it is said. But as we have sensibly started our stroll in the cool of morning, the world seems a graspable place. Your Florsheims are sparkling now; let those dogs lead the way. You are not hallucinating, no matter how much giggle juice you imbibed last night: what you think you see a few blocks down is what is truly there—an ocean liner docked curbside. A block-long Coca-Cola bottling plant, inexplicably designed in the shape of a great Art Deco cruise ship, stands along our path.

Soon arrives the corner of 18th and Central, and a structure somehow inadequate in the wake of a luxury liner. Just a house. Musicians Union Local #767 occupies what once was the home of a well-off family, and though they are long gone, their place retains its broad, shady front porch. The angels and clouds painted on the ceilings inside remain as well, though the musicians who now occupy the dwelling have added their own imagery: one room bears an oil painting of poker-playing hounds.

Many facets of Los Angeles were built on segregation: beneath the hardened eyes of cigar-chomping mutts here is simply one more, the Negro musician's union. Whites have their union local in Hollywood, and through its offices they enjoy a lock on most of the nightclub gigs and film work show business has to offer. But on Central Avenue, Local 767 offers far less and far more. Denied a role beyond the neighborhood, it has cultivated a dominant position within that extends past the mere apportionment of jobs. The building is a community center, school, clubhouse. Great parades down the Avenue begin here, featuring the bands of Lionel Hampton and Count Basie playing on flatbed trucks. Great pig roasts blaze into the night, beer sucked out of tin cans, poker upstairs. All day long ensembles and soloists practice, and kids drift in to listen. You can wander through the house; if you are a young musician you are *supposed* to wander in off the street and ponder the Ellington band's rehearsal, ask saxophonist Johnny Hodges or bassist Jimmy Blanton why they played that note, that phrase.

Homeboy Al Adams and crew are rehearsing today; tonight they'll play a few blocks down the street at the Lincoln Theater. The Lincoln is the westernmost stop on the black theater circuit, another feature of segregation. The building evokes a Middle Eastern landscape, with minarets and towers in relief on the Lincoln's surface, as if they are tattooed onto its skin. We stop briefly at the Haitian Coffee Company, round the corner at 22nd Street, sip a hot, muddy concoction, and watch the passing scene. The sun is coming up over the Avenue. A streetcar, jangling its bells as it glides before us, is a red clangor blurring our view. Steam curls above our cups; a mist floats out of a vent in a wall; from the open door of a laundry a nimbus of vapor mingles with the foot traffic. Momentarily we are lost in a fog.

A Victrola plays from beyond a torn lace curtain on the second floor of a wooden storefront. It's a song recorded a few years ago, featuring an affecting girl singer.

"Shoe shine boy, you find joy in the things you do, shoe shine boy, seldom ever blue." Duke Ellington and his orchestra back Ivie Anderson, a California-born singer who is no stranger to the Avenue. She lives here.

"You keep walking up and down the street, pleading with each one you meet, brother, can you spare a dime?"

The song parts the lace, splits the steam edging over our Haitian coffee, too, and penetrates our sidewalk daze. It's a two-sided record, somehow playing both top and bottom at once. The happy shoeshine boy, seldom ever blue, versus the ragged urchin calling out, "Brother, can you spare a dime?" The smile triumphant—then turned inside out.

Gallop over to the Elks Temple, one of the more florid ornaments of the street, paying equal tribute to piety and excess. Fraternal societies thrive up and down Central, lodges like the Household of Ruth, the United Brothers of Friendship and Sisters of the Mysterious Ten. At 52nd street is the Thomas Waller Masonic Lodge, the local franchise named after jazz pianist Fats Waller, composer of "The Jitterbug Waltz" and a 23rd-degree Mason.

But situated near 34th, the Elks Temple is by far the leading fraternal organization in the community. The membership has furnished the brotherhood with a building of their own, the Golden West Lodge, which houses a ballroom and dance floors on two stories and rooms upstairs for private rites lasting past sunrise. The Exalted Ruler of the Golden West Lodge is Eugene Sorrell, esteemed owner of a popular liquor store. Sorrell knows what the citizenry are capable of at their best and worst, and the lodge is where respectable people gather and celebrate their respectability until, as the night wears on, dignity like an ice cube loses its form. The well-to-do and the ambitious, the life-insurance salesmen and the cooks, porters and maids on their night off, all come and frolic. Vanity is in full preen, and the mix of grasp and stumble makes the scene rich material for satirists. A newspaper columnist tweaks the pretense of those who gather one night: "I can't for the life of me be convinced that the bald little guy with the tubby front is one of the town's leading doctors, and not the headwaiter of the Cocktail Lounge sneaking in a spot of jitterbugging between courses. . . . Those prewar tuxedos our men are wearing have got to go, gals."

The costumes get flashier and more modern as we amble south. Lately the menswear shops are featuring pastel colors and impossibly vivid hues in their windows, styles that one fashion critic says make "eyebrows east of the Rockies fly up like frightened windowshades." The sudden appearance of knee-length coats on men is also a shock; the Eastern-Columbia clothing store stocks $35 Bradbury Super-Drapes, high-rise trousers, Long Drape Finger Tip coats, and full pleated trousers. The zoot suit has arrived.

A cardboard sign in a window at 42nd Street:

It's Here! THE NEW MEMO CLUB
   Choice viands served from morning throughout the evening
   Now playing: Kathryn La Mar at the Solovox Organ and the Memo's Kings of Syncopation
   Drink Hill & Hill Kentucky Bourbon

Step lively, friend, the pace quickens. For we have arrived at the center of the middle, the reason the whole street swings. See that homely hulk of a building yonder? Descend the front steps and you enter the Club Alabam, formerly dubbed the Apex. The ballroom is oval-shaped, and terraced loges hang over the dance floor. Fake palm trees loiter at the back, providing a merry mood that makes the room feel far larger than it is. Now playing: Count Leroy, roller-skating tap dancer; Harry Fiddler, Chinese impersonator; Patsy Hunter & Her Streamline Cuties. "In the daylight, one could see that it was not really what one might call a sumptuous place. But when you went in at night and the lights were all on, it covered up a multitude of evils," explained one visitor.

"The working man just coming off of a job wouldn't dare try to walk into the Club Alabam in his work clothes. Number one, he had more self-respect than that, and number two, he would be out of place. Nobody wanted to sit next to someone in dirty work clothes." Women at the Alabam wear long gowns and the men take to three-piece suits and raglan topcoats.

Flush beside the Alabam is the Dunbar Hotel. And here, in a sense, is Central's biggest stage. It is afternoon now; the curbstone cowboys and plum-coated pimps have yet to gather along the way. A few celebrities collect at one end of the block: the Four Rockets, stunt dancers, chat up a female bystander while boxer Jack Johnson leans silently against the brick wall, wearing a huge belt buckle that spells out his initials in diamonds. They are leisurely in their motions. But at noontime, most of those on the block have come in hopes of getting paid.

Surely you've noticed the ones pounding their chests and snorting. Standing nonchalantly in a line, some reading newspapers, others staring off into the distance. The Dunbar Hotel is a de facto recruitment center for Hollywood studios in need of black extras. A studio places a call to a man roosting by a phone at the hotel, and within minutes the casting call is out: young entrepreneurs hustle to the Dunbar hoping they'll get to play a jungle savage, perhaps a sharecropper. Stunt dancer and spear carrier, everyone around the Dunbar has their costume, it seems, and they all have perfected a style mixing liberty and labor. The sidewalk of the Dunbar is both rostrum and pulpit: big stuff happens here. Standing in front is like resting at the center of a giant, whirling wheel; if everything around you is swinging like mad, the block is perhaps the single place where things are in such a state of flux that, paradoxically, they seem at rest.

Like the Pullman porter in his fine-pressed clothes, the aspiring actors in front of the Dunbar portray the neighborhood to the world at large. The face they present, well, it is vexatious and limited, a mask impeding enough to suffocate. Yet by assembling your countenance and projecting it to passersby, you can project some small part of yourself onto a larger audience. The area around the Dunbar is a place where people love to congregate and have a good time, check out the new models and pick up on the latest lingo. The blocks around the Dunbar are among the most concentrated of the Avenue. Numerous jazz clubs are within a stone's throw, the two biggest newspapers, barbershops and pool halls. The whole community comes to bear here, and a density of conversation, style and invective is guaranteed upon this spot. It is as if these few blocks are an enormous, theoretical crystal set, a radio honing a message, waiting for someone to tune in.

Blacks are kept out of white-owned hotels around the city and the Dunbar is, at the most fundamental level, simply a place to stay. A massive brick edifice, its inner spaces cool in the hottest summer days. It has a restaurant, cocktail lounge, piano bar, and barbershop. The Dunbar symbolizes luxury and respect even at the worst of times, its 100 rooms over four floors favored by the elite of Negro America. Joe Louis stays here, and Billy Strayhorn, W. E. B. Du Bois, Billie Holiday and Stepin Fetchit.

Plastered to the brick wall, a row of signs:

For President of Central Avenue
     Vote for EDDIE 'ROCHESTER' ANDERSON. Office in the Dunbar Hotel.

It was owned in the late 1930s by the Nelson family, or at least that was the official story; many wondered who was really behind the Dunbar and the Alabam next door. In 1939 National Association for the Advancement of Colored People (NAACP) assistant executive secretary Roy Wilkins celebrated the hotel in New York's *Amsterdam News:*

Everything was just the opposite from what we have come to expect in "Negro" hotels, the bell boy was intelligent, polite and efficient. The desk clerk was courtesy itself, we arrived in the city before midnight on a Saturday, but did not get to the hotel until after 1:30. Nevertheless, we were able to have sandwiches sent to the room promptly from the grill downstairs. An all night valet service took care of the wrinkled suits and dresses and delivered them next morning as soon as we were awake. The bathroom was spotless, as was the linen. The curtains were fresh and neat. The Sunday morning paper was brought to our door. The rates were reasonable.

A few blocks down brings us to Vernon Avenue, another place where two streetcar lines intersect, and business booms along the diagonal. Here is where Ivie Anderson of the Duke Ellington band recently opened Ivie's Chicken Shack. The supper club proclaims two slogans: "Keep 'Em Frying" and "Fresh Killed Daily."

Central and Vernon is also where Julius Juarez holds forth behind the shutters of his Bombay Incense Company. The Cuban-born Juarez is the man to see when you want to put a hex on somebody. His store carries lucky charms, *van van* floor wash, John the Conqueror root, rosaries, lodestones, holy oil. And if the spirit world doesn't proffer the desired result, you can always visit the room in the back, where Juarez operates a bookie joint. When goofer dust and holy oil fail, perhaps a wisely invested fiver can redirect your fate.

Close by are the Bronze Recording Studios and Flash Electronic Laboratories, a pair of businesses bankrolled by suave songster Herb Jeffries. Bronze is one of the earliest record labels in the black community, and together these businesses are an indication that music works on more frequencies than we ever fully know. In the Flash Electronic Laboratories, engineers strive to perfect their "color organ," an instrument that can take sound from a radio and translate it into visual energy. Sound is seen; the invisible becomes indigo in your living room. There is a gold rush aspect to the Vernon-Central neighborhood, a sense that ideas won't stay in place and faiths are bound to be unbounded. A neighbor of Flash Electronic Laboratories is Professor George W. Phillips, a Christian holy man who bills himself as the "Spiro-electronic Messenger." If we had more time we might see what messages the professor is sending this afternoon, but the shadows grow long and we need be on our way.

Let us walk down a few more blocks, and then let us walk no more. South to Slauson, and then, I'm telling you, we take the streetcar. For

Slauson Avenue is the blood latitude, and Slauson is a bitch. The word is out, man, and I don't care to inquire about it. Though Negroes have moved south to the neighborhood around Vernon and Central, all motion stops here. Mister Jones heard the Klan claimed Slauson and everything below; Lady Creswell heard about the kids put in the county hospital after the police caught them playing on the swings south of the line. Everybody's got a tale of what happens to those detained in this white man's land, and enough of it is true that the street has acquired a supernatural power. You and I will acquire a seat on the streetcar.

The Red Cap lets us out at 103rd street, end of the line. At the corner of Central and 103rd are various shops and movie theaters, but walk just a few blocks away and you feel like you are in some other place—Mexico, perhaps, or Mississippi—a long way off from the bright lights of Central. The dirt streets turn to mud when it rains, and cesspools are dug behind many of the houses. Chickens, goats, horses, hogs and cows graze in backyards and on the numerous empty lots. Jackrabbits race through fields of celery. Not for nothing do citizens of Watts call it Plum Nelly—plum out of the city and nelly out of the world.

If the area around the Dunbar Hotel is pure swing music, the Avenue in Watts is the blues. At 118th Street just off Central is the Little Harlem Club, a jook joint run by the Brown sisters. Like the rest of the clubs in Watts, the Little Harlem is not favored by whites visiting from Hollywood, is unknown to the tourists who would avidly trek to the Alabam. It is a fine place to hide out. Fights jump off here so often they don't always bother to pick up the blood and the police are a sometime thing. Local favorites like the Woodman Brothers Biggest Little Band in the World play here, and a frequent master of ceremonies is bluesman T-Bone Walker.

Night, now. We slouch upon a stool at the Little Harlem and confront the technical skill Walker exhibits on his new contraption, an experimental guitar with electrical amplification. His playing is fine, but let us put it aside and instead marvel at something truly incredible.

The greatest blues guitarist alive can lift a chair, put it in his mouth, and balance it on end as he plays a frenetic shuffle. It is all well and good to master your tool, but at the Little Harlem Mr. Walker shows a mastery of gravity itself. His is a zeal that gives until it hurts, a self-denial that makes him the favorite of Watts patrons.

A man playing guitar with a chair clenched in his jaws might be the ultimate attraction on most streets. But there is one more stop for us, one last landmark to our tour. To the terminus. There's something you really ought to see.

All the way south now to Long Beach, to the charming mess of seaside attractions planted at land's edge. The funhouse and the roller coaster, guess-your-weight games and kooch dancers, to each their own. You and I proceed to the Bobo. A time-honored carnival figure, he is as familiar as the lion tamer or the clown; the Bobo is the guy you love to hate, teasing the crowd as he sits on a ducking stool, taunting you to hit the plunger and drop him into the icy cold water. At Long Beach, his name is Hard-Headed Sam.

All you see is that noggin, shaved and shiny beneath the white light bulbs, Sam's dark black head poking through a round hole at the rear of the attraction. What you hear is his gruff voice talking: "What are you two waiting for? Step up to the line. Hit my hard head and win a prize!" He makes eye contact—creepy, as if he knows us personally, knows why we are here. And way past creepy because, as he calls out insults, Sam *smiles*. A black spot against a white field, he has no body just a skull, that eager shine, that look that sizes up the passerby so clearly. We know him, and he knows us. "Shut your trap," a fat guy yells back. Sam lights up, the dome bobbles around in the hole, and . . . he . . . laughs. It's a crazy howl, angry and jubilant pouring out of the aperture. "Hit the bull's-eye! Right now, right now! I want more throws!" All we see is a smooth face, a bull's-eye, a black porthole.

And that is Central Avenue by shoe leather. Businesses are flourishing, the streets are safe, and the neon gleams in the clear night air like the pearls at Gold's Department Store. Central Avenue: towering over all of it is one man, a small figure in a gaudy pinstriped suit. He knows how to dance and he sure is good with the white folks.

Eddie Anderson grew up in Oakland and was raised in a show business family—his father was a song and dance man, his mother a circus tightrope walker. As a teenager Anderson made a name for himself on the black theatrical circuit. He got his start with his feet—he was a talented hoofer—but Anderson's secret weapon was a rasp that boomed like a bulletin from hell. His voice was torn up at an early age—selling newspapers as a boy on busy Oakland streets took its toll—but from the surviving tones and tissues he coaxed an ungodly cry. His noise commanded attention, and his humor made a connection reaching across racial lines.

"I like white folks and they like me. We know how to get along with each othah," Anderson was quoted in a 1943 *Saturday Evening Post* story. "A colored man's just nacherly gotta laugh. Take me. If I don't laugh I reckon pretty quick I'd die. And other folks ain't no different."

He knew the unmarked doors of Central, having lived in the neighborhood since he came in the 1930s in search of a Hollywood break. Eddie Anderson's star could have flickered out then, one more talent unable to find work in the movies that wasn't demeaning. Heck—demeaning work was all right too, and Anderson did his share. He might have gone on this way, bowing and scraping together a living from the kind of eye-rolling, afraid-of-his-shadow lackey roles that were a black comic actor's stock in trade. But then a one-off appearance as a Pullman porter on the popular Jack Benny radio show struck a chord with a national audience; he and Benny found an instant rapport, and his timing was nearby as sharp as Benny's. Knowing a good thing when he heard it, Benny made him a regular. As Rochester Van Jones, Mr. Benny's manservant, Anderson stormed into millions of homes. His charisma was tangible, his pumice-like orations undeniable, and a neighborhood listened as one of its own made good. He became a Spiro-electronic Messenger of the black city, a rasp unstoppable.

Debuting on Benny's *The Jell-O Program* in 1937, Rochester was the first black character with a regular role on a national radio show. In basic ways no new ground was broken—Rochester waited on Benny's beck and call as chauffeur, dresser, cook and housekeeper; he was practically an index of the black domestic workforce. But if the *idea* of Rochester seems like a more perfect stereotype, as played by Anderson the character was something new. He routinely got the better of his boss. He served Benny as a laborer, but Benny also served Rochester as a comic foil. The focus of ridicule was usually Benny, and Anderson's guilelessness, his ability to seem sly and oblivious at the same moment, won over an audience that easily might have resented him.

Within the confines of his servitude, Rochester was a breath of fresh air. First of all, he really *was* a black man, unlike the whites who mimicked blacks on *Amos and Andy*. His success was a crucial turning away from stereotypes. In one show, when Benny asks Rochester to sing, the valet begs off, explaining, "I can't do that blackface stuff." The son of a black man who had performed in blackface, Anderson must have given thought to the quip. It had special meaning to his black listeners, too, who were themselves turning away from blackface performers. Once, black comics were all but required to wear burnt cork makeup when they took the stage, and though many still did so in the 1930s, a younger generation was vocal in its criticism of the custom. As Anderson became a national star, blacks followed his career, and they certainly noticed the name he gave to the racehorse he bought with the fruits of his labor: Burnt Cork. Anderson made minstrelsy work for *him*, the appellation seemed to imply. Burnt Cork suggested that although it was a shared legacy, the mask was not the man.

Every detail of Rochester's character was scrutinized by the Central Avenue community; that he called his employer not Sir but simply Boss, for instance, was viewed as a step forward—one man speaking more directly to another. When he mentioned Central Avenue, which Rochester often did, the neighborhood went wild. Guest star Orson Welles asked Rochester to teach him "Central Avenue shuffleboard," by which he meant shooting craps. "On Central Avenue," Rochester explained knowingly to Benny, "Father Time lingers till we get rollin'." Obviously, old stereotypes were being trotted out. And the jokes occasionally offended; when Rochester mocked the fashion sense of Avenue morticians, the local funeral industry loudly complained. Still, all that was something new. Rochester, it was clear, did not belong to his white employer—he had his own life on the Avenue and he didn't "act white." If blackface was a mask, the show made clear that so was the face Rochester presented to the white world embodied by Benny. It was when he went home to Central Avenue that he became himself.

Every appearance on the Benny show was likely to simultaneously further and undermine stereotypes, like the time Rochester called Benny to report on Carmichael, the boss's new pet polar bear:

Rochester: I don't mind opening doors, running errands, driving your car and cleaning the house, but when you expect me to be lady in waiting to that North Pole kitten, I quit!

Benny: Now don't get excited, Rochester. In the first place, you can't quit this minute—I haven't paid you yet.

Rochester: That's all right. I'll just take some spoons.

The thieving housekeeper, a cliché white America savored in the 1930s, comes through loud and clear. But not just:

Rochester: Say Boss, if you win the Academy Award, will you give me a raise?

Benny: I certainly will—you'll get a nice, substantial increase.

Rochester: Man, I sure wish you was a better actor.

Rochester freely mocked the boss and was free to laugh at his foibles, like Benny's miserliness and vanity. It was this license to speak openly that made Rochester a hero on Central Avenue. Or maybe the truth was simpler. Maybe it was the show in which Benny prepares for a boxing match. Benny and Rochester spar, and the valet accidentally knocks his boss out cold. Wit and banter have their place, but when it comes to cinching celebrity on the Avenue, perhaps they are as nothing compared to a rock-hard jab to the boss man's head.

On May 23, 1940, an advertisement appeared in the *California Eagle*:

Vote for Eddie "Rochester" Anderson
　for mayor of Central Avenue in the ELECTION TODAY

The mock election of a black leader had long been a rite on the street. In the ad Rochester vows, "If I am elected, I will pave Central Avenue with pancakes and flood it with molasses!"

His platform ascends from there. "I believe the people of the East-side are entitled to the same Civil, Political and Social Rights as people of other communities. . . . I believe that our streets should be cleaned, that we should have more efficient police protection, that po-lice officers should be promoted according to Ability, not because of Race or Creed." The ad finishes with, "A vote for Rochester is a vote for yourself."

A flash flood of flapjacks. A rasp for civil rights two decades before the civil rights era. A police force ruthlessly efficient. Several months later, a plainclothes officer attempted to arrest a Mexican girl near the Rossmore Hotel, a Negro-only business on Central. Several black men defended her and fought the officer. At ten that night over a dozen vice squad cops returned, entered the Rossmore café, and or-dered all Negroes in the place to line up outside. Officer J. R. Stew-ard walked down the line beating each man, most of them hotel porters, and cursing them out while other cops made sure no one broke the line.

In Los Angeles there were things more starkly surreal than a comic running for mayor. Rochester was a work of fiction stepping into a real political void. He took his campaign more or less seriously, headquar-tering his effort in the Dunbar Hotel. His main competition was Eu-gene Sorrell, Exalted Ruler of the Golden West Lodge of the Elks. Rochester's platform promoted the recruitment of blacks into aviation jobs, and after the campaign he continued to advocate the creation of a training school for Negro aviators, even calling for Congress to estab-lish a Negro flying corps. Rochester felt so strongly about the issue, he was taking a flying course himself and lecturing with a representative from the Tuskegee Institute. The push for black aviators was one more example of his canniness; the same month Rochester announced his run for mayor, President Franklin D. Roosevelt called upon the nation to build a 50,000-plane air force and suggested the industry retool to generate a subsequent 50,000 aircraft a year—this at a time when the Army Air Corps only had 2,400 planes. America was heading toward war, and it was clear the aviation industry, centered in Southern California, would play a huge role. To workers all over the region, but particularly to black workers, aviation symbolized new opportunity.

In the end, Rochester won the honorific title of mayor of Central Avenue. Being mayor was not without meaning. It was a safe way to register criticism of police tactics, of the lack of black political representation, of the city's neglect of Central Avenue. Rochester bamboozled Benny on radio and in movies that gave him as much face time as the boss, and then invested his wealth in a parachute company, part of his aviation dream. His symbolism had weight. Still, while his fame grew events were transpiring that would alter the dynamics of black power in Los Angeles. Real leaders were emerging. The smile was turning inside out, and Rochester would be, if not turned out of office, then replaced by leaders who were more than symbols.

CHAPTER 1

A Brand New Suit of Clothes

JOHN KINLOCH WAS AN OUTGOING PERSON WITH A GOING-OUT OUTFIT. His mother made it; she was a seamstress back in Harlem. He brought it to Los Angeles, and in the early 1940s, when he wasn't writing columns in the offices of the *California Eagle*, Kinloch dressed properly for the Central Avenue stroll.

"That gorgeous green suit is my pride and joy," he told his mother. "Madame"—a pet name for Kinloch's aunt, Charlotta Bass—"says I try to wear it on the slightest pretext,—I do. It's in a style that's one up on the folks out here. My friend, Martin, wants to know what firm he can write to for information about where they are sold on the West Coast."

Flash green suits and clothes far more outlandish were arriving in Los Angeles by 1940. The zoot suit had been a part of the jazz scene since the late 1930s, particularly among blacks in the East. Now it was hitting Los Angeles and hard, so hard that not just black kids like Kinloch but also young Mexican Americans and Filipino Americans were trying it on. Downtown haberdashers were selling getups starting at $20, although a full ensemble could easily cost more than that. Working out of their homes and garages, a handful of Avenue tailors were supplementing their incomes by sewing zoot suits of their own.

Kinloch had arrived on the West Coast at the same moment as the zoot suit. Handsome, light-skinned, he had a jutting jaw and a disarming smile, and there was mischief behind it: "He's no boy to go around in a car with," a woman who worked at the *Eagle* recalled. He was friendly in print and knew many up and down the street. Yet although he was extremely active socially, few knew him well. Kinloch was a man who attended to appearances and presented a polished surface beneath which much remained uncertain, perhaps because much remained unformed.

He was 16 years old when he began working for his aunt, Charlotta Bass, who was editor and publisher of the *California Eagle*. Madame's husband, one of the founders of the *Eagle*, had died in 1934 and she was determined to keep the paper afloat. Bass weathered the Depression by getting maximum work out of a skeletal staff. Kinloch's arrival was a godsend, and she quickly started grooming him to take over the paper. He started writing for the paper and soon became its managing editor, which hardly exhausted his energy. He organized a Junior Council of the NAACP and wrote and performed on a nightly radio program. Kinloch's youthfulness shocked folks: "Almost every colored person you meet listens [to the radio show]," he wrote home in a letter, "and, when introduced, people look at me sort of wry-like and say, 'Kinloch? Kinloch? Are you the son of that fellow who's on the radio?'"

With or without his fly green ensemble, Kinloch contravened the established order of Central Avenue, where newcomers were encouraged to shut their mouths and learn their place. The Negro leaders of Los Angeles were methodical elders who chose their words carefully, and those who raised their voices where whites might hear, as well as those who were too pointed in their comments, received the dour scorn of the grand old men. One observer of the enclave in the early decades of the twentieth century has suggested that the most pronounced tension wasn't between blacks and whites, but among longtime black residents and newcomers.

"Some Negroes entering Los Angeles during the Depression met greater hostility within their own community than from any outside groups," wrote historian Lawrence de Graaf in 1962. He noted how a divide grew "between established residents and the newest migrants who were regarded as a threat to the economic position of resident Negroes."

The *Eagle* itself had much to say on the matter. "If only as a simple measure for self-preservation, veteran black citizens of California must take an active part in training incoming Negroes from the South in basic rules of culture. This problem, however, cannot be approached with any false ideas of superiority and condescension," the paper editorialized in 1939. "By instilling in these people, especially the youth, an appreciation for inconspicuous conduct in public places, local residents will be safeguarding their liberties in the most practical and intelligent manner."

Rowdy, gullible, unskilled, overall-wearing, Southern—these were the stereotypes attributed to fresh arrivals. Such characterizations bore small connection to reality. By 1940, Texas and Oklahoma supplied the most newcomers, and more than 40 percent of arrivals were from the North or West. According to Loren Miller, a black lawyer who came to Los Angeles from Topeka around 1931, they

> were not peasants or sharecroppers. They were apt to have been persons who had lived in if not cities, at least in towns of some size and who had some experience with urban life, even if their urban life was not as great as it was here in Los Angeles. And they were not entirely ignorant and unlearned. Most of them had rudimentary education because both Texas and Oklahoma paid some attention at least to the *equal* in the separate but equal formula. And so their students and persons who had graduated from their schools, when they came to L.A., didn't come here steeped in the same ignorance [as] the peasants [who] flooded up from Mississippi to Chicago.

Kinloch was one more Easterner come to the city, and if that hardly made him unusual, less common was the way he acted. He didn't hold to the black part of town; he was not obsequious to his elders. He had been brash in Harlem, and working at the *Eagle* only encouraged him to raise his voice. The *Eagle*'s offices filled several rooms in a building at 40th and Central. A plate-glass window facing the Avenue spelled out the newspaper's name in hand-painted letters. Inside the old building, one ground-floor room was filled with desks and typewriters, and behind that was the room where the linotype machines clattered, and behind them was the staircase that led to Madame's apartment. Kinloch accompanied Madame everywhere: "She's too afraid to stay anyplace by herself," he said in a letter home. He felt a need to protect her, a tiny woman—5 feet tall—living alone: "certain individuals out here thought they had the Madame all tied up so far as falling heir to the paper was concerned. Just my presence keeps off so many of the schemers who would like to get in with her and take everything she has."

Kinloch was Madame's protector and the *Eagle* was his home, the place where he cultivated his voice and a growing audience. He edited, wrote reviews and editorials, and ghostwrote Bass's column; on the small staff he was the consummate polish man, the stylist who would take the raw copy from others and give it a snap that could be heard round the corner. He also ran a linotype machine and was known to toss on a coat and chase sirens screeching down Central Avenue.

One August day in 1941, a man of Kinloch's generation stopped by the *Eagle* offices. The story he told was front-page news. His name was Clarence Woods.

Woods was a member of the Army's 94th Engineer's Battalion, stationed for war games at Gurdon, Arkansas. Composed of northern blacks, the 94th was unprepared for what this small town had in store. In a rural area outside city limits, about 200 black soldiers were marching along a road when Gurdon's sheriff and a convoy of deputies blocked their path.

"Who the hell is in charge of these goddam niggers?" the sheriff asked. "Get these black bastards off the concrete." He ordered their white lieutenant to have the soldiers march back to town in a muddy ditch. "If so much as one black bastard opens his mouth, I will kill all of them."

The lieutenant protested the command and was beaten by sheriffs and machine-gun-toting military police. The soldiers marched back in the mud to Gurdon, where they discovered that 15 blacks left behind on cleanup duty had been assaulted by locals. Fearing an even larger attack, and denied ammunition by an Army careful not to inflame Southern whites, 50 black soldiers, including Woods, fled the base. Woods put on civilian clothes and affected a Southern accent— "smart" Negroes were objects of hatred in the South. He hoboed to Los Angeles, riding the rails, a deserter from the Jim Crow Army.

When they met, Woods and Kinloch were kindred spirits. Kinloch was 21, Woods 23. Woods was a founder of Detroit's Junior Council of the NAACP; Kinloch was president of Los Angeles's Junior Council. In words and deeds, both expressed a new spirit rising among the young black men who knew America was headed into war. They were raising fresh questions about the value of their loyalty. Why attack a brutal tyrant overseas when Negroes faced brutality at home? Why join armed forces that denied its black soldiers rights in order to fight for the rights of others? These arguments were surfacing even before the United States entered World War II. Once the fight began, they would explode into the open.

An unsigned *Eagle* editorial on Woods's flight from Arkansas, probably written by Kinloch, defined the mood emerging: "The issue faces America fairly and squarely. She must give justice to the black boys in khaki or the black boys won't stay in it."

The candor might have felt like a cold slap to the old Negro elite, but how could Kinloch act otherwise? From birth his parents had encouraged him to speak, question, argue. His father, James Kinloch, was an Episcopalian and Republican, a cigar maker who was a friend of Harlem Renaissance writer James Weldon Johnson. His mother, Victorine Spears, was a dressmaker and a Christian Scientist; her sister was Charlotta Spears Bass, the *Eagle*'s editor. John Kinloch was born in New Jersey in 1920 and raised to feel comfortable both in 1930s Harlem and the white Manhattan to the South. Kinloch went to the Ethical Culture School, a liberal humanist institution that taught social justice and racial equality, and also attended DeWitt Clinton High School. He wandered freely as a child, skipping school to go to the library, taking trolleys to surrounding suburbs, and even witnessing the 1935 trial of the Lindbergh baby kidnapper Bruno Richard Hauptmann.

The adolescent Kinloch wrote plays and performed them in his backyard; his school papers included essays on Frederick Douglass and the power of the Southern black vote. These writings are precocious, witty, and steeped in Depression-era progressive politics. A short story from 1935, "Two Blocks East of Broadway," tells the story of two white urchins who meet in the New York subway and become pals. In fractured Krazy Kat English, one explains to his buddy why he has become a member of "da commonistic party": "Dis gumment has been founded, er losted, er somethin', on a very ingracious basis, which is foin—democracy. Democracy, a gumment fer da public, by day people, an' of da public. . . . But dis same democracy has been discontorted, an' miscastrued, an' sich, an' is been gobbled up by big bizniz. Democracy in dis country is becoming nuttin but a bidder joke. . . . "

Kinloch's Harlem was near the end of the Harlem Renaissance. By the mid-1930s this cultural upwelling had come and mostly gone, having cemented Harlem's reputation as black America's premiere district and the summit of black achievement. Yet the Renaissance was as much symbol as reality, as the contradictions at its core reveal. Many of its major figures—James Weldon Johnson, Jessie Fauset, Charles Johnson, Walter White and Alain Locke, among others—either spent little time in Harlem or shunned it altogether, yet Harlem—a population center near the publishing industry and the white cultural elite—was a convenient focus.

At the root of the Harlem Renaissance was the notion of the Talented Tenth, a concept delineated by W. E. B. Du Bois. They were the cream at the top of the bottle, the educated elite that would lift up the backward, former sharecroppers settling by the thousands in northern cities during the Great Migration. "I believed in the higher education of a Talented Tenth who through their knowledge of modern culture could guide the American Negro into a higher civilization," explained Du Bois.

Guidance was required because nationally the situation for blacks was worsening. In the years following World War I, a white supremacy dampened by wartime solidarity came out in the open. Lynching exploded across the South, and a wave of urban attacks on blacks struck Washington D.C., Chicago, Omaha, Knoxville and elsewhere. The black vote in the South had largely been dismantled, and trade unions mostly barred black membership. The grand strategists of the Harlem Renaissance noted these impediments and sensed one glaring vulnerability in the armor of white supremacy. The political process was off limits, the mass media firmly in the hands of whites, but culture presented a means to communicate an appeal for equal rights. Literature, like Harlem itself, was a convenient focus, providing a frame for what was in essence a political appeal. The verdict arrived simultaneously with the evidence: a literary movement was needed, so a movement must be at hand.

The masterminds of the Renaissance believed they were erecting a New Negro, an individual who manifested liberation on the cultural plane, and who might somehow therefore manifest earthly liberation as well. That was the wish; the reality was that the Harlem Renaissance was about the black Talented Tenth speaking to educated whites. They hoped fine words and pictures might help the message of equality reach the masses. Sometimes it did. But before all else, the Renaissance existed as symbol and myth—in the words of historian David Levering Lewis, as "artifice imitating likelihood." The fabled Harlem of the 1920s existed as much in the mind as on the map.

The minders of the movement were hardly strangers to jazz or the crush of Lenox Avenue, Harlem's swing street. Still, there was a great distance between them and the masses they aimed to lift up. The New Negroes were bohemians and academics sharing a high-minded sense of culture's potential; they were disengaged from the public rallying around boxer Jack Johnson or musician Duke Ellington. Thinkers such as Walter White and Alain Locke were comfortable in their conviction that they themselves were the crests of the wave, bringing news of the masses—the worth of the masses—*to* the masses. American realities made it necessary for their arguments to be framed this way, but all the same, the situation was fraught with ironies that didn't escape its protagonists. As Langston Hughes wrote, "the ordinary Negroes hadn't heard of the Negro Renaissance. And if they had, it hadn't raised their wages any."

Writing to Hughes, Negro lawyer and newspaperman Loren Miller offered a West Coast perspective.

Anybody looking critically at the output of the NEW NEGRO ARTISTS must have been struck with the thought that the stuff has been written too much with a main eye on the good White Folks [and] the other eye cocked on the synthetic black bourgeoisie who heard that they had been emancipated from something or other and hence were in need of ART, in capitals. That this product has failed to make much of a dent on the nation is my own conclusion. Written to a pre-conceived pattern, it suffered exactly as did the output of the old academicians. If the generation before spent its ability by trying to impress the Negro into the mold of the slave-mammy stuff, the newer art failed no less as it fitted us into a new and equally artificial mold of either gin-swigging so-phisticates or sad young men with a far away back-to-Africa-with-scarlet-birds-in-the-offing look in our eyes and hearts.

The Los Angeles that Kinloch moved to in 1936 was a bewilderingly unfamiliar place. Even as it was a growing Western hub for blacks, it was to any self-respecting New Yorker unmistakably an outpost. Nei-ther the intellectual nor communications center that it would become after World War II, Los Angeles was not at the top of the list of places an aspirant activist would go in hopes of hijacking the public platform.

In Los Angeles white and black elites focused on business and civic order, and they viewed culture as bad for both. Some clichés at least start out true: this booster's paradise was not even a cultural backwa-ter. Here the masses were not going to be reached through artists and the intelligentsia: few listened to them. The power centers—the *Los Angeles Times*, downtown WASPs and Hollywood Jews—ignored black life. Save for the Communist Party, no institution supported promising artists, as had happened in Harlem. For blacks and whites there was instead a sense of lockstep business accomplishment.

Black Los Angeles was a buttoned-down place where everybody knew everybody else. As one local explained, "it was said that if you went to 12th and Central and stood there long enough, you'd see every black person in the city of Los Angeles." Many older community members owned their own homes, having purchased them during a flurry of early-twentieth-century tract development sometimes called the "bungalow boom." Black Los Angeles in the 1930s, Charlotta Bass wrote, was "a sober residential and business settlement."

Figureheads had elected one another to represent those below: men like Thomas Griffith of the Second Baptist Church, composer William Grant Still, architect Paul Revere Williams, businessmen William Nickerson Jr., George Beavers Jr. and Norman O. Houston all held a certain sway. Nickerson, Beavers and Houston's Golden State Mutual Life Insurance Company was the largest single employer in the community, a juggernaut with far more sway than the NAACP; Golden State's board had helped put the NAACP leaders in power. Yet their dominance would be fleeting; their grasp was weakening by the minute.

By the end of the 1940s these leaders would seem as remote from the life of the community as Eskimos. By decade's end the enclave would break open, and a new mass culture would roil. Unlike in Harlem, it moved up from the lower ranks. Du Bois had a name for the bottom dwellers, too: the Debauched Tenth. In black Los Angeles in the 1940s, it was the debauched, those presumed irredeemably untouched by culture, who came together to build a society. And make history. What was about to happen in Los Angeles was a working-class uproar, a coalescing of those who would disobey, mock, outrun and make followers of their leaders.

The Harlem Renaissance was cracking up on Central Avenue, its onetime elitists dropping by to cash a Hollywood check. Langston Hughes, Zora Neale Hurston, Arna Bontemps, Countee Cullen and Wallace Thurman had all been on its periphery between the early 1930s and the early 1940s, as they performed lucrative if fruitless writing tasks for the picture business. Taking Hollywood money might for them have been a guilt-inducing expedient. But Kinloch loved movies, and it wasn't slumming when he knocked on Hollywood's door. He worked at MGM, writing a script about a lynching for director Julien Duvivier. He rubbed elbows with Hollywood liberals like Edward G. Robinson and had the ear of Orson Welles, who suggested they work together on a project.

"Langston Hughes invited me to dinner yesterday," Kinloch wrote in a letter.

> We talked for about two and a half hours on the possibilities of Negro development in the movies. . . . Hughes feels that the only way really good Negro flickers can be made is to have them subsidized by some great white foundation or individual philanthropist. I don't think so. There is a wide enough market for the production—at a profit—of commendable commercial films for Negroes. Hughes also believes that Negro writers by and large are a somber lot, forever weeping in their beard. He thinks we need a "three Musketeers" spirit in Negro literature—the creation of dashing popular idols. He thinks my greatest opportunity is to develop my assertedly humorous work.

Kinloch adored the movies, and tortured Madame by disappearing without notice for days at a time, haunting all-night theaters, watching film after film, sleeping and then watching still more. His conflicted feelings about movies weren't induced by high-art ambitions pitted against the vulgar need to make the rent; rather, they were a case of unrequited love. Kinloch saw firsthand how the industry treated blacks, excluding them on the one hand and humiliating them through clichés on the other. In the early 1940s Kinloch spearheaded a boycott of the white-owned movie theaters of Central Avenue, pressuring them to screen all-black productions for their all-black ticket-buying public. He and other young activists realized that in a Jim Crow system where black consumers were steered to businesses along the Avenue, they wielded disproportionate power. Jim Crow concentrated black purchasing power, a power that could be used to communicate a demand for civil rights.

A man given to wisecracks as much as to poetry, a man such as Kinloch, was living in the right town. He gathered with those like himself: wearers of zoot suits, viewers of the low-budget black western "The Bronze Buckaroo," fans of local drummer Cee Pee Johnson's show band. Such men and women expected to find something of their lives on screen and in the music coming from jukeboxes and radios. Engaged, active consumers of popular culture, they were expressing an identity in the marketplace. In their hands, style became a kind of protest.

The zoot suit symbolized a generation filling the streets, taking up more than the space allotted them by the Golden State Mutual Life Insurance Company. It was bountiful, but first of all it was big. The zoot contravened wisdom and challenged physics. The jacket had more padding than a cell at Camarillo State Hospital; the sleeves overachieved all the way to the fingertips. The slacks hoisted almost to the armpits, and the seat was super loose, as were the legs—all the way down to the ankles. There generosity ran out, the cuffs neatly holding the ankles. Coast-to-coast this outfit spoke the same vernacular, but Southern California customized the array with a crucial element: thick-soled oxford shoes.

"They were about 12 inches at the knees and maybe 6 inches at the cuffs," remembered neighborhood resident Richard Dunn. "Some of them had zippers in them. They were that drastic, you couldn't get your foot in them." A teenager when the suit first arrived, Dunn delivered newspapers along Central to pay for his zoot suit.

"Glover was a tailor; he had a shop in the back of his home," recalled Dunn. "Over the years he'd built up a couple of little rooms and he would have people back there like 10 or 11 o'clock the day before Christmas, and until 1 or 2 o'clock the day before Easter. Working on those suits."

They were called "streamlined," a term signaling grand proportions. They were called "drapes," perhaps derived from the 1930s English drape suit, perhaps simply a nod to their grand expenditure of fabric falling about one's frame. Not least they were called "shameful," "wicked": the crux of their sin that they sung their uselessness. Zoot suits celebrated leisure at a time when in some parts of the country Negroes spotted wearing something other than work clothes risked a beating from affronted whites. The outfit was sybaritic, voluptuous, cryptic, mute and formidable at once. On the street, where older folks reflexively worried about what whites thought, here was a generation scrambling the codes, silently signaling they couldn't care less what "ofays"—hepster pig Latin for "foes," or white people—thought.

"You were assumed not to be really clean—you got grease on you, dirt, and the kind of work that most of us did was a job that you would end up dirty," remembered Dunn. "Like, if you were a mechanic you would have grease on you and like that. Wearing a zoot suit gave you identity, and it gave you pride; not wearing work clothes probably boosted your ego."

The sidewalks of Central were a stage, never more than on Sunday. Whatever else Sunday was for, the parades along the Avenue were an instinctive rejection of the white judgment that black bodies existed for work. There and on the streets of black American cities—at least outside of the Deep South—the sidewalks became, as one writer put it, a "private world of [the] African American's own making." On this spot and on this day, a suit of clothes signified ownership of one's own body, and one's own soul.

Traditional Sunday clothes raised one's standing; a zoot suit raised eyebrows, questions, catcalls. They were not church finery and challenged not just the white stare, but the gaze of black elders as well. Zoot suit wearers asked for no man's blessing, and asked why every day could not be Sunday.

No wonder church leaders fumed. "Surely there is much clowning going on," lamented Reverend J. L. Caston. "Those extreme fashions called drapes and their clownish accessories, the clowning that goes on with the carefree exhibition of disregard for any probability of danger in the course they pursue and the reckless determination of many youth to grab off an easy living and spurn all advice to the contrary. . . . these are but symptoms of tragedy which may lurk in a clown's suit." It was a heavy burden of meaning to lay on a set of threads. Caston saw in them a whimsical disrespect for all the Castons of the world and a disregard for order itself. To the reverend, the zoot challenged the very fabric of the world. He was not wrong.

Though their arrival was not an overnight thing, these gaudy outfits came into their own at the beginning of the decade. Perhaps their coming-out party occurred on the evening of July 10, 1941, opening night of Duke Ellington's stage show *Jump for Joy* at the Mayan Theater in the heart of downtown. The Duke had all but moved from his beloved Harlem to the Dunbar Hotel for the sake of a show that was dear to his heart. *Jump for Joy*, he knew, was something special, more than merely another revue: it was conceived as a race-conscious production, an expression of a new sensibility among African Americans. At the same time that Kinloch was criticizing representation of Negroes in Hollywood films, Ellington was writing a show that aimed, he said, "to take Uncle Tom out of the theater, to eliminate the stereotyped image."

Born out of conversations among Ellington, Langston Hughes and a group of Hollywood radicals, *Jump for Joy* declared the emergence of a New New Negro. It celebrated the sweep of black popular culture, using the talents of performers like balladeer Herb Jeffries, blues singer Big Joe Turner, and comic Wonderful Smith. Ellington singer Ivie Anderson performed her classic "I've Got It Bad (And That Ain't Good)," while a young dancer from the neighborhood, Dorothy Dandridge, captured much attention. In his autobiography, *Music Is My Mistress,* Ellington called the show a "suntanned revue-sical," one meant to "eliminate the stereotyped image that had been exploited by Hollywood and Broadway, and say things that would make the audience think." He harnessed local songwriters and entertainers to hone his vision and drew on their own work for inspiration. One tune imagined Uncle Tom's Cabin as a Hollywood drive-in restaurant, illustrating Jim Crow's successful transplant to the Promised Land. "I've Got a Passport from Georgia (and I'm Going to the U.S.A.)" mocked Southern segregation and brought bomb threats to the Mayan. Unlike many public venues in Los Angeles, the Mayan Theater was an integrated space. The audience was, Ellington wrote later, "of unusual composition, for it included the most celebrated Hollywoodians, middle-class ofays, the sweet-and-low scuffling-type Negroes, and dicty Negroes as well (doctors, lawyers, etc.). The Negroes always left proudly, with their chests sticking out."

Ellington seemed to be everywhere that autumn. He was hanging out with John Garfield at Culver City's Casa Manana, where his band was headlining. He delivered a radio talk on civil rights titled "We, Too, Sing America," its name derived from a poem of the same title by Langston Hughes. The Duke even caused a zoot suit–like clamor of his own when he played selections from *Jump for Joy* as part of a series of religious concerts in Pasadena. Members of the clergy revolted.

Jump for Joy opened at precisely the wrong moment: the Depression was still on and now America was in the middle of war preparations, a jittery time when attentions were turned in a hundred different directions. And if today the production is viewed as a high point of Ellington's career, in 1941 *Jump for Joy* was a modest success, lasting a mere 101 performances at the Mayan. Ellington never attempted a show as socially ambitious again.

Musically it pushed his orchestra in new directions. This was probably the greatest group of musicians he ever assembled, featuring bassist Jimmy Blanton and alto saxophonist Ben Webster. Arranger Billy Strayhorn lurked behind the scenes, attending Hollywood cocktail parties and Eastside soirees, fine-tuning a score that swayed from lush swing to earthy stomp.

Central Avenue regular Richard Dunn attended most every night. "I think *Jump for Joy* was the best there was to offer," he recalled. "I guess you get a certain vibration when you walk into a place. Do you ever feel it? You feel like you're walking on air. I can go into certain people's homes and I say 'oh, this home's got love. It's got peace. It's got harmony.' I can feel it. *Jump for Joy* had all of that."

John Kinloch was there, praising the production for the *Eagle*. One of the most-celebrated scenes from *Jump for Joy* came near the end, a bit called "Made to Order" that featured the comedy team of Pot, Pan and Skillet. "Made to Order" opened with Pan and Skillet playing two tailors at work in their shop. Pot arrives, announcing he's in the market for a can't-miss suit to wear on Easter Sunday. He gets measured, then places a request for an outfit with "shoulders eighteen inches this-away and eighteen inches that-away . . ." The Ellington band falls in, vamping as Pot, Pan and Skillet break off a set of clipped rhymes that clatter like a tap-dance routine.

You've got a zoot suit with a reet pleat and a stuff cuff and a drape shape, shoulders extended, eighteen as intended; padding—Gibraltar; shiny as a halter; streamlined alignment; pipeline the pocket; drape it, drop it, sock it, and lock it—fifty-three at the knee and seven at the cuff.

Is there anything else?

Hell no, that's enough!

What color cloth do you want to cover your hide?

Daddy, let the rainbow be your guide!

Their banter defined zoot style for all time.

Set change. A sidewalk parade crosses the stage as the band swings into Ellington's "Sharp Easter." A quartet sings: "Easter Sunday is the one day/when the sun-tanned tenth of the nation/Celebratin', start creatin'/A sartorial sensation." Sunday—the day when work stopped and black workers owned their own bodies, showing them off in clothes that outlandishly proclaimed style and play. The procession continues, the two tailors appearing at last in brilliant gold and purple confections. Then arrives Pot, wearing what a writer for the show described as "the loudest, most outrageous checkered suit ever constructed. The pants came up to his armpits, the vest was two or three inches long, even the lining was blinding." That was the apex of *Jump for Joy:* a glorious parade of black artistry, culminating with the arrival of the zoot suit beyond all knowing.

Jump for Joy closed on September 27. Pearl Harbor was bombed on December 7. America was now at war. In an undated letter, John Kinloch wrote his mother, "Last night, for the first time in months, I went to a dance. Mom, you should have *seen* the women! Oh, my!"

"Have to go down to the draft board tomorrow. Will let you know how it comes out."

CHAPTER 2

Tearing Up the Double V

AMERICA WAS HEADING FOR WAR: EVERYONE COULD SEE THAT. BLACK Angelenos knew the draft was coming, and among them there grew both support and skepticism. Even before the United States escalated war preparations, many were expressing reluctance and feelings far stronger, but the imposition of a draft in the autumn of 1940 crystal-lized dissent. Black protest stepped out of the shadows and began tak-ing shape.

As part of the enlistment paperwork, blacks were supposed to check a box marked "Negro." Identifying yourself meant consenting to a Jim Crow military, a federal system of segregation. It meant digging ditches, building roads, cleaning latrines and serving white people. Nothing brought resentment more to the surface than conscription. The Marines didn't accept blacks at all, the Navy allowed them only to work in menial positions, and the Army had no intention of letting them fight on the front line. The California National Guard banned black membership.

Many shared the feelings of trumpeter Howard McGhee, who was playing in the Charlie Barnet band when the draft board caught up with him. He described his experience years later in an oral history:

They called me up for the induction meeting to the Army and shit, and I told them, "I ain't fighting for nobody. Are you kidding me? I must be crazy." But they told me, "Well, either you fight or you go to jail." So I said, "I ain't going to jail and I ain't gonna fight. Now what are you gonna do about that?" so the cat said, "Send him in and let him talk to the psychiatrist." So I went in to the psychiatrist, and I said, "Well, man, why should I fight? I ain't mad at nobody over there." . . . I said, "Shit, I'll shoot any son of a bitch that's white that comes up in front of me." And they said, "No, we can't use you."

I wasn't ready to go dodge no bullets for nobody, I'll tell you that. I really wasn't for that. And I like America, but I didn't like it that much! I mean, it's all right to be a second-class citizen, but shit, to be *shot at*, that's another damn story. No, I couldn't make that.

To understand such resistance, stronger and more vocal than ever before, it helps to recall the previous generation of black soldiers, the ones who returned from World War I. For the dissent of World War II was built on the failures of the past. Negro soldiers had fought and died in World War I. Their prevailing philosophy had been one of stoicism, a policy of keeping dissent sheathed.

In 1917, on the verge of the United States entering the fight, W. E. B. Du Bois wrote a clarion editorial in the *Crisis*, the NAACP's official magazine. The influential column inspired what came to be called the "Close Ranks" strategy, arguing that blacks should hold nothing back in fighting for the American flag; by demonstrating their loyalty and bravery they would prove their worth. "Let us, while this war lasts, forget our special grievances and close our ranks shoulder to shoulder with our own white fellow citizens and the allied nations that are fighting for democracy," wrote Du Bois. "We make no ordinary sacrifice, but make it gladly and willingly with our eyes lifted to the hills."

Surely a grateful country would appreciate those dark-skinned soldiers who had fought in Europe. Surely the bravery of blacks would deal a blow to segregation. Asking race warriors to hold their fire, Du Bois suggested that symbols were sometimes more effective than action. Ultimately, Negro protest would be more powerful for taking the high road of steadfastness, he wagered. His words resonated across the country, and beyond that, the thinking they embodied—the necessity of restraint, the dependency upon symbolism when so few weapons were at hand—was echoed by those who might not even have read the "Close Ranks" editorial.

Soldiers in Los Angeles heard the message. "The Negro has done his part in this war," said Journee White, a black real estate dealer who put his career on hold to enlist. "He does not claim to have done any more than any one else, but he does want the world to know and give him credit for what he actually achieved. If he gets that it will be much." For black Angelenos returning from the European battlefront, there was a celebratory banquet at Patriotic Hall in May 1919, followed by a jazz concert from the Reb Spikes band. A mass assembly of uniformed veterans, featuring a parade and military band, formed at the corner of 12th and Central. This being Los Angeles, the assembly also served a second purpose: it was filmed for use in a movie titled *Injustice*.

Gathering at the intersection was a generation expecting its battlefield sacrifice to translate into equality at home. No such credit would be tendered. The Negro soldier did not receive what White and others had hoped was coming. Southern veterans were quickly delivered a postwar message: as they arrived home, some as they stepped off trains, they were stripped of their uniforms, beaten and warned to expect no new treatment. Their uniforms were viewed as presumption, and presumption was met with retribution. Georgia alone saw 22 blacks lynched in 1919, including a veteran who was killed by a Blakely mob for "wearing his uniform too long." A wave of racial violence surged in what came to be called the Red Summer; there were more lynchings in 1919 than there had been in years, and racial violence flared in Chicago, Oklahoma, Washington D.C., and dozens of other places. If there was any doubt that the "Close Ranks" strategy had grossly misjudged white sympathies, it was laid to rest when Du Bois himself declared a year later that "*we return fighting*" and admitted privately that he hadn't foreseen the war's "wide impotence as a method of social reform."

As a formal strategy "Close Ranks" died on the vine, but black Los Angeles maintained a policy of quiet humility after the war, exhorting the citizenry to keep their heads down and trust in leaders. High-minded rules of etiquette and politesse prevailed, and displaying one's good faith and standards to the white city over the long haul was expected to convince city fathers of black worthiness. A sense held sway among the old guard that race problems could be solved through letting a handful of educated, successful elites—Du Bois's "Talented Tenth"—speak for all. Strategy, cunning and survival skills made for battlefield heroes in World War I; privilege, tact and survival skills made for civic leaders in postwar Los Angeles. White Angelenos were not paying any attention at all, but in the black community the pantomime of black leaders dramatizing their good intentions, their good faith with whites, certified their role as spokesmen of the race.

The response from whites would certainly be less wrenching than what was happening in the South. Yet over the next few decades Los Angeles would become a far more segregated place than it had been, a markedly less safe place to be black. Racial progress began running in reverse.

• • •

LOS ANGELES WAS FOUNDED in 1781 by a group of black and biracial settlers. Of the 46 original settlers, 26 were of African or part-African extraction. From the beginning the city was a black place. That quickly changed as the population grew, but for a long time racial relations were relaxed. Indeed, a town as small as Los Angeles in its first decades, resting in a landscape so huge, gave convenient cover to the city's black population. Growth was assured and battles over scarce resources were deferred. Into the early twentieth century, furthermore, white enmity was focused mostly on the Chinese, allowing the Avenue community to quietly grow.

Resident and scholar J. Max Bond described turn-of-the-century black L.A. as "without leadership . . . poor . . . scattered [but] with no restrictions against them." Reporting in the *Crisis* on a 1913 West Coast visit, Du Bois agreed, noting that although there was racism, "Out here in this matchless Southern California there would seem to be no limit to your opportunities, your possibilities." The rise of restrictive covenants had not yet deeply affected the community; blacks lived in assorted neighborhoods, enjoying mobility and relative anonymity.

By the end of World War I, however, the city had unpacked enough that white Angelenos—only now really seeing themselves as Angelenos, as members of the same city—first gave blacks the respect of their hatred. The day-to-day indignities of Jim Crow coalesced. The result was an elevated indignation, a sense that freedoms were melting away. Boundaries that had not existed were defined and suddenly became matters of life and death.

In the years just prior to U.S. entry into World War II, black status had fully emerged before the eyes of white Los Angeles, and with it came open discrimination. City council districts were drawn to divide black political power, and school districts were drawn to quarantine black students. In the police division that patrolled Central Avenue, the white commanding officer declared that no white cop would ever take orders from a Negro. Meanwhile the Los Angeles Police Department brutally established order up and down the street, invading homes, shooting suspects in the back. Blacks appeared before downtown judges like Ray Brockman, who in ruling on a tenant dispute explained: "Negroes are like sleek, fat dogs; when they have full bellies, they lick each other, but take their bones from them, in this case their house, and they are ready to fight." Restaurants refused to seat black patrons, some displaying signs that declared "No Negroes" and worse. Public swimming pools were off limits to blacks, save those that provided a day of the week when they alone were allowed to swim (pools were then drained and refilled). Restrictive covenants were becoming a favorite new tool of discrimination; as the frontier collapsed and development tracts popped up all around the metropolis, a new social contract also emerged by which communities agreed to keep blacks and others—Jews, Indians, Asians, Mexicans—out. Mocking posters of Ubangi women were tacked up at sheriff stations; a book titled *Ten Little Nigger Boys* circulated at a local school. In 1940, bowling alleys, boxing matches, ice rinks, ballrooms, even pet cemeteries were segregated.

In the South an armature of laws gave form to racism. Tangible, rendered "rational" through their expression on the printed page, their statutory basis gave them a sense of permanence. Southern laws gave order to hate. But the California Constitution of 1849 declared slavery illegal, and in 1893 a sweeping statewide antidiscrimination law was passed. In California, legal structure gave shape to tolerance, but alas, tolerance was inchoate and melting in the heat of the twentieth century. In Los Angeles, racism grew as a native expression of power—in the dark, in agreements made between gentlemen behind closed doors. Restrictive covenants were pacts among private partners that the courts faithfully backed up. There was no law against a restaurant overlooking a black couple; it was just that explicitly refusing service was technically illegal. In Los Angeles a quiet understanding was observed. White supremacy here was vast but incomplete, and its subtleties mystified even those who felt it most harshly. An evasive waiter could be ambiguous, while a sign above a water fountain was definitive. Strange as it may sound, racism could be counted on in the South; it was no less real, but far less dependable, graspable, on the West Coast.

Hatred was not a quantifiable system as it was in Dixie: it was an organism growing, testing its limits, measuring its strength by overreaching. It lived. Or: it lived here and hid *there*. The restaurant on one side of the street was friendly, and you'd get the boot from the one across the way. This side of the street was restricted, but that one wasn't. Gravity worked somewhere and not somewhere else; the pistol butt fell randomly. The rules were spoken sotto voce, yet they were heard. There was something about the uncertainty of the organism, about its clumsy steps toward self-recognition, that defined its character.

At the west end of Pico Boulevard, where the street reached the Santa Monica beach, stood a hot dog stand of modest proportions. A vendor worked there on weekends. "We knew which side we were able to lay a blanket on, and which side was where people were not going to be friendly to us," said an African American woman who grew up in Los Angeles in the 1930s. "That hot dog stand marked the line." A blanket on the wrong side of the umbrella was an open invitation to a brawl.

Who belonged where: that was the essence of the race war in the late 1930s Los Angeles. Everywhere there were borders, as dangerous to breach as if they were electrified. Everywhere there were lines burned into minds. The bones of L.A. segregation came before words posted in public and thrived in places where words lost their meaning. A hot dog stand that was an outpost. An ironic remark that had to be turned 180 degrees to be understood, a downward casting of the eyes. The angle of a hat. A mark on a playing card. A newcomer quickly learned the cues and learned how to read them. Those who were going to make it in the new West interpreted the invisible and discerned where they couldn't go, what they couldn't buy, where the other man lived. *Avoid that block, that cop, that hour.* A brand new oral tradition floated on the orange-scented breeze, and you learned it bit by bit. And lived.

Skirmishes: The Palomar Ballroom, a swing club on Vermont Avenue, burned to the ground one hot night in 1937, torched, it was whispered, to keep Negroes from attending an appearance of the Count Basie band. The Klan resurfaced in Los Angeles three years later after a 10-year hiatus, marching around city hall. In 1940 more than 1,000 whites attacked 50 Negro members of the Pleasant Hills Baptist Church choir while they picnicked on the beach in Santa Monica. Police arrived and arrested the beaten. A few months later, a more troubling incident occurred at Fremont High School, in a white neighborhood sandwiched between two black areas. Fremont had long steered black students to outlying high schools; after six blacks sought to attend classes, six black effigies were burned on a campus bonfire. "This is no coon's day!" warned a poster. When the fires burned out, the charred figures were used in a mock lynching.

Rancor was emerging, and in this setting a community that for years had led the nation in smiles suddenly stirred. Stories, gossip, news all flowed along Central Avenue like it was the Los Angeles River. Whether you wanted it so or not, you were up to your ears before breakfast. In May 1940, Angelenos were talking about a letter printed in the *Pittsburgh Courier*, the most popular black newspaper in the country. Written by 15 mess attendants stationed on the U.S.S. *Philadelphia*, the letter expressed the cold shock of the damaged innocent, as well as a warning to other innocents. These men knew that by addressing the nationally distributed *Courier*, they would be addressing all of black America.

"Our main reason [for writing] is to let all of our colored mothers and fathers know how their sons are treated after taking an oath and pledging allegiance and loyalty to their flag and country," declared the letter writers. They were protesting the lack of opportunity for advancement in the Navy and an unequal pay scale.

> On this ship, out of a crew of 750, there are 18 colored boys, ranging in ages from 18 to 25. They are fresh out of high school and some have a year of college education.
>
> Their work is limited to waiting on tables and making beds for the officers. . . .
>
> In the last nine months there have been nine mess attendants given solitary confinement on bread and water.
>
> Five of the nine were given brig time because of fighting and arguments with other enlisted men. From this you will probably think we are a pretty bad bunch. We are not.
>
> With the treading on and kicking around we receive here (without being able to do anything about it), every last one of us becomes bitter enough to fight a member of our own family.
>
> We, the mess attendants of the *Philadelphia*, are not merely stating these facts because of our own plight. In doing so, we sincerely hope to discourage any other colored boys who might have planned to join the Navy and make the same mistake we did.
>
> All they would become is seagoing bell hops, chambermaids and dishwashers.

A pair of messages had landed. To the *Courier*'s readers, there was a metaphor for the Negro soldier's lot: they were domestic servants picking up after the white man. To the federal government came a warning: that the status quo produced discouragement, and discouragement would lead many to turn their back on the war. What was new wasn't the complaint, but that the sailors felt emboldened to say it out loud.

Soon the fate of the *Philadelphia*'s crew was also widely reported—the 15 letter writers were arrested, and two were imprisoned. The rest were held in the ship's brig as the *Philadelphia* docked in San Diego, California.

Chester Himes came to Los Angeles in 1941, taking up work in the defense factories and writing fiction. In his 1945 novel, *If He Hollers Let Him Go*, Himes's protagonist works in the shipyards of San Pedro. One day he takes a break from welding and glances out at the water, spotting a passing Navy ship. This is a novel, but it might have been the *Philadelphia* he saw for the thoughts that it stirred.

> I stood there on the deck looking out across the harbor. A cruiser was silhouetted against the skyline. The white folks are still going strong, I thought; then I thought about the black sailors aboard waiting on the white. In the good old American tradition, I thought; the good old American way.
>
> My face felt drawn in, thin, skin-tight on the bone. I wondered what would happen if all the Negroes in America would refuse to serve in the armed forces, refuse to work in war production until the Jim Crow pattern was abolished. The white folks would no doubt go right on fighting the war without us, I thought—and no doubt win it. They'd kill us maybe; but they couldn't kill us all. And if they did they'd have one hell of a job of burying us.

There was a new turn in the consciousness of black America, a notion that this time loyalty was conditional. The issue for black leaders was how to erect a mass movement, how to build on past defeats, bargain from a position of weakness. Labor organizer A. Philip Randolph focused on these questions. The Harlem-based Randolph was no stranger to Los Angeles; as the head of the sleeping car porters union, he'd long visited this important railroad town. In 1927 Randolph had spoken at the opening of Central Avenue's Lincoln

Theater, sharing the stage with blues singer Sarah Martin. Randolph's politics were all about harnessing the power of the unruly millions who put nickels in dive bar jukeboxes. He challenged them to surpass their leaders. "We need not depend on big names, for ours is a 'little people's' movement," he told his Los Angeles supporters.

"I met him in 1936, but he used to come out here every year," recalled Abie Robinson, a longtime journalist on the Avenue.

I heard him talk in a house on 24th Street. Couldn't afford no hall. It was like a rent party house that was made available to him. And the people would come.

He's the one that would instruct us how we should be planning our future, and what we should be thinking of in terms of advancing ourselves. You'd look at him—strong, neat, well dressed, well mannered, articulate. He was a real role model. He was our inspiration when he came to town, because he understood what we were up against.

A shrewd bargainer, Randolph understood how powerful symbols could be in a struggle. Early in 1941, the 51-year-old Randolph planned a mass movement that was essentially symbolic, existing most fully not in the streets—though it lived there—but in the mass media.

Randolph was an unlikely messenger to the masses, snappily appointed and erudite in a way that some people found mannered. Yet he sensed looming, in the balcony rows of theaters and in the breadlines, a black populace capable of forcing change. "Power and pressure do not reside in the few, the intelligentsia, they lie and flow from the masses," he wrote. "Power does not even rest with the masses as such. Power is the active principle of only the organized masses, the masses united for a definite purpose."

Late in January 1941, a call to arms written by Randolph appeared on the front page of the *California Eagle*. In a piece syndicated throughout the Negro press, he threw down the gauntlet to both the federal government and the black working class.

The whole National Defense setup reeks and stinks with race prejudice, hatred and discrimination.

It is obvious to anyone who is not deaf, dumb and blind that the
South, with its attitude that the Negro is inferior, worthless and simply
doesn't count, is in the saddle. It is a matter of common knowledge that
the Army, Navy and Air Corps are dominated and virtually controlled
by southerners.

Daringly, he linked his protest of racism in the armed forces with a
protest of racism in defense factories. Symbolism was fine, but jobs
could lead a man to eat.

I suggest that 10,000 Negroes march on Washington, with the slogan:
WE LOYAL NEGRO AMERICAN CITIZENS DEMAND THE
RIGHT TO WORK AND FIGHT FOR OUR COUNTRY.

Negroes could join this march from various sections of the country,
from all trades, professions and callings, such as laborers, doctors,
nurses, lawyers, teachers, preachers, mechanics, soldiers, women and
youth groups. . . .

Such a pilgrimage of 10,000 Negroes would wake up and shock Official Washington as it has never been shocked before. Why? The answer is clear. Nobody expects 10,000 Negroes to get together and
march anywhere for anything at any time. Negroes are supposed not to
have sufficient iron in their blood for this type of struggle. In common
parlance, they are supposed to be scared and unorganizable. Is this
true? I contend it is not.

A July 1 date was set for the demonstration, and a name established
for Randolph's rabble: the March on Washington Movement. The
group was conceived as an expression of blackness; white support
might be accepted, but the marchers and organizers would all be
black, for Randolph recognized an opportunity to create a new sense
of Negro possibility. While its circumvention of black leadership was
hard to miss—both the NAACP and the National Urban League were

agnostic, even subtly undermining of Randolph until it was clear the movement was gathering momentum—the call to march was spontaneously picked up and echoed on street corners and in beauty shops coast to coast. This was a shout-out ringing far above the heads of the elites and leaders, falling on the ears of "laborers, doctors, nurses, lawyers, teachers, preachers, mechanics, soldiers, women and youth groups."

In June, another article by Randolph appeared in the *Eagle*. The government had yet to accede to his demands, so Randolph upped the ante and called for a cool 100,000 marchers. This was hardball straight from the Negro leagues, brinksmanship aimed at the White House. "In a democracy every citizen has a right to express his opinion about the policies of the government," Randolph began, drawing in a breath. "He has a right, lawfully and orderly, to seek to change these policies when he deems them inadequate and unjust." At the onset of the last world war blacks felt a need to make a show of their loyalty; this time Randolph was calling for the government to demonstrate its own good citizenship.

The president had resolved to wage war, and black protest threatened to undermine Roosevelt's ability to fight. If a march occurred, it would signal to the world that Americans were not united and would catch the president between the pincers of two contradictory wings of his party—Southern white segregationists and Northern blacks. From the start government officials viewed Negro anger as subversive, for it conflicted with a federal imperative. A handful of sailors could be thrown into the brig: 100,000 black folks from Los Angeles and D.C. and everywhere in between were a harder thing to make disappear. At a time when the gloss of unity was at a premium, Randolph had discovered that the gloss of dissent held unusual powers of persuasion. This might be the moment when the president had to listen to a black man.

"Mass power is the chief form of power Negroes possess if they mobilize it," Randolph wrote in June.

It is a matter of common knowledge, however, that Negro mass power has never been really tested, measured and utilized to even its approximate maximum pressure possibilities. The Negro masses have always been discounted, underrated and undervalued. The stress and emphasis and importance have always been put upon the moneyed, educated and talented Negro.

Plans were in place for late June rallies in Los Angeles, Detroit, Chicago and New York, building momentum to a July 1 demonstration at the Lincoln Memorial. Local March on Washington Movement offices sprouted up around the country; Los Angeles had one. Nowhere in the country were both of Randolph's goals—integrating defense factories and the military—more intertwined in the minds of Negroes than in Los Angeles. The chance to upend this dual segregation inspired among those standing on the curb of Central Avenue, draft cards in their pockets and available for work, an unstable mix of hope and cynicism.

A new belligerence was in the air. It could communicate unequivocally, as in the letters mailed anonymously to the LAPD Vice Squad in 1939. After a series of police raids on Avenue homes in which officers arrived without warrants and shot up the premises, blacks mailed threats to "meet force with force." The belligerence could take more elliptical forms, as in the case of the 300 extras on the set of the Bob Hope–Bing Crosby picture *The Road to Zanzibar*. They had been hired to play African natives but, irked at the demand they put on minstrel-style blackface makeup, they went on strike. Claiming they feared "makeup poisoning," the natives insisted that the white makeup artists try the cosmetics first. Turning the tables on Hollywood, perhaps these extras shared a private laugh at the blackface performance unwittingly put on for their enjoyment.

The new belligerence didn't always have much of a point, nor was it always phrased in front-page diatribes. It might not "add up to something." But it held meaning. Street violence was on the rise: it was not planned, but it had meanings the participants themselves might not even understand. At the corner of 5th Street and Main, young black men were arrested for brawling with a pair of white baseball players from Seattle. The blacks were wearing zoot suits.

From pitching a ruckus to disobeying police orders, from cursing to vandalism, from graffiti to loud talk at the movies, acts of defiance bubbled out of the black district. They came from people who felt little connection to the political structure or the leadership class. Blacks were fighting back like never before, and more publicly than ever. You would only know it, however, if you understood the symbolism.

Everyone could see war was coming. It was just a matter of time, Negro Angelenos knew, before they would be asked to "do their part." The imminent need to do one's part filled some with a sense of duty and others with dread. America was petitioning its citizens to put aside disagreements for the sake of defeating fascism overseas. Only this time many held their allegiance in check. This time, it would not be a sure thing.

Randolph was a multitude of figures: orator, organizer, teacher, poker player. He was not a magician, however, and here is what he had created on the verge of July 1, 1941: nothing. What looked as if it had suddenly appeared had long quietly existed, and what had expressed itself had merely been looking for the words. A fine mix of hope and despair were everywhere in the era. It was Randolph's gift to see the moment for what it was, and put himself at its service.

Into the summer of 1941, Randolph picked up speed as the slights multiplied. By the end of May, he had succeeded in linking the integration of the armed forces and the defense plants: that month he called upon Roosevelt to issue a formal executive order banning discrimination in both instances.

Across the country buses and trains were chartered for the July 1 march, and buckets were passed from coast to coast to raise money for the effort. Yet it was far from clear that Randolph could marshal his projected 100,000, or even the 10,000 he'd first called for. Nobody, frankly, knew for sure. What was most real about the march was the optimism it stirred in the black press and the fears it triggered in Washington. Randolph's plan had meant for local rallies in major cities to build a fire under the New Dealers. But when local rallies failed to materialize that summer, Randolph chose to ignore that reality and respect the reality of optimism and fear. Faced with complicated questions about his ability to achieve his goals, Randolph upped the number of marchers he was urging to D.C. and urged them on all the more.

If Roosevelt had simply refused to negotiate with the movement he might have engineered its undoing, since it is unclear how many marchers would have shown up. But the risks were greater on his side; he simply could not afford to gamble with national unity by calling Randolph's bluff. Instead the president directed First Lady Eleanor Roosevelt and New York City mayor Fiorello Laguardia to urge Randolph to call off the demonstration. It was a cordial meeting, but Randolph could not be persuaded. "I'm certain it will do some good," he told Laguardia and Roosevelt. "In fact it has already done some good; for if you were not concerned about it you wouldn't be here now." Days later the president personally lobbied Randolph, also to no avail.

Finally, Roosevelt blinked. On June 25, 1941, he signed Executive Order 8802, declaring discrimination based on race (as well as creed, color or national origin) in defense industries to be illegal and setting up a Fair Employment Practices Commission (FEPC) to investigate and expose discrimination. It was a great, if partial, triumph for Randolph and the March on Washington Movement. The order was a huge step forward for ending Jim Crow in the workplace, and it seemed to echo Randolph's contention that racism was unpatriotic. However, the order said nothing about integrating the armed forces, a move that would have turned Southern Democrats against the president. Randolph quickly called off the march and declared a solid victory. A new climate of protest had been released, mobilizing the people who passed through the bus stations, storefront churches and taverns of black America. "It demonstrates the capacity of Negro people themselves," Randolph said. "The masses of Negro people must take over their leadership."

Another executive order, issued in February 1942, ultimately had perhaps even greater impact on L.A.'s blacks. Time would reveal Roosevelt's order to intern Japanese Americans on the West Coast as accidentally rebounding to the great profit of local blacks. But in 1941 the FEPC seemed about to transform the Avenue. The *Eagle* compared the order to the Emancipation Proclamation. Local activists pointed to the FEPC as "proof our voices are being heard." Soon after, Randolph visited Los Angeles and addressed a large crowd at what was unmistakably a victory celebration. He savored the triumph and continued to push for the building of an all-black mass movement. Randolph told a gathering at Second Baptist Church how he had turned down an offer of $50,000 from a well-intentioned white benefactor.

I refused that $50,000 because I knew that Negroes could only be emancipated by themselves.

If you take $50,000 from a white liberal, you've got the $50,000 and the white liberal's got you. If you take a nickel from a Negro on the corner. . . . you've got the Negro and the nickel, too.

The march was called off, yet columns of phantom protestors continued to amass. Maybe Randolph was a magician after all, because he turned one illusion (the depth of his army) into a whole field of them. Allegorical thinking cropped up all over black America, as people started taking their illusions very seriously. A 26-year-old cafeteria worker from Wichita, Kansas, named James Thompson composed a letter to the editor of the *Pittsburgh Courier*. It ran in the January 31, 1942, edition:

Being an American of dark complexion, these questions flash through my mind. Should I sacrifice my life to live half-American? Would it be demanding too much to demand full citizenship rights in exchange for the sacrifice of my life? Will colored Americans suffer still the indignities that have been heaped upon them in the past?

Leaving his own question hanging, Thompson then suggested a bit of symbolism he called "the Double V."

Let's have victory over these totalitarian forces overseas—meaning the
Germans, and the Japanese, and the Italians—and let's have victories
over the same types of forces in this country.

The notion was clean, simple and spring-loaded: two Vs-for-
Victory. We will fight for freedom overseas—We will fight for freedom
at home. The principles worth shedding blood for in one place were
no less elemental in another. The Double V's easy duality echoed Randolph's pairing of integration overseas and at home.

The Double V flowed out of the same dissatisfaction and hope as the
March on Washington Movement. Among the rank and file who picked
up its meaning instantly, the Double V was—like a trumpeter revising a
Tin Pan Alley pop tune—an example of black culture riffing on white
symbols. Among blacks, "the war incited militancy," Los Angeles attorney Loren Miller noted. "The Negroes used it in a way which I thought
was effective and ingenious. They had what they called the Double V
sign, you know, victory over the Fascists in Europe and victory over discrimination here. So when another person would go around giving the
V sign for victory, the Negroes were giving the Double V sign."

Black America ran with Thompson's words, turned them into a
movement, a force that was expressed and understood not as rhetoric
or philosophy but as popular culture. The Double V traveled by word
of mouth and by radio; it floated through the air. Black soldiers shelled
out for Double V tattoos; there were Double V dresses, pins, and hats.
Lucky Millinder's swing band traveled the country with two Vs
painted on his bus. Songwriters Andy Razaf and J. C. Johnson composed a Double V anthem, "Yankee Doodle Tan," which debuted on a
national broadcast on NBC radio. It was performed by L.A.'s Lionel
Hampton band, billing itself as the Double V Orchestra.

The Double V had special implications in Southern California. Over
$10 billion in war-related federal spending came to Los Angeles during
the course of the war. With its huge aviation industry and its Pacific
ports, steel and rubber factories and more, the area was a key weapon in

the fight. But with its Jim Crow hiring policies and whites-only unions, the Los Angeles defense factories would also be a battleground for the Double V fight. Along the Avenue, citizens geared up for combat and embraced the new movement.

Local boxing stars Chalky Wright and Jackie Wilson told reporters they endorsed the Double V, and the black newspaper the *Los Angeles Sentinel* plugged it weekly. Just off Central there was an after-hours joint run by a local gambler and sportsman: its name was the Double V. At the crook of the Double V movement, hypocrisy and hope were welded together; here was a dynamo waiting to be tapped; here was a dynamo speaking to itself, in a voice that cackled, whooped, shouted and surged.

Cackle, whoop, shout, surge: in the pages of the *Eagle*, John Kinloch raised a ruckus for the Double V. He was writing editorials that flipped the script on hometown members of the master race. While taking classes at the University of Southern California, he noticed, for instance, when a USC fraternity geared up for the big football game against UCLA by building a mock slave ship on its front lawn and nailing effigies of three black UCLA players—Woody Strode, Kenny Washington, and Jackie Robinson—to a palm tree. The *Eagle* called this display "Nazism . . . big as life and twice as natural." After a black-owned restaurant had "nigger" splashed across its front in red paint, the *Eagle* ran a photograph of the restaurant, the caption asking "Berlin or Los Angeles?" In an editorial, the *Eagle* noted that Los Angeles was "95 percent Nazi," because that much of the city was now covered by restrictive covenants.

Kinloch and the *Eagle* pounded away at home-front racists, using the Double V as their weapon. They applied the democratic principles and the rhetoric of Roosevelt's "Four Freedoms" speech to the city in which they published. Yes, Hitlerism must be fought. But "instead of fighting an English war, black America would prefer finishing one of our own— the Civil War," he wrote. The language and the principles of the American mission would be inverted, and in this way the V became a wedge.

Like blacks elsewhere, Kinloch wrestled with his sense of patriotism, pondered what it meant to the nation, what it might cost him. Unlike most people he knew, he didn't mind if others watched him battle with his ambivalence.

A Pome. For Folks. Who Wonder. What. The Hell.

By John Kinloch

Have you.
Sometimes felt.
That the guys.
Who shout.
Wegottawindawar!
And the sign boards.
In Red. White and Blue.
And the radio commercials.
Fulla patriotism.
And the jumping.
Up to salute.
In the show.
And speeches.
Lip heavy.
With Democracy and.
Freedom.
And Any Bonds Today?
And cracks like.
Don't Rock The Boat.
And big shots saying.
We can depend upon.
You good, colored folks.
Well, have you ever.
Felt.
That altogether.
This is so much.
Bull?
We remember.
Another war . . .
Greedy men.
Who thought.
The world's a big, fat jug.

And said.
Gimme my swig.
And we remember.
RIOTS.
TULSA, NEW YORK.
CHICAGO, WASHINGTON.
Bloody black bodies.
In khaki.
And bitter, black thoughts.
In mourning.
And so we decided.
They all lie.
In their teeth.
And the kids.
Who died.
Were damfools.
Yet, here we are.
In the middle.
Of another mess.
And the words.
They say.
Are the same words.
They said before.
And we are lonely.
For something.
To hold on to.
And live and die for.
BE NOBLE ABOUT.
AND COURAGEOUS.
AND BIG.
AND STRONG ABOUT.
But we can't.
Be these.
If this is the same.
As last time.

BUT . . .
But this time out.
It is we who.
Have the biggest stake.
Because Hitler.
Is against us.
As no man.
Has ever been.
Against the human race.
And if we.
Let him win.
Every revolution.
From Massachusetts.
To Moscow.
Will be lost.
And the people's.
Inch by inch.
Fight for freedom.
Will be lost.
And the right.
To fight for freedom.
Will be lost.
And that right.
Is the foot we've got.
Stuck.
In tomorrow's doorway.
And this is something.
To hold on to.
That's true.
AND BIG.
AND COURAGEOUS.
AND STRONG.
AND TO LIVE.
AND DIE FOR.

CHAPTER 3

Flying Home

COMING SOON!

THE DOUGLAS MINSTRELS OF 1943

"Minstrel Days Are Here Again" will be the opening number of the great
Minstrel Show coming soon to Douglas and the public under the direction
of D. Y. Cole of Forms and Procedure department. 'Lasses White, famed
minstrel and radio star, will sing ... everything in the show will picture the
aircraft industry of today in minstrel form.

—*Douglas Airview, November–December 1942*

THE KID HAD MOVED TO LOS ANGELES IN 1941. A TENOR SAXOPHONIST
not much bigger than his horn, he soon landed a gig in a no-name trio
playing in a no-name club. They'd had mixed success. "What are you
niggers doing here?" some guy in the crowd shouted at them; the bass
player cracked him in the head with his instrument. That job they lost.

Soon the 20-year-old Illinois Jacquet landed a better gig, with the
up-and-coming Lionel Hampton Band. In 1942 Jacquet found himself
recording for the first time in his life, stepping onto a makeshift studio
platform Hampton had built for him—Jacquet was too short to reach

the microphone stand. On his way up to record his first-ever solo, he passed the sage alto saxophonist Marshall Royal. The mentor had advice for the pup. "Go for yourself," Royal whispered to Jacquet.

"What did he mean?" Jacquet wondered.

Go for yourself. Jacquet's solo was a paroxysm of self-ness, of self-ishness, of doing for self and shouting from the deepest recesses of a self that had until that moment no sense of what it might have to say—no clue that it had *anything* to say. It was a bass to the head, that solo, and a shock to the system: the song was called "Flying Home," but it sounded like running away from home. At its apex Jacquet wailed the same note lined up 12 times in a fit of keening, erotic squeals that explored a range of the saxophone and of human sexuality rarely surveyed before. "Flying Home" was bump and grind music, it would divide jazz fans into camps of prudes and libertines, and it became the solo every tenor player memorized. Here was skywriting in an unknown language, brought to you by an L.A.–based band that called itself the Double V Orchestra. It was a jukebox smash.

In no time, a young writer and swing fan named Ralph Ellison was working on a short story, titled, with a wink, "Flying Home." In it a black aviator crash lands on a Southern farm. He waits for help to arrive and talks to a local tenant farmer who finds him lying injured in a field. The black sharecropper is perplexed by his discovery. "Lawd, I'd done heard about you boys but I haven't never *seen* one o' you all. Caint tell you how it felt to see somebody what looks like me in a airplane."

At the beginning of World War II, Negro eyes were turned to the sky. Bandleader Jimmie Lunceford wasn't just celebrated for his swing group's musical prowess; he was looked up to because he was a licensed pilot who flew to his shows. When Lunceford played a date in Wichita, Kansas, in 1942, he made a splash in the Negro press by visiting James Thompson, originator of the Double V movement, and taking Thompson up for his first airplane ride. Maceo Sheffield, a black police detective along Central Avenue, was already one of the biggest characters on the street; when he retired from the force in the 1930s and became a commercial pilot, his legend became larger than life. Even Jack Benny's sidekick Rochester yearned to fly. While attending the premiere of his 1940 movie *Buck Benny Rides Again*, Eddie Anderson, who was studying to get his pilot's license, took advantage of the press before him to call for the creation of a Negro Army Air Corps. Less than a year later, the Army would authorize training of black fighter pilots through the Tuskegee Institute.

The aviator in Ellison's 1944 story was a member of the Tuskegee airmen, the first black fliers permitted training—albeit segregated training—in the U.S. military. The Tuskegee aviators were heroes to blacks across the country, and included among their ranks were Angelenos like Roger Terry and Celestus King. Their comings and goings were avidly tracked in the local press.

But if winged flight had symbolic resonance in Southern California, the practical implications were no less considerable. Los Angeles was the seat of American aviation, and by 1940 aviation was at once the biggest industry in the region and the fastest growing. The business was a generation old, having gained a hold in the 1920s and then recouping after the Depression wiped most local firms out. Land was cheap and abundant in farm areas just beyond L.A., in Inglewood, Santa Monica, Downey, Hawthorne and Burbank. Skilled labor came cheap, too, cheaper than in the East thanks to anti-union practices prevalent in Southern California. The result was the rapid rise of firms like Douglas, Northrop, Hughes, North American Aviation, and Lockheed, all headquartered in Los Angeles.

The imminence of war paved the way for industrial expansion. France and Great Britain began placing large orders with L.A. firms, and indications from overseas suggested more were on the way. The federal government began to unsubtly prod production. Roosevelt's May 1940 call for the aircraft industry to turn out 50,000 a year was greeted by industry leaders with eagerness and disbelief. That was about as many planes as had been built in all the years since the airplane's 1903 invention. The goal was preposterous, but it underscored the need for defense to get in gear, and it warmed the hearts of local moguls. As war began, everyone's eyes were turned to the sky.

Even with the boom in purchase orders, unemployment endured in Southern California. In 1940 13.7 percent were out of work, but though that suggested a considerable pool from which to stock factories, the reality was markedly different. Aviation required approximately 90 percent skilled and semiskilled labor, and in Los Angeles, a town built on hype and tourism, movies and citrus, industry was a small part of the economy—only 20 percent of employment before Pearl Harbor came from manufacturing. Locally, there was shockingly little skilled labor available for the job at hand. So when the aviation boom came, defense production quickly depleted the marginal reserves, and skilled workers were recruited in huge numbers from the East and Midwest, where they existed in much higher numbers. "Perhaps 90 percent of the skilled men being hired in the aircraft industry in late 1940 came not from the ranks of the unemployed, but from steady employment elsewhere," says James Wilburn, a historian of the L.A. aviation industry.

For black Angelenos, the promise of flight didn't simply symbolize a chance for respect or distinction; aircraft held out the simple possibility of making a living as the Depression dragged on. It would be a while, however, before a black man would see the inside of an airplane factory, unless he was pushing a broom. Private trade schools quickly flourished to feed the need for workers, but they refused to train blacks, explaining that since factories did not hire blacks, what was the point of training them? Industrialists, naturally, explained there was no reason to waste resources on hiring blacks who lacked proper training.

Labor unions barred black membership; management didn't need to hire nonwhites, given the surplus of workers arriving from elsewhere in 1940 and 1941. Both wings thus in proper alignment, aviation racism chased the horizon. At the birth of the boom in 1940, there were but 186 nonwhite workers in the aircraft industry. A year later, some 8,769 skilled and semiskilled aircraft jobs were filled between January and March. Thirteen went to nonwhite workers.

An accident of candor brought the issue into the open. On the phone in his office in Inglewood, J. H. "Dutch" Kindelberger was describing the enterprise to a newspaper reporter in Kansas. President and general manager of North American Aviation, Kindelberger was handling huge government orders for new aircraft—allotments so big, in fact, that in 1940 he had to open a brand new factory in Wichita. In the interview Kindelberger explained that his new plant would follow previous North American practices in not hiring skilled black workers.

While we are in complete sympathy with the Negro, it is against the company policy to employ them as mechanics or aircraft workers. We use none except white workers in the plant here in Inglewood. There will be some jobs as janitors for Negroes. Regardless of their training as aircraft workers, we will not employ them in the North American plant.

A spokesman for the local Vultee corporation put his company's policy similarly on the public record: "We do not believe it advisable to include colored people in our regular working force. We may at a later date be in a position to add some colored people in minor capacities such as porters and cleaners."

The words of these industrialists were widely reported in the Negro press, as were those of A. R. Clifton, Los Angeles County superintendent of schools. Clifton started a controversy when he suggested that the city would soon need to import *unskilled* white workers from other parts of the country to attend training schools. Blacks heard these words and felt a slap. We are here, they said. Are we not Americans?

In the wake of the creation of the Fair Employment Practices Commission, at least one thing was new: now government representatives were scrutinizing the words of bigots, too, and expressing their criticism. After Roosevelt's five-member FEPC was empanelled, it fittingly scheduled its first hearings in Los Angeles in the fall of 1941. Los Angeles was a focus of job discrimination; Los Angeles was also far away from the Dixie Democrats crucial to Roosevelt and thus a good place to root out racism. Yet if the creation of the FEPC was a sizable victory, activists in Los Angeles were torn between celebration and criticism. No sudden wave of opportunity arrived with the October 1941 hearings. During the second half of that year, more than 60,000 black workers remained unemployed citywide. The federal government might be interested in stemming discrimination, but not past the point where it hampered war production. FEPC panelists quickly discovered that

there was little in the way of punishment they could bring upon violators. Their weakness was emphasized from the beginning, when intran-
sigent representatives of Vultee refused to even show up as requested
for the hearings. They got along fine without the FEPC.

As preparations continued for the October hearings, a local group
called the Allied Organizations, composed of leaders from the black
community, moved to place black workers in the airplane factories.
The Allied Organizations documented discrimination, gathering statistics and assembling petitions. They held a few rallies in 1941, but
they were desultory affairs, the antithesis of the March on Washington
Movement. There can't be rallies without the masses, and the Allied
Organizations—led by the zoot-suit-hating Reverend J. L. Caston and
George Beavers, vice president of the Golden State Mutual Life Insurance Company—were not entirely comfortable with the people. They
were well-off burghers with an anxious grasp on status. Their public
statements seemed to ask if the masses were truly deserving of their
benevolence; Beavers lectured black workers: "Some of our men have
already been fired from good jobs in defense industries which the efforts of this community had opened up." Elsewhere he urged patience
from the anxious working class:

> Our aircraft petitions are in such a delicate state just at this moment,
> that prudence dictates that I say no more as to our activities. Please be-
> lieve me when I say we are definitely on our way to complete victory in
> this field. If you know the character of our operations, you would with-
> hold all questions in this direction.

In other words: trust us to do the right thing.

Trust was in short supply. How short was driven home one clear
night in February 1942, as air raid sirens went off all over town in anticipation of a Japanese attack. Searchlights hatch-marked the sky, and
shells boomed from anti-aircraft cannons. Civil defense demanded
that the whole city observe a blackout, shutting off every light that
might be seen by an approaching Imperial pilot. Central Avenue went
dark, too—except for the neon sign of the Golden State Mutual Life

Insurance Company. Beavers and the firm were rightly proud of their landmark, an ornate glass clock that spilled colored light down upon the street. Perhaps they were forgetful, or perhaps arrogant. In any case the light stayed on as sirens wailed. Golden State's illumination poured down on civilian defense teams, assembled from patriotic members of the community, until common citizens did their duty and smashed the light to bits. Perhaps they did so with glee; without doubt, Central Avenue denizens could touch their leaders like never before.

About a month later, John Kinloch published a column titled "Advice Fo' Colored Folks." He was mocking all those who believed in such benevolent radiance.

Dear folks, have you ever felt that your life is a banana split without a banana? Do you think you are now living fully, with freedom and abundance? Are you worried? Do you suffer from an inferiority complex, defeatism, heartburn or housemaid's knee? Have you missed Love, Marriage, SUCCESS?

If so, Dr. Kinloch speaks to YOU! You will find new courage, vision, DETERMINATION in this fascinating article. Read twice and gargle with spirits of gin.

So the columnist begins. Adopting a Miss Lonelyhearts manner, Kinloch targets the public image of blacks, and does so by taking aim at Booker T. Washington, the most widely revered Negro of the early twentieth century. Educator and author, Washington was the first president of the prestigious Tuskegee Institute in Alabama. In the column Kinloch parodies a famous oration delivered to a white Atlanta audience in 1895, in which Washington gave notice that blacks should work hard and build their own institutions rather than attempt to reform white ones. This philosophy had been lucrative for the likes of Golden State Mutual Life insurance man George A. Beavers.

Washington: "No race can prosper till it learns that there is as much dignity in tilling a field as in writing a poem. It is at the bottom of life we must begin, and not at the top. Nor should we permit our grievances to overshadow our opportunities."

Kinloch: "The firm foundation upon which colored individuals may base their success in the American way of life can be found in the theory, philosophy and sociological outlook of Professor Adolphus Q. Yassuh of the Alabama State University for Darkies and Institution for the Insane."

Washington: "You can be sure in the future, as in the past, that you and your families will be surrounded by the most patient, faithful, law-abiding, and unresentful people that the world has seen. As we have proved our loyalty to you in the past, in nursing your children, watching by the sick bed of your mothers and fathers, and often following them with tear-dimmed eyes to their graves, so in the future, in our humble way, we shall stand by you with a devotion that no foreigner can approach, ready to lay down our lives, if need be, in defense of yours."

Kinloch: "[Blacks] may consider [themselves] fortunate to live in a land of such bountiful patronage, affection and condescension on the part of our dearly beloved White Friends, whose singular magnanimity has given us the glorious freedom for which we would bleed; yea, even die!"

At the end of "Advice Fo' Colored Folks," Kinloch's Professor Yassuh offers "TEN EASY RULES ON HOW TO WIN PECKERWOODS AND INFLUENCE OFAYS" ("peckerwood" was slang for redneck):

1. Stay in your Place.
    A. Don't mess with ofay chicks.
    B. Don't get caught.
2. Hate the damn Reds.
3. Stay in your Place.
4. Ask for a donation to our struggling institutions.
5. Make little jokes about your last crap game.
6. Stay in your Place.

7. Think that what's wrong with Negroes is their bad leadership and don't support it.
8. Laugh, kyahkyahkyah, at regular intervals.

In this early 1940s column we see Kinloch's compulsive desire to connect with those young enough to see the clay shoes of old leaders. Kinloch was flying high, his writing earning him lots of attention, though not always the kind he liked. Politicians were angry, elderly readers offended. For his agitated parents the problem wasn't just that he used language no Christian Scientist could countenance; it was that he never came home. They weren't shy about letting him know it, either. He wrote that although he felt "lower than the Times Square subway," he still couldn't get back to Harlem. Madame needed him too much.

He was the *Eagle*'s managing editor and circulation manager, one of its two reporters, and one of two linotype machine operators. In late 1942, all of Aunt Charlotta Bass's money had been swept "down the drain" in an effort to keep the *Eagle* from "actual dismantling." At the last minute the newspaper got an influx of money from an unnamed source that kept Bass at the helm.

Worse than the creditors, the paper had dangerous enemies. In 1942 FBI agents made ostentatious appearances downtown and on the Avenue, asking pointed questions about the paper and its staff. The F.B. Eyes, as one *Eagle* columnist called them, were scanning the paper for indications of disloyalty at a time when an angry blast at racism might be interpreted on the federal level as subversion. Political forces, Kinloch believed, were attempting to bring the *Eagle* down: "if there was ever dirty work at the crossroads, we had it here," he wrote in a letter. "They tried to run us out of business."

The FBI had started a file on Bass and the *Eagle*. It was widely rumored that Madame was taking money from the California Communist Party, and the government was aware of the talk. Investigators were concerned that criticism leveled in papers like the *Pittsburgh Courier* and the *Eagle* could damage the war machine, and Roosevelt even pondered shutting certain Negro papers down for the war's duration. He held back, however, and in 1942 the Eagle went on the offensive, blasting agents for asking questions about Bass. It chose the same moment to loudly endorse the Double V:

> Although no other citizen can destroy our common enemy with greater vigor, no other one can match the Negro's lack of enthusiasm concerning the conduct of the agencies which organize our resistance to fascism on a Jim Crow basis. . . . no other one is so frequently disgusted with the petty, home grown fascism which permeates the thinking of persons in supreme command of the war effort.

With a trimmed staff and secret benefactors, Madame and Kinloch kept the paper running. They'd go to movies on Sunday nights, but the rest of the week they were likely to be found at the office. Some *Eagle* employees were asked to do more for less pay; others received draft notices. One after another of Kinloch's friends was disappearing, and the outgoing, preternaturally composed young man was becoming frayed by events. He was dating women in Los Angeles but still nursing an attraction to Yvonne Shepherd, a New Yorker he'd known since they were both children. To Shepherd, Kinloch confided his feelings of watching chums offer farewells: "For the first time since I first came here nearly six years ago, I feel a dead weight of loneliness. I guess it's just a mood—but I'm not a moody guy."

He was growing as a writer, composing long stream-of-consciousness columns, parodies, and rants along with ghostwriting Madame's column and editorials. Cultivating a sharpness and voicing a militancy at the forefront of wartime culture, Kinloch exuded bonhomie and confidence, an unnervingly assured sense of himself. A sense perhaps of destiny, or at least of forward motion. Here was a writer who signed letters "John (The Great) Kinloch."

By 1942 the *Eagle*'s tiny staff was losing workers to better-paying jobs in defense plants. All around the Avenue employment opportunities began brightening, and by 1943 substantial numbers of blacks were working for the aircraft industry. Jobs were opening in part because of the War Manpower Commission and its local minority employment division based in Los Angeles. Aggressively investigating aircraft companies, the

WMC warned those practicing bias they would not be listed for job referrals. With defense contractors hiring the elderly and handicapped to meet production needs, in the end it was simple hunger for bodies that turned the tide. Starting in 1942 it became impossible to keep factory shifts running around the clock on white labor alone, and black men and women began to find substantial employment in defense.

In 1944, 40,772 blacks had been placed in jobs through the largest government job placement agency—the United States Employment Service. By that summer there were 7,186 blacks hired in the aviation industry, and across the board blacks constituted, on average, between 3 and 7 percent of the industry's workforce.

In "A Pome of Love and War and Death and Marv's Sweet Shop," Kinloch assumed the voice of an aviation worker:

> You are.
> A young snot.
> Who don't know.
> What the war's about.
> Or the peace.
> That was.
> For that matter.
> And life is.
> A blazing, bright.
> Thing.
> With a lot of parts.
> That don't.
> Add up. [. . .]
> Life is.
> A job.
> At North American.
> It is. The banging.
> And busting.
> Of big machines.
> That you can run.
> You like.

The noise.
And the being a part.
Of something so.
Damn big.
The machines—
The planes they make.
And the men.
Okies and Chinks.
Jigs and the.
Mexican cats.
With their draped britches.
Who gotta.
Run the machines.
That bang out.
The planes.

Here's the New Deal coalition, white and black and brown and yellow thriving on the shop floor, ethnicities dissolving into a totality far bigger than themselves. In the poem Kinloch describes sitting at Marv's Sweet Shop, a Central Avenue soda fountain he favored, and listening to a record of bluesman Jimmie Rushing singing "Mr. Five by Five." With his pals at Marv's, he's again lost in a looming clatter, in something far bigger than individual experience. At the North American Aviation plant and off-the-clock at Marv's, a generation understood there was a world to be won, and yet another world to be won after airplanes and bombs won the first, a world in which impatient kids who dropped nickels in the jukebox might run down Central smashing the signs of their parents' munificent brightness.

FROM "YOU AND ME AND WHERE
WE CAME FROM AND HOW":

. . . the white kids think.
They're better.
And the black kids think.
Their folks were jerks. . . .

The coalition Kinloch envisioned was coming together on the shop floor; laborers were needed, and aircraft companies grew desperate to keep up with government demands. Radio commercials advertised opportunities in the field: "It's fun to work in an aircraft factory." But it wasn't fun for everybody. Some of the plants that hired Negroes segregated them, setting up separate black dances and sports teams at the factories. At Douglas there were blackface minstrel shows put on for the benefit of white workers, many freshly arrived from the South. In a magazine published for Lockheed employees, an interview with a black worker was printed in what was meant to be Negro dialect— before he worked at Lockheed, the account said he had been "wukkin' on the railroad."

Making fun of black workers had its pleasures, perhaps, but they were nothing compared to the spectacles staged at lunch hour at one factory. According to historian Wilburn, at Douglas a boxing ring was set up in a commons area and black workers were compelled to fight one another. Having battled their way into the defense factories of Los Angeles, Negro workers were now induced to fight for the lunchtime amusement of white coworkers.

CHAPTER 4

Changelings

To you who in seven long, long years have led us toward our goal,
We lift our voices very loud, in praise to unfold.
We do not praise you as we would our Father on high,
But as a man who has accomplished much as days go swiftly by.
The faith we have in you is strong—As you stand up to fight,
Shoulder to shoulder against the wrongs, to get us our rights.
So we have now this day resolved—To get up and hustle,
And a million strong we will unite and fight with Clayton D. Russell.
—"A Song of Praise," Nell Saunders, sung to the tune of "Auld Lang Syne"

SOMETHING BIZARRE HAPPENED IN 1942. JOHN KINLOCH STARTED GOING to church.

He found his way to the People's Independent Church of Christ, a substantial edifice at 18th and Paloma streets. Kinloch's reasons for joining were earthly ones. He was hoping to make social connections for his newspaper work, and Independent had long been one of the most important churches in town, its membership boasting stars of black Hollywood, politicos, doctors, lawyers and teachers. When actress Hattie McDaniel won an Oscar for her performance in *Gone with the Wind*, she celebrated that night at Independent. Young athlete Jackie Robinson had his wedding there, and when Harlem's rising star the Reverend Adam Clayton Powell Jr. was in town, he preached there. Independent was at the center of the social swirl.

Independent's main attraction was its brash young pastor, Clayton Donovan Russell. In the early years of the war, Russell was the most sought-after man in the Negro city, his church offering entrée to the ambitious, finding work for the jobless. Like Kinloch, Russell was unrestrained and restless, looking for ways around the problem of compromised leadership. He projected self-confidence and an urban sophistication startling to many newcomers.

"The first time I visited his church, he was informing the black people they should vote, that it was the only resource they had," said Boyd Dickey, who became a deacon at Independent. "I had been in church all my life and that was the first time I ever heard a minister telling his congregation how to do these things. Coming from Texas, out in the country, we came up under segregation. He made me feel great."

No fulminator, Russell was a polished public speaker who drew from events in the news to make his point. But his stature in the pulpit was only one source of Russell's strength; the figure he cut in the street was equally essential to his reputation. Round-faced with cherubic features, possessing a mischievous smile, it was impossible to imagine him sweating away on a Northrop swing shift. He was sharp and soberly dressed, a man who liked his hats and expected those around him to dress well too; Russell chastised boys who wore brown shoes with blue suits. Every hair was in place, his image one of neatness and gravity, which was surprising given how quick he was on his feet and how many decisions he made on the fly.

"My first memory of him was when I was a little guy," said family friend Leslie Bellamy.

> I was an altar boy, and so we would be outside waiting for him to arrive, and he'd come swinging around the corner in his Packard—he always

had Packards back then—and he'd jump out of the car as it would be rolling down the street, the deacons would be chasing the car and he'd walk up and put his arms out and they'd throw his robe on. "Yeah," I said, "I want to be like that when I grow up!"

Some pastors saw themselves as protectors of church tradition; Russell saw himself as a force for change and had little time for iterations of habit. He attacked as "pulpit cowards" those who did not see their calling as a commitment to improve conditions. He switched directions as fast as he hopped off his Packard; he was a master of change who embraced the methods of the moment. He was a modernist. Russell sponsored a Duke Ellington performance in 1941, earning the scorn of elders who felt the Spirit and swing did not belong together. When a local appearance by poet Langston Hughes was picketed by white Christian revivalist Aimee Semple McPherson—she'd objected to his incendiary poem "Goodbye Christ," calling Hughes a "black devil"—Russell built a sermon around his measured reading of the work. Like Kinloch, he had his own weekly radio show and was one of the first Negro ministers to grasp the medium's potential. A special concern were Central Avenue youth, for whom he had set up welfare programs, employment and housing. "Several young people have been sent through college on grants from the church and really a very fine work is going forward," noted Kinloch in a letter.

Russell was a natural charmer whose light shone from an early age. Born in Los Angeles in 1910, he was raised in Boyle Heights, a neighborhood that was a mixture of Jews, Negroes and Japanese. This background early on gave him ease in talking with people of other races. At the age of 7 he was labeled the "Boy Preacher," standing on a wooden box and orating at Independent. He was a regular at the 28th street YMCA, another spot where social connections were made, boxing and playing basketball with the young Ralph Bunche. "As a youth he was a very likeable chap but you would not have anticipated his becoming a prominent leader," said Augustus Hawkins, a state assemblyman who went on to become the first black congressman from California. "He was great for telling little stories and jokes and whatnot. Eventually he became a minister, but I would have thought he would have become an entertainer."

Russell attended Jefferson High and spent one year at the University of Southern California and another at Chapman College, a church-oriented private university. Then he worked as an insurance salesman at Golden State. In 1934 an organization of independent and community churches made him a field evangelist; for the next 13 months he traveled throughout the Midwest, before he took a job preaching at a small church in Detroit.

A family story has it that one night in 1935, Russell saw a long-deceased grandmother in a dream. She shook his bed and said, "It's time to go home." That same night, the pastor at the Independent Church had taken ill; soon Russell would leave Detroit to assume responsibilities for the church he'd grown up in.

Independent was already an important fundament before Russell came home. Its first pastor, Napoleon P. Greggs, and a group of churchmen had split with the oldest Negro church in town, the First African Methodist Episcopal, in 1915. "The people were motivated by a spirit of democracy and felt that something must be done to bring a Christian democracy into the church government," explained a founding Independent Church document. Over the next several decades Greggs built Independent into a community institution with more than 3,000 active members. Now he was dead and a native son had come home to replace him. It was a huge responsibility for a 24-year-old. "It is believed that Reverend Russell is the youngest colored minister in the country ever to be placed at the head of such a large and popular church," reported the *Eagle*.

He returned to a late-1930s Central Avenue marinated in corruption, with a leadership in the pay of a criminal bunch in city hall fronted by Mayor Frank Shaw. The Shaw machine reached deep into the Avenue, bribing churchmen, influencing the election of NAACP leadership, doling out public jobs to those who proved their loyalty. It was Russell's good fortune to come home just as a reform movement was gathering momentum to turn the scoundrels out—a recall ousted Frank Shaw and Fletcher Bowron, a conservative Republican, was the reform movement's choice to clean up city hall. Russell's critique of entrenched black leadership caught the spirit of the moment and spoke to a younger generation frozen out by a spoils system that punished the unaffiliated. He hadn't come up through established ranks, which made him suspect to the old guard. That was fine with him: launching a critique of local clergy, Russell blasted unnamed figures, calling for rank-and-file Negroes to seize power for themselves. "Negroes should revolt against any religious leaders, including myself, who do not take a definite stand against all conditions that are destructive to the values of life," he sermonized in 1938. He demanded a new activism, one that was beholden only to one's conscience: "We should openly rebel against those of us who stand in the pulpit before you and are unable to hit unseemly conditions because they are cramped and bottled up by the pay-off route."

He had married well, wedding Gwendolyn Diggs, the beautiful daughter of a prominent doctor, in 1938. He had social status inside the city, and the force of his oratory—his style was clear, unadorned with metaphor—gave Russell a prominence far beyond Los Angeles. At a 1939 meeting of the National Council of Community Churches in New York City, Mary McLeod Bethune, an educator and adviser to President Franklin D. Roosevelt, addressed the delegates. Unaware that Russell was in the room, she described a recent visit to Los Angeles that included a stop at Independent. "I was thrilled at this young dynamo whose Christian influence is so far-reaching," said Bethune.

The dynamo made a considerable racket. When he returned that same year from a trip to Europe, he suggested to reporters that Adolf Hitler treated Negroes better than did Uncle Sam. The statement stirred up considerable criticism and debate on the street. So did recurrent rumors of his lavish spending, rumors that would follow him for years to come. "He did a good job, except he had a devil of a time trying to keep his books straight," remembered Augustus Hawkins. As disquiet mounted between Russell and the church board of directors, he made a startling announcement in October 1939, one sure to inspire consternation and fill the pews that Sunday. In his weekly church notice, Russell announced the subject of his next talk: "My Resignation

Sermon." Could that be? Supporters were heartsick, and a small set of enemies was likely in high anticipation.

A record crowd filled the huge church that Sunday. Even the choir loft overflowed with the curious. "[You] thought I was going to quit," he teased the congregation. "I am not a quitter!"

"My resignation is a spiritual resignation to the will of God, not to please you or me, but God," he roared. He chided his critics, taking the steam out of their whispering campaign by making the gossip about his finances seem petty and pompous. He took credit for bringing stability to the church after Greggs died and for raising considerable money for church programs. "Everything went fine until we got on our feet and got a few hundred dollars in the treasury," he rebuked, "then everybody wanted to be a big shot, to run the church and the pastor." Only God could run him out, Russell said, and this was not his time to pass from the public's gaze. At the end of the service, with Independent's choir singing "Take Another Stand," Russell stalked the church's aisles, up and down and up again, a lion victorious. This was his house, his time. Russell didn't reason with his enemies, didn't ultimately dispute them—he just mocked and belittled them, daring them to try it again, rolling right over them. Those enemies would remain, but his power was greater than ever. A trickster came of age that day.

Here was a box office star, which was fitting as Independent was something of a pop culture church. Back when Russell was a teenage pastor, Greggs had already defined Independent as open to the world around it, setting up a screen in the pulpit and showing movies on Sunday nights to the congregation. While some churches frowned on dancing, Greggs believed young people were *supposed* to dance, and sponsored musicals, operettas and plays. Independent was a natural fit for the Avenue's growing film community, and they made up a key constituency for Russell.

He learned the Hollywood language of voracious optimism. Part of the community church movement, Independent was nondenominational, and Russell's sermons were steeped in nonsectarianism, tinted with the anything-is-possible individualism of the New Thought movement. New Thought disciple Ernest Holmes was a Los Angeles–based metaphysician who in 1927 wrote the popular *The Science of Mind*, a book that Russell referred to often throughout his life. The "science of mind" philosophy celebrated the power of a driven individual to triumph over his surroundings; Russell's recasting of it melded Booker T. Washington–style uplift with Southern California spiritual yearning. New Thought's message that mind power could control one's destiny—that if you believed in yourself you were going to win—was well suited for a town full of newcomers remaking themselves. "God is a living spirit," believed Russell, "a universal spirit that is able to meet all occasions and dwells in all of us. If you have a problem, release it, come to the church, come see me. If I can't help you, I will put you in touch with those who can." Here was the minister as fixer, the boy preacher grown up to become a mogul.

His strategy was to keep moving. In the spring of 1942 Russell organized meetings with a small group of liberals, unionists, and Communist Party activists, discussing a range of civil rights issues heating up with the war. They were looking for a way to build on the Fair Employment Practices Commission mandate, a way to hold local industries accountable for their discrimination. More meaningful, perhaps, than who attended the meetings was who was absent: the Eastside Chamber of Commerce figures, the Urban League perennials, the mainstream church leaders who had achieved little success in bringing Negroes into the defense industry. Russell and the others were acutely aware of the early failure of the FEPC to increase black employment and had watched as tactics like leaving lists of available workers with hostile employers had amounted to nil. Russell was assembling a team that was tuned to the frequencies of the Double V; aspiring to will out of thin air a mass movement like the one that Randolph had prophesied. He was looking for a way to use power, not appeals to conscience, to leverage change.

By mid-1942 the shortcomings of the FEPC were apparent: the panel set up to administer the presidential order couldn't penalize those who didn't hire Negroes and couldn't take violators to court. They couldn't even cancel a contract of those that discriminated. What they could do was hold public hearings and try to shame wrongdoers into compliance. In the breach between good intentions and results, Russell pulled together a crew. They called themselves the Negro Victory Committee. In April they held their first public meeting, a mass rally staged at Independent, with speakers including state assemblyman Augustus Hawkins and a surprise appearance by Harry Bridges, leader of the longshoremen's union and West Coast director for the Congress of Industrial Organizations. Russell's keynote was a nuanced history lesson aimed at disaffected Negro listeners, all those who wondered how much of a stake they had in the war. He invoked figures from black history, and drew a line from slave rebellion leader Denmark Vesey to Dorie Miller, the Negro hero of Pearl Harbor, a Navy cook who manned a machine gun during the attack. Russell asserted that Negroes had an inordinate investment in this war, that their history of oppression had bestowed on them a special burden and, potentially, a special reward.

"This is the essence of today's warfare, whether freedom shall be the goal of mankind or whether slavery shall be the law," he said. Who better to understand what is being fought for than those who had borne the burden of slavery? "If America falls, the Italian-German-Japanese combination will become the rulers of the world with Hitler as the master. Democracy will die and the same slavery that now holds the conquered of Europe will be that fate of America and we Negroes in America will face racial extinction. It will be as if the KKK had taken over the White House and Congress, and lynching, instead of being a blot on the nation's honor, will be the lawful practice of the land as is the persecution of the Jews in Germany." The Democratic Party, under the influence of its Southern wing, was a problematic messenger of democratic values, as were labor unions, many of which prohibited Negro membership. It was Negroes themselves—maybe even Negroes alone—who possessed sufficient moral integrity, Russell was saying, and thus it was Negroes who could best articulate a critique of racial supremacy.

The NAACP deliberated over the smallest matters; the Negro Victory Committee moved quickly and depended on surprise. On his

Sunday radio broadcast one July morning in 1942, Russell mysteriously urged listeners to attend an emergency meeting that night at the church. There he criticized the lack of defense jobs available for black women and the lack of training that was the common excuse for filling jobs with white female workers. At his rally Russell referred to a currently circulating rumor, something said at the downtown office of the federal employment agency that filled job orders. The hearsay was that an official said that black women didn't want to work in defense factories and were better suited anyway to be maids and cooks. With less than a day's planning, Russell announced a march on the downtown office the following morning, calling on protestors to turn the agency into a "little Africa."

"This is our war. We've got to win it," one woman said. "We cannot win it in the kitchen. We must win it on the assembly line."

The next morning a snaking line of hundreds of Negro women queued up to request employment forms. In case anybody thought these women wanted to be cooks and maids, Russell handed over pages of testimony given the night before, including the words of one woman whose husband was killed at Pearl Harbor—and who was then turned down for work by several aircraft companies. Representatives—including John Kinloch—met with federal officials, and Washington responded by sending a team to investigate Victory Committee claims and then affirmed a policy of nondiscrimination.

"I remember a woman who was a deaconess at Independent, an old woman," said Welford Wilson, an insider at the employment agency who was also working with Russell. "She heard the call on the radio same as everyone else and came down to the employment service. I saw her there and she said, 'I can't do anything but pray, and I'm praying.'"

Less than a month later, the Negro Victory Committee turned the spotlight on the Board of Education, interrupting their proceedings to demand training centers for Negro women. "We haven't come here for explanations or promises," Russell told the board. "We simply want to know: are there going to be beginners' classes in defense training on the Eastside or aren't there?"

"You people have come up here for a show," a board member shot back. "We're interested in no show," said Russell. "We're interested in a showdown. Hitler's putting on the show!"

One week later, the Board of Education announced machine shop, welding and riveting classes would be offered at Jefferson and Manual Arts high schools, just off the Avenue. L.A.'s Negro Rosie the Riveters had become a workplace force. "We [got] them out of the domestic fields into certain low-skilled, and then more skilled jobs," remembered Augustus Hawkins. "That was a great opening. To get a black woman in as a welder in a shipyard was a tremendous battle. Seems simple now, but looking back on it that was a great struggle."

Creating job opportunities wasn't the biggest achievement. More meaningful was the shock of black bodies marching en masse. The March on Washington Movement had raised the specter of throngs of Negro marchers raising their voices in the streets, and that was what it took to compel the government to take action. Russell honed Randolph's rhetoric and gave it a Central Avenue locution—they weren't marching *against* anything, they were just marching to apply for a job. *You don't think we want to work in the shipyards; we're here to straighten you out.* Taboos were being broken, and onetime domestic workers and cooks were sensing a new political power. A long line of angry women was discovering new latitude.

That March FBI agents began interviewing Avenue sources about Russell.

His instincts led him to amass power, to believe that it was most of all a show of force that convinced people. He was a master of the ambush, not nearly so interested in defusing a situation as he was in catching unawares those who had underestimated him and then letting the moment play out in full. A group of ministers once came to his door to share their criticism of his methods. In a 1975 interview, Russell recalled what he said to them: "I consider it a sin to stand up in the pulpit and preach to hungry people and not help them get a job or to get some food. I said, you don't hesitate to collect money to pay your salaries and pay your debts and if that is not a sin, then what is a sin? I said, you go your way and I'll go mine."

Working with Russell were three aides-de-camp who formed Negro Victory Committee strategy. Walter Williams was a plainspoken welder who was building a movement among the shipyard workers, an up-and-comer whom national CIO officials were watching. Welford Wilson was a champion student orator from Harlem who, once he came west after graduating from City College, worked a variety of government jobs that gave him connections in city hall and Sacramento. Lou Rosser was the mensch, a gay Communist, one-time actor and street-corner rabble-rouser well known on the Avenue. They called themselves "the Rustlers," and together Williams, Wilson and Rosser had a varied set of tools at their disposal—union clout and organizing know-how, knowledge of local and federal bureaucracy, a deep understanding of the community. Through his Sunday morning radio show *The Visitor*, Russell could get the word out in an instant, and Independent, now the most popular Negro church in the city, was able to direct bodies to where they were needed.

Late in 1942, Russell turned his attention to the hiring practices of the private company running the public streetcar system. The Los Angeles Railway Company—LARY, as it was called—refused to promote Negroes to the rank of motorman or conductor, restricting them mostly to janitorial work. The discrimination was bad enough, but the symbolism made it worse. That the bias was happening out in the open, on the streets of L.A., made for a very public humiliation. Blacks couldn't be conductors, but on the sides of the cars were ads featuring Aunt Jemimah and watermelon-eating darkies. Streetcars were essential to the war effort, a way for workers to get to the shipyards and factories. Crisscrossing the city, public places where black and white passengers were treated as equals, the cars were vehicles of social unity turned into symbols of discrimination, and as such they cut deep into the psyche.

The kicker was that L.A. was desperate for more conductors and motormen. Military service and job opportunities had depleted their ranks to the point at which cars were being taken out of service for want of skilled workers to drive them. By late 1942, hundreds of cars were laid up in transit barns, and tens of thousands of war workers were showing up late for their jobs. On Central Avenue, eight cars were mothballed because the company would not hire blacks.

The skipper of a streetcar was no grinning entertainer, he was a calm, uniformed navigator of the city, an ambassador of social mobility, and the rail company balked at electing a Negro to the role. Rail officials predicted white mob violence if blacks were upgraded to skilled positions. At a meeting with Russell, a company spokesman said white workers would never go for integration. "I'll have to build separate toilets at the end of the lines. I'm not going to have white women going to the same toilets as colored men."

"Well," Russell replied, "urination is your problem; transportation is ours." According to a family member, Russell also warned officials he was speaking to some blacks who were mad enough to torch buildings where out-of-circulation cars idled. For all the meetings and threats, integrating the streetcar force seemed a long way off at the end of 1942.

That December a gala entertainment was set for Pershing Square, the park in the heart of downtown. Months before, a "Victory House" had been constructed in the square, a staging area for rallies to buy war bonds. Now, during the holiday season, Victory House had been handed over to Negro organizers, and a production featuring the cream of Avenue show business had been assembled for the delectation of white Angelenos. "This program will present to the city of Los Angeles the full unity of the Negro people aligned behind the government's Win the War Program," announced Russell's aide Welford Wilson. Doubtless the unity message would be heard by many who might not otherwise listen, what with the likes of Mantan Moreland—Hollywood's favorite pop-eyed butler—on hand, along with singer Herb "Flamingo" Jeffries.

Film and recording star Ethel Waters sang the National Anthem, and revered bandleader Noble Sissle performed for the assembled 1,500. Actors Nicodemus and Clarence Muse entertained. Finally it was time for the featured speaker, Reverend Russell, to take the microphone. Pershing Square was as close to a town commons as Los Angeles had, and the young black leader had scored a lofty assignment, addressing the assembled townspeople. According to the convention of such events, he would voice the expected patriotism, seasoned with pitches to buy bonds. Such, at least, was the belief of Victory House's keepers.

But Russell, knowing the possibilities of the moment, had other plans. "You have heard about Dorie Miller," he began as he spoke to the assembly.

> You have seen how we feel about this war against barbarians and those who would re-enslave us all over the world. But I tell you, while we fight Hitler abroad we had better watch Hitlerism at home, lest we fight in vain.
>
> Thousands of Los Angeles war workers, white and black, are jammed into inadequate transportation facilities every day—300 cars are off the lines of the Los Angeles Railway Company because of a so-called "manpower shortage"—yet that firm refuses to employ as conductors and motormen loyal, patriotic Negroes. I think that is Hitlerism at home. What do you think?

According to the *Eagle*, the response was "a great, sweeping ovation from the Aryan lips of literally hundreds of Angelenos."

> I submit that if Dorie Miller, a Negro who had never before touched firearms, could grab a machine gun in the height of battle and down four Jap planes, the contention that Negroes cannot serve their country as motormen and conductors of the Los Angeles Railway Company is pure malarkey!

They raised $62,000 in war bonds on New Year's Eve, 1942. And a group of white Angelenos who thought they'd be crooned and tap-danced at by black folks got a lecture in patriotism many were unlikely to forget. Russell's sucker punch had fast results. Within weeks, the railroad company agreed to open all positions to black men and women.

All in all, it was a fine season for tricksters. Not every one of them had access to a microphone; in 1943, some were flocking to the Avenue, revealing themselves wherever people looked the other way. Many announced their presence with a sparkle and noise that instantly distinguished them from the group. Rhythm and blues music turned their movements into choppy choreography, pomades and konked hair turned their heads into reflective ornament, hip argot replaced the shared tongue of parents. They threw light back onto the street, deflected questions, and wore the official uniform of the 1940s trickster: the zoot suit.

This was not Duke Ellington's merry suit of clothes. It might even have been out loud for years, but by 1943 something about it had muted. Its colors were tuned down; some of the garish tailoring had been excised: it started looking less like fun and even more like a provocation, no longer an invitation to a groovy scene but a door slammed shut on the mainstream. No longer celebrating pop excess, its new form placed limits on what was shared. This outfit marked lines. To be a young Latino representing on a downtown corner, or to be black and wearing it on the Avenue, was to draw attention and, after that, contempt. Look at me: hate me now. Black Los Angeles was flooded with newcomers in the summer of 1943, some 3,500 to 5,000 arriving per month by one estimate. White Southerners, too, flocked to the city, bringing Southern codes of behavior with them, including the Dixie practice of acting out social hierarchy in the open, on the street. The sidewalk was where social order was policed, and in this shifting context it began to contest the received wisdom of social order and threw it into a strange new dimension.

Some resisted its effects. Seventeen young Mexican American gang members had been convicted in the wake of the murder of another gang member in 1942. In the aftermath of what was called the "Sleepy Lagoon Murder," newspapers whipped up convulsions of rage and focused on the handy image of the zoot suit. Zoot suiters were called "sinister clowns" and "baby hoodlums" in the press; in the spring of 1943, the principal of Dorsey High, a formerly all-white school now enrolling blacks and Latinos, banned the outfit. "I don't want any of that low zoot suit stuff from the eastside on this campus," G. M. Montgomery told a student assembly. Judgment was promptly hurled back at him: John Kinloch and the Junior Council of the NAACP formed a delegation of students and pledged "unity with Mexican youth in fighting waves of police brutality." They charged that the principal's edict was "an open attempt to attack Negro students of the school."

Some purported originators of the zoot suit: a busboy from Gainesville, Georgia; a Jewish tailor from Chicago; Cab Calloway; Clark Gable; the Mexican film star Tin Tan; the Duke of Windsor; scat singer Leo Watson. Who invented it, nobody really knew. But by 1943, *ownership* of the zoot suit was all but settled. It belonged to a dark-skinned subculture whose identity stretched across racial lines.

John Kinloch, 1942:

WHY ARE WE NEGROES INTERESTED IN WHAT HAPPENS TO OUR MEXICAN NEIGHBORS?
Well, we've had a lot of experience along the same lines. We've felt the whiplash of oppression and we know how and where it stings. Besides, it would be us if the Mexicans weren't more convenient.

Negro empathy flourished in June 1943, during what came to be called the zoot suit riots. Over several days and nights servicemen left nearby bases and roamed downtown and East L.A., beating an assortment of targets. The attacks were cheered on by white bystanders under the detached gaze of the police department. Though the riots were reported in the press as a series of brawls between Mexican Americans and whites, at bottom they were attacks on young men of color. Many of those attacked weren't even wearing the costume that the media alleged was the instigator of the melee. The title of an eyewitness piece, written by novelist Chester Himes for the NAACP magazine the *Crisis*, expressed the feelings of many Negroes: "Zoot Riots Are Race Riots." "The South has won Los Angeles," wrote Himes.

The worst injured during the riot was a black man, 23-year-old Lewis Jackson. Jackson was fresh to the city, having arrived from Louisiana four months before to take a job in the shipyards. While walking to his home, he encountered a mob of more than 100 servicemen on the edge of downtown. The throng held him down and one of them pulled a knife and gouged out his eye. Jackson wasn't wearing a zoot suit.

Radio stations provided rioters with daily reports on where brawls would happen that night. Monday, June 7, word was out that mobs of soldiers, sailors and marines were heading for the intersection of 12th Street and Central Avenue. After days of focusing on Mexican Los Angeles, the attackers were preparing to cross into the Negro city.

Lawyer and journalist Loren Miller was working at the *Los Angeles Sentinel* in 1943, when he heard that blacks and Mexican Americans were teaming up along 12th Street. He called the mayor's office, warning Mayor Bowron of what was coming. "We were going to raise hell and see that anybody that came over in the Negro community looking around for any trouble was going to find plenty of trouble," he said. "[I] told them that if anybody came up to 12th and Central somebody was going to get killed and I didn't think it was going to be Negroes."

At least 500 Latino gang members came into the neighborhood, including members of the Jug Town, Adams, Clanton, Watts, 38th Street, and Jardine crews. The battle of 12th Street was on. Almena Lomax was an editor of the black paper the *Tribune*; she heard the call and headed for 12th Street, digging in at a soda fountain near the intersection. "The little Mexican girls were ferocious. They had much more, they were much more tigers than Negro girls and they went with a lot of Mexican and Negro boys. They were all there sitting in the soda parlor, waiting."

Participant Rudy Leyvas described the scene later to a *Los Angeles Times* reporter:

All day we were just transferring guys from the neighborhoods into the city. The black people loaned us their cars to use. We used to call them "neighborhoods," not gangs.

Toward evening, we started hiding in alleys. Then we sent about twenty guys right out into the middle of the street as decoys. Then they came up in U.S. Navy trucks. There were many civilians, too. There was at least as many of them as us. They started coming after the decoys, then we came out. They were surprised. It was the first time anybody was organized to fight back. Lots of people were hurt on both sides. I was about 15 at the time, and I had a baseball bat. I came out ok, but I know I hurt a lot of people.

Servicemen were mounting a retreat when Mexican Americans tried a rear-guard action to cut them off before they could get out of the neighborhood. At that moment busloads of police arrived, and only the dark-skinned combatants were rounded up and taken to the station.

After the battle of 12th Street, military officials took actions to stop the rampage, declaring all Los Angeles off-limits and confining servicemen to their bases. Perhaps theirs was a delayed reaction to days of violence. Or perhaps 12th Street, where black and brown working-class kids came together at malt stands and in the alleys to defend common interests, sent a message authorities couldn't afford to ignore. Suddenly, putting people in their place became a little harder than it had been a week before.

"The recent rioting," Russell said afterward, "has welded us ever closer to the Mexican community of this city." The surprise, he said, was not that there were so many zoot suit gangs but that there were so few, given the damaging social conditions shared by many Mexican American youths. In spirit he was the black leader closest to the zoot suiters. He lived in the moment and fed off the mood of the streets. He fought back. "Most churches were saying you'll get your reward when you die. He said get it now," recalled E. Frederic Anderson, who grew up a member of Russell's church. Russell did not look down on those who stayed up all night plying one trade or another. "He had a jazz musician playing the organ," said Anderson. "He told the guy once he got through playing at the Tail of the Cock at 2 in the morning, 'go get four hours of sleep in and then come play at church services.' You could tell it too, because he was really swinging."

In the pulpit there was a coolness to Russell's manner; not for him the foot-stomping, chest-pounding fury of some services. His sermons were conversational; his delight in misdirection kept people guessing. People *were* guessing, for Russell had a way of saying contradictory

things and offering bland reassurances that left in doubt what ultimately was on his mind. Like the zoot suit, he was very loud and very
quiet at the same time. He too was disconnected, revealing different
guises to different people. Some on the right called him a Communist,
while some on the left called him a government informer. He was a
lady's man; he was secretly into men. As the decade progressed, Russell's image would take on the shape of a Möbius strip, every surface or
quality smoothly disappearing into its opposite.

Attorney Walter Gordon remembers his friend Russell driving past
his office in his Packard. "We'd be standing out in front of the office,
and he had his car laden down with beautiful women." Abie Robinson,
a journalist on the Avenue, knew about Russell and his car. "The rumor was that some of the women in the church had all got together and
had the inside all done in velvet," said Robinson. "He knew how to
make himself popular with the ladies."

Except that others say he wasn't quite the romancer he appeared.
Hadda Brooks was a singer and piano player from Russell's Boyle
Heights neighborhood; she was a young member of the Independent
Church. "All the girls wanted him, but the hell of it is he was, the word
is 'open' now—he was on the gay side," Brooks said. "He didn't flaunt
it. I don't think very many people knew."

Clarence H. Cobbs was a flamboyant preacher from Chicago whose
First Church of Divine Guidance was recently described in Wallace D.
Best's religious history of black Chicago as "a major stop on the gay
nightlife circuit of the 1930s and 40s." Cobbs and the Reverend Adam
Clayton Powell Jr. would come to Los Angeles and stay at the Dunbar
Hotel; Russell would join them for a night in, recalled Russell's cousin
Clifton Russell. "When Clayton Powell and Reverend Cobbs from
Chicago would come to town, they would have the entire second floor
of the Dunbar. There was a woman officer, I've forgotten her name,
who saw to it that no one interrupted their little frolicking." (Biogra-
phies of Powell give no indication of homosexuality; in fact, he was a
known critic of homosexuality.)

In years to come, as Russell's enemies grew, those who opposed him
sought to use his appetites against him. "They even planted nude

white women on his lawn to try to entice him," recalled family friend
Vivian Hodge. "He wouldn't let them in," said his son, Clayton Russell
Jr. "He'd get one of my mother's dresses, and I remember one time he
dropped it out of my window to her!" Russell Jr. even believes there
were efforts to kill his father and remembers driving on a mountain
road when the wheels came off the family car. A later examination
showed they had been tampered with, said the son.

At the beginning of 1942, Russell began raising money for a chain
of black-owned, cooperatively run groceries that he called Victory
Markets. He explained that he could have easily opened markets
with a few investors but wanted to make working people the share-
holders. "It is time for the group to own, for the group to control," he
declared. "The Negro must become a vital economic factor during
this world conflict or a nonentity when it is over!" he said. This was
vintage Russell—grasping that right now, when blacks had jobs and
money, was the time to build something. He knew a downturn was
coming when the war ended and the factories and shipyards slowed
down.

Shares were sold to community members. The markets provided
fresh produce so Negroes could do their shopping in the neighborhood. There was a nascent idea here of building a coalition of consumers, of teaching consumers to be active in the economic process
through ownership. Russell had picked up these ideas in the late
1930s, when he toured Europe and was impressed by the cooperative
movement flourishing there. A year after starting, the markets had 17
employees, grossed $173,000 and had seen $26,000 in profits. By the
end of the war there were five Victory Markets. Decades before the
Black Panthers and other activists sought to build black-owned institutions in the ghetto, Russell assembled a chain of markets that show-
cased black spending power.

He sailed above most folks' heads. In three years, Russell had won
important victories in defense training and reformed hiring practices
in several sectors of the local economy. He had held high-profile
protests against police brutality, opened markets, given shelter to Navy
Seabees protesting mistreatment at a nearby base, and more. His star

was in ascendance and some were urging him to run for office. He would never sail beyond this moment.

In 1944, he left town for several months on a trip east. He stayed with the Powells in New York and spent some time in Chicago and Washington, D.C. After he returned, his profile diminished throughout the rest of the decade.

"He was an honorable guy," said Walter Gordon. "He became debauched. That is, so many excesses kind of got to him. He was well received; he was loved by people. He wasn't a mean man at all. He was probably the most flamboyant minister of all, but he did a lot of good social work."

"Clayton Russell marched in the 40s and got people jobs here when it was hard, when there was no television, no government behind you," said Vivian Hodge. "Martin Luther King had media coverage, he had government behind him. Clayton Russell did all that and he did it on his own. He never got the credit he should have. I don't know why. . . . maybe it was his private life. That got involved. People look at your private life and see 'oh, you're doing this.' But that has nothing to do with the good that you're doing—it's *your* life."

Gay, straight; insider, outsider; radical, informant; icon, debauchee. Everybody knew Clayton Russell. It was a fine season for tricksters.

CHAPTER 5

Iron and Steel

A DASHING YOUNG MAN FROM A GOOD EAST COAST FAMILY, GERALD Edwards came to Los Angeles and found steady work in the shipyards of San Pedro. His larger ambitions were artistic, and he spent mornings reading poetry with his wife before heading to work.

The shipyards were rough places for Negro laborers like the 19-year-old Edwards. The ships themselves were huge, but workers were often squeezed against each other in tiny work compartments. Blacks, whites, men and women came from all over the country to labor in the yards and they brought their resentments with them. The mood was twitchy; the yards were full of white Southerners, and some blacks showed up for work packing pistols.

One November morning in 1944, Edwards and his wife read William Cullen Bryant's poem "Thanatopsis," and then he went to the yard. At the end of the workday as he left the vast complex owned by the California Shipbuilding Company (Calship for short), he had an argument with a watchman, perhaps over his leaving through the wrong gate. The white guard barked an order at Edwards, then fired a warning shot into the ground in front of him. The next shot was aimed a few feet higher. A jury acquitted the guard of manslaughter.

What happened in broad daylight at the Calship gate? It sounds like a noir plot and in a way it was, the gripping story of a stranger stumbling head-on into his fate. (William Cullen Bryant: "And what if thou withdraw/In silence from the living and no friend/Take note of thy departure?") In the shipyard enclaves thousands of newcomers were thrown together in a vortex of pressure and noise; tense standoffs were commonplace. Isolated by government security measures and numerous barricades, the yards squelched news of confrontations before it reached outsiders' ears.

In a flickering a whole factory town had been assembled on the sandy swamp of Terminal Island, transforming a hinterland into a little city with more than 90,000 workers at the wartime peak. Southern California was the main producer of "liberty ships," as cargo vessels were called. Terminal Island, lying just off the coast of San Pedro and about 18 miles south of the Dunbar Hotel, was the focal point of liberty ship construction. The Big Three companies—Western Pipe and Steel, Consolidated Steel's shipbuilding division, and Calship—were all based there. Orbiting around them were numerous smaller yards and floating dry docks that repaired ships in the harbor.

In the air were barrage balloons and fighter planes scouting for enemy aircraft. On the ground were thousands of newcomers struggling to understand their tasks and yard managers grappling with ever-changing government orders. Explosions and fires were routine occupational hazards; as a shipyard rhyme told by Negroes put it, "This is iron, this is steel, and if they don't get you, the flying debris will." Add in the racial tensions brought from the outside world and it was no wonder government officials began watching the yards closely as potential riot zones. After a wave of assaults on Negro workers in 1942, blacks began entering and exiting in pairs. White crew leaders regularly refused to upgrade job status for blacks and filed bogus charges of loafing to get them fired. Negroes were ordered to pull swing shifts and threatened with firing if they declined. John N. Grimes, a black employee at Terminal Island, described the feelings of many in a complaint he filed with the government:

Ever since I have been at the dry docks I have tried to satisfy everyone that I worked for but it seems as if I have failed miserable. This is due largely to the fact that supervision is corrupted with prejudice, discrimination, ignorance and stupidity, so much so until justice is a thing of the past. This yard is full of self made rules and each supervisor runs his gang with his own rules. After watching them in operation the only description of them is, the blind trying to lead the blind.

Disquieting incidents piled up. A pair of whites jumped a Negro Calship worker; he was jailed for fighting. At Consolidated Shipbuilding, a Klan membership form was posted in a washroom. Also at Consolidated, a black chipper named Osborne Moore was talking to a coworker when his white lead man cursed him out and told him to shut up. Moore objected to his tone, and the white then angrily called him "nigger" while advancing on him. Moore pulled a knife and slashed at the lead man, and a mob picked up two-by-fours and chased him through the yard, the pursuit ending with Moore literally running into a white police officer. He was arrested for assault. Witnesses raised the possibility that Moore might have been killed, and that a race riot would have resulted.

The FBI quietly monitored the shipyards with concern, as classified memos indicated: "It was reported in April 1943 that racial trouble appeared imminent in several industrial plants in the Los Angeles area, particularly in the California Shipbuilding Corporation, the Western Pipe and Steel Company and the Bethlehem Shipbuilding Corporations. Negroes at the first two named plants were reportedly showing up for work with guns and liquor concealed in their clothing. It has been stated that a part of the difficulty appears to be that the Negroes insisted that they be allowed to join regular unions rather than auxiliary unions." This is iron, this is steel, and if they don't get you the plant security will.

You could write a letter about the injustice, you could even pull a knife on the lead man who was calling you "nigger." But how to stick a shiv into a whole union? What most insulted black dignity was the bigotry inherent in shipyard hiring, which was largely controlled by a single union, the International Brotherhood of Boilermakers, Iron Shipbuilders and Helpers. Years before the attack on Pearl Harbor the Boilermakers had banned Negroes from its regular membership. When war broke out and derrick towers and barbed wire went up on Terminal Island, the discrimination became institutionalized in an agreement drawn up among labor, manufacturing and government officials eager to expedite ship construction. The pact gave authority over hiring, firing and promotion in West Coast shipyards largely to the Boilermakers and gave them official sanction to establish an "auxiliary system" of membership exclusively applicable to Negroes. With manpower desperately needed and blacks streaming into L.A., Negro workers could not be kept out altogether without damaging the war effort, so under the watch of business agent E. V. Blackwell, the union conspired to shunt them into unequal Jim Crow locals that were the next best thing to outright banishment.

Flimsy contrivances, the Negro auxiliaries were subordinate to the white locals in matters regarding union policies and expenditures from their treasury. They provided black members with worse benefits than whites received, allowed for no grievance procedures, and gave blacks no representation at national conventions. Dues, however, were the same as those taken from whites' paychecks. In essence, blacks were being taxed for the privilege of being segregated. The Negro auxiliaries also meant it would be easier to lop off black membership wholesale in the postwar era, when the need for transport ships declined. The system put control of most Los Angeles hires (perhaps 80 percent) in the hands of whites bent on installing a Southern-style employment structure.

For a time the Boilermakers successfully kept the setup quiet. But in early 1943 a 25-year-old Calship welder named Walter Williams looked at his receipt for union dues and saw the word "auxiliary" printed on it; that, he thought to himself, was something new. It's likely black workers didn't even realize they were barred from the white local, since so many had just recently signed on and since *somebody* was deducting union dues from their paychecks. Williams and others started making inquiries and discovered they were part of a segregated union.

He was already breaking down barriers to black employment as a strategist for Clayton Russell's Negro Victory Committee. Now, in response to the Boilermakers he organized the Shipyard Workers Committee for Equal Participation (SWCEP) and began to fight for full membership in an integrated union.

Walter Williams was "a tall, fine looking rather mild Negro lad," according to one government observer. He had arrived in L.A. from Atlanta around 1919, and was raised by a single mother. At the age of 11 he was unloading trucks in a downtown produce market and by 15 Williams was driving a Mack truck for the Teamsters Union. One day a Teamster official decided his job should go to a white man, and Williams was fired. With his own family to support in the heart of the Depression, Williams took an unskilled job at a brass and lead foundry. He began signing up black workers to form a CIO union local in the factory; after he signed up a few white workers, he was fired on the spot. From these experiences he learned much; chiefly, perhaps, Williams would say he learned the limits of language.

"I learned one thing, that as far as racism was concerned, that unless you were really aggressive in trying to bring about a change that changes weren't gonna just come because there were laws on the books," he told an interviewer. Words alone wouldn't protect your job. "Whether they were in contracts, whether they were in the union constitution, whether they were lawfully legislated by Congress." What was needed were strong bodies organizing to give words meaning.

And folks willing to raise the level of discourse. When he arrived at Calship in 1941, Williams realized mainstream Negro leadership wouldn't support the shipyard workers; many thought well-paying jobs in a segregated union were acceptable compared to no jobs at all. (Garner Grayson, selected by whites to lead the auxiliary, was an established business leader on the Avenue.) This battle was going to be fought by those with the most to lose—their paycheck—and the most to win—dignity and self-respect. It was going to be fought by the black shipyard workers themselves, and before they were done they workers would become the first rank-and-file movement of black working people in L.A.

The SWCEP called for the government to investigate the yards, urged Negro workers to withhold dues from the shadow local and collected signatures on a statement that declared, "I shall continue to work for victory on the production front as long as I am permitted to do so, but I will not pay for Fascism." In response to the claim of some Boilermakers that whites in the union wouldn't tolerate integration, Williams turned over to the government petitions with more than 1,000 signatures from sympathetic whites calling for a single local.

The Boilermakers went all-out with their Potemkin auxiliary, opening an office for the black local at 41st Place and Main—they knew better than to show up on Central—in the summer of 1943. Protestors greeted their appearance, a scene that John Kinloch covered for the *Eagle*. "Bright and early, scores of pickets, many of them weary from a full night's work building ships, appeared in front of the gold lettered Jim Crow office," he wrote. "They carried signs stating, 'Jim Crow Belongs in Germany—Not in America, We Won't Pay Dues for Hitlerism.' Their numbers grew throughout the day."

At one point Boilermakers representative E. V. Blackwell offered Williams a blank check. There were three zeroes drawn to the left of the decimal point; Williams was told he could write any two figures he wanted to the left of that—if he'd accept the auxiliary. Williams declined what was essentially a $99,000 bribe ("I like to try to live with myself," he later explained).

The picketing continued for several days. Blackwell threatened federal officials that he might break up the demonstration. "If an assault were made on the picket line either through police intervention or by opposing elements, it might be the start of a general race clash," a worried federal official wrote in a memo.

Although he didn't make good on his threat, Blackwell and the Boilermakers ordered the mass firing of approximately 500 Negro workers. "Regardless of whether you want it, you're going to have the auxiliary," he told a group of demonstrators.

Well, boys, this is going to be short and sweet. I'm pressing charges against you for the propaganda you are putting out against the Boiler-makers. . . . I know you won't be able to carry a case into court. We've got all the money, anyhow.

All this campaign you're putting on—taking this thing to the NAACP, the Victory Committee, Clarence Johnson—won't do any good. You can't win. We got all the damn money!

Among the fired shipyard workers was a jazz trumpeter named Andrew Blakeney, a welder at Calship. Blakeney had played with Lionel Hampton, Les Hite and the cream of L.A.'s first generation of jazz musicians. He made a better living as a trumpeter than a shipyard worker, Blakeney told federal officials investigating the Boilermakers. But he was too old for the draft and he wanted to do his part for the war effort. Walter Williams had personally recruited Blakeney to lead a group that was suing the Big Three shipbuilders and asking for a temporary injunction against the ongoing firing of black employees who were refusing to pay their dues to the segregated union.

While he waited for his case to work its way through the courts, Blakeney got his horn out and started practicing again.

• • •

A DASHING YOUNG MAN from a good Midwestern family, Chester Himes came to Los Angeles and found a job at the shipyards of San Pedro. His ambitions were artistic, and Himes spent what spare time he had between shifts writing fiction.

Himes came to Los Angeles with a mind to write about working people like Gerald Edwards and Walter Williams. He came to the city—despite a mistrusting nature—with a large measure of optimism, an urge to get the most out of a fresh start. When Himes arrived, probably in late 1941, he was a straight-ahead realist writer, working in the gritty proletarian style of the day. While pursuing a career as a Hollywood writer, he worked in the yards as a shipwright's helper, as well as many other places. Negro Los Angeles quickly became his subject. No writer was more alive to what was going on in the city during the

1940s, and Himes dropped in on the after-hours jam sessions and the political debates in Pershing Square, visited Hollywood sets and avant-garde parties and wrote it all down, sizing up a city that, like himself, was toiling dusk to dawn. From *If He Hollers Let Him Go*, his 1945 novel set in and around the Terminal Island shipyards:

> It was a bright June morning. The sun was already high. . . . The huge industrial plants flanking the ribbon of road—shipyards, refineries, oil wells, steel mills, construction companies—the thousands of rushing workers, the low-hanging barrage balloons, the close hard roar of Diesel trucks and the distant drone of patrolling planes, the sharp, pungent smell of exhaust that used to send me driving clear across Ohio on a sunny summer morning, and the snowcapped mountains in the background, like picture-postcards.

Few writers have ever sounded so intoxicated by Los Angeles.

In the early 1940s Himes traveled in some of the same circles as Walter Williams. Langston Hughes, an acquaintance from back east, introduced him to his political contacts on the Avenue. Himes met the black union organizers and became a roommate of Welford Wilson, like Williams a member of the Negro Victory Committee. The Communist Party made an effort to recruit him and he sought a place in the world of left-wing activism, but Himes was a problematic man of the people—quick to anger, easy with a grudge, he was anything but a joiner. His agitation would continue, but any coalition-building impulse died fast.

"Chester Himes is a working writer I admire for not heeding our distracting how-dee-do. Occupying a cozy home overlooking Hollywood, I'm told," an *Eagle* society columnist noted, while relaying that tongues were wagging about what this secretive presence was up to. "Himes's career reminds us we've long appreciated the number of creative artists in our section who won't allow aimless bridge games, barstools and telephone sessions to interfere with their calling!"

Chester Himes began his stay in Los Angeles with the loftiest literary ambitions, but by the time his stay was done and the dust had settled, he was a writer whose work would be found on dime-store paperback racks and in ghetto bus stations, when it was found at all. This trajectory makes him both one of the most influential writers of post–World War II America and one of the least understood. He's best known for a series of detective novels written in the 1950s and 1960s (*Cotton Comes to Harlem* and *The Real Cool Killers*, among them), featuring two brutal black cops named Coffin Ed Johnson and Grave Digger Jones. They have earned him the title of father of the black crime novel, and no doubt he helped create the modern pulp sensibility. His biographer, James Sallis, calls him "America's central black writer." "He was an original, with a prickly and ungovernable disposition," wrote the critic Luc Sante. The *Financial Times* of London once compared him to Ernest Hemingway, Eudora Welty, and James Baldwin. Far more precisely, he is linked to tormented realists like Raymond Chandler and Richard Wright. He's one of the few writers to have any impact on hip-hop—the most important cultural movement of the last quarter of the twentieth century—and his influence there has been considerable. Himes created the template for keeping it real—he was a chronicler of black street life who knew all about scuffling, a creator of violent art who had lived a violent life. As hip-hop journalist Nelson George has written, "Ice Cube, The Notorious B.I.G., Scarface and many other of the genre's master storytellers are heirs to Himes' Technicolor prose."

His finest work includes two novels, *If He Hollers Let Him Go* and *Lonely Crusade*, as well as a raft of short stories and essays in which Los Angeles is the main character. He described the Avenue from a beer joint, from a seat on the bus. In his first novel, *If He Hollers Let Him Go*, he looks at the city the way any Angeleno does—through a windshield, mapping intersections, commutes, distances between stops. He is a newcomer taking it all in, and what a contemporary reader is most likely to take from *If He Hollers* is his shock at what he saw.

L.A. coldcocked Himes. "It wasn't being refused employment in the plants so much," the narrator, a shipyard worker named Bob Jones, says.

When I got here practically the only job a Negro could get was service in the white folks' kitchens. But it wasn't that so much. It was the look on the people's faces when you asked them about a job. Most of 'em didn't say right out they wouldn't hire me. They just looked so god-damned startled that I'd even asked. As if some friendly dog had come in through the door and said, "I can talk." It shook me.

When Himes wrote his autobiography, *The Quality of Hurt*, he quoted the passage because, he said, it explained how he felt about Los Angeles.

He'd taken magazine stories he'd written and the manuscript of a novel around to the movie studios, but there was no interest in his work. He was involved with a group of white screenwriters crafting a film based on the life of inventor George Washington Carver, but their well-intended liberal pieties drove him off—as did, perhaps, their valorizing of a stereotypically "good Negro" rather than a flesh-and-blood Negro. Himes was more likely to write about a factory worker or a convict than a role model. Among the screenwriters the conversation got around to what a humble man Carver was; why, he even ironed his own shirts. That's when Himes bolted from the room.

He tried out for a $47-a-week job at Warner Brothers, writing one-page synopses of novels that producers were pondering. They gave him the job, until the day his boss bumped into studio mogul Jack Warner on the lot. "I have a new man, Mr. Warner, and I think he's going to work out very well indeed," the man said. "Who is he?" asked Warner. "He's a young black man." To which Warner said, "I don't want no niggers on this lot."

Life in L.A. stacked humiliation upon hardship for Himes, same as it did for the characters in his fiction. From *If He Hollers:*

It was the look in the white people's faces when I walked down the streets. It was that crazy, wild-eyed, unleashed hatred that the first Jap bomb on Pearl Harbor let loose in a flood. All that tight, crazy feeling of race as thick in the street as gas fumes. Every time I stepped outside I saw a challenge I had to accept or ignore. Every day I had to make one decision a thousand times: *Is it now? Is now the time?*

This was fiction, but it was also Himes's personal temperature. It was God's little joke: drop a tightly wrapped man with a violent streak into a tightly wrapped town with violence flaring up all around and then watch him write. He was a black crack-up artist who never recovered from living along the Avenue. Nobody wrote better about Los Angeles in the 1940s. Maybe that even makes what happened to him worth it.

Himes was born in Jefferson City, Missouri, in 1909. Here's how he described his family in an autobiographical letter: "My parents were bourgeoisie school teachers, and that finishes that." He meant it, too. His parents were who they were, but they weren't him. Himes turned his back on the ways of schoolteachers and upward mobility. There was an aura of menace about him, and it came from practice. Novelist John A. Williams says he always kept alert when Himes was around, because Himes was good with a knife and he relished an argument. While briefly attending Ohio State University, Himes started hanging out in whorehouses and running with hustlers, and soon enough he'd forgotten about college. He was arrested for stealing guns from an armory and passing bad checks, and then an armed robbery in 1928 landed him 20 to 25 years of hard labor in the Ohio State Penitentiary. A year later, a fire broke out on Easter morning, killing some 300 inmates. The incident pushed Himes to take up writing; he bought a Remington typewriter and while imprisoned began a series of short stories based on his prison experiences. Success came shockingly fast, and soon he was selling stories to *Esquire*, at a time when it was publishing fiction from F. Scott Fitzgerald, Hemingway, and Theodore Dreiser.

After he had spent seven and a half years in prison, Ohio commuted Himes's sentence in 1936, and he began working for Louis Bromfield, a now-forgotten but once hugely popular Midwestern novelist. Bromfield came west in 1939, and Himes and his wife, Jean, followed. It was the era of the Popular Front, when black writers like Richard Wright, Ralph Ellison, and Hughes traveled in Communist Party circles. The communists aggressively encouraged black protest—at least until Russia was attacked by Nazi Germany, after which party policy squashed anything that stood in the way of winning the war. Suddenly, civil rights fell off the agenda, and many blacks like Himes who saw the hypocrisy up close never forgot it.

His wife worked for the USO, and Himes wrote of feeling humiliated that she was the breadwinner. Guilt was probably running deeper than that. Perhaps Himes's most autobiographical book is his prison novel, *Yesterday Will Make You Cry*. It's impossible to read the book, in which the narrator describes his loving relationship with another convict, without pondering Himes's own sexuality. It is probably the only positive sexual relationship he ever wrote about. Indeed, some who knew him are convinced he was deep in the closet.

Chester and Jean Himes lived in a tiny house in City Terrace, the hilly area north of Boyle Heights. They got the home from a Japanese family who had been sent to the internment camps; they grew beets, radishes and carrots. "We are by the purest of luck, living in the cutest little house in L.A.," he wrote in a letter. The hill was mostly theirs, a perfect place to write in peace. Even so: "I [keep] my Winchester rifle within reach at all times."

Himes came down from the hill to work at a warehouse and check out the action on the Avenue. One day, he descended to deliver an inspired, angry review to the editor of the *California Eagle*. His article attacks a simple-minded black musical featuring Avenue talent, but beneath the criticism is a call for the kind of art Himes wanted to make:

> In the midst of this huge chaotic war (which so badly needs defining), beset on every side with the death struggles of varying ideologies (in only one of which we have a hope), living each moment on the very crest of abrupt and violent change, all of which affects the Negro in America more than any other race in any other land, it seems utterly nonsensical and stupid to produce a show that does not try to capture some essence of this tremendous scene. . . .
>
> The ignorance of the Negro is no longer as funny as the Negro thinks it is; it is not even funny to the white folks anymore.

Nothing in this forgotten show matters, he writes.

And the reason for this, no doubt, is the one rigid rule of Negro show business; Whatever you do, don't offend the white folks. This graciousness of all our characteristics I have never been able to understand. . . .

What our producers don't seem to realize is that the white folks are now taking sides. Those that are on the other side are not going to support a Negro show even if we gave them a seven-course spread of Hollywood mammies. And those who are on our side want us to come out with the best we got, hard, fast, and timely: they expect us to speak up, to voice our desires and protests in songs, dance, and otherwise.

Hard, fast and timely is the way Himes wrote about Los Angeles, and his review was probably the most explicit declaration of his aesthetic he ever came up with. He was a protest artist who put craft in the service of rage. But notice how Himes calls both for a mirror to be held up to the world and for the black artist to take sides. He was balanced on an electrified rail—too much realism or too much agitation would knock him off balance. That balance was the source of his art—as millions of volts flowed through him.

"I adore him but he tells everybody what he thinks and they hate him for it," said his friend Carl Van Vechten. He did so in his life and in his work; Himes shatters the mirror by hurling a rage as unforgettable as it was unstable. It's so overpowering it risks turning his Los Angeles fiction into pathological case studies—this is a man who, before making *If He Hollers* a story of life in the shipyards, considered writing a novel about an unsolved series of murders of white people. His FBI file starts at about this time. His fiction gave paranoid readers plenty of reason to worry.

He was also capable of an easy charm, as Van Vechten knew. A wealthy white patron who bankrolled many Harlem Renaissance artists, Van Vechten was a socialite and aesthete from New York City who favored his intimates by asking them to pose for a photographic portrait. One day in the mid-1940s it was Himes's turn for a sitting. After he received his picture, however, Himes communicated his concern to Van Vechten.

Dear Carl:

Thanks for your letter and the photographs which were very fine indeed. However, there is a smoothness in the facial lines which I do not quite like. I would like for all the blemishes, marks, scars, and lines of the face to show, even at the risk of appearing like a thug.

The realist began dabbling in masquerade. Holding up a mirror would never do, would never stop the humiliation. Holding up a mirror wasn't paying the bills—his second novel, 1947's *Lonely Crusade*, wasn't selling—and it wasn't pleasing the critics, either. *Lonely Crusade* follows a black activist in an aircraft factory butting heads with communists and industrialists. Himes gleefully caricatured his Marxist associates, and when the book came out it was his targets' turn to attack. In the radical journal *New Masses*, a critic wrote, "I cannot recall ever having read a worse book on the Negro theme." A review in *Ebony* magazine declared:

> Chester Himes followed up his recent malevolent *If He Hollers Let Him Go* with an invidious, shocking, incendiary work which he appropriately calls *Lonely Crusade*. It is a virulent, malicious book full of rancor and venom.

The best he could hope for, Himes realized after a few years in the city, was a wicked, surreal—*evil*—tone. He turned toward a style that couched his punishing malice in a wildly entertaining sarcasm. Looking like a thug wasn't to be avoided—actually, it was something to be courted, though discretion kept Himes from admitting as much. He liked thugs.

Long before hip-hop MCs obsessed over the proper menacing scowl, Himes was probing lines and fissures for all they were worth. The last thing he was interested in was being a role model, in "representing the race." That was the burden of those elegant Harlem Renaissance writers whose pictures he was turning to the wall. His writing frequently appalled black critics (including the Renaissance bunch), who felt he was showing white readers things they weren't meant to see. An *Ebony* writer even said Himes was as much a racist as Hitler or the notorious Mississippi senator Theodore Bilbo.

A member of the bourgeoisie turned hood. A lefty who assaulted political correctness. A husband with doubts. Maybe in the end, Himes's arrival in Los Angeles amounts to that unkillable cliché, a man who goes west to find out who he really is. Soon, this is who he is: a man with blemishes, marks and scars.

"I'm getting jittery in this town," he wrote.

CHAPTER 6

Black Noir

The Mayor says these Negroes with their new-found freedom become at
times demonstrably arrogant in restaurants, etc.
—*internal Fair Employment Practices Commission document*

THE FIRST SUMMER WEATHER OF THE YEAR ARRIVED JUST IN TIME FOR
the "I Am an American Day" celebration in May 1943. There were parades and picnics and, at the Coliseum, a star-packed rally promoting
unity and tolerance to a mostly white crowd. Irving Berlin played his
songs and comic Joe E. Brown shared the dais with Governor Earl
Warren and Mayor Fletcher Bowron. Singing to the thousands who
packed the stadium, one performer offered a little improvisation during a rendition of "Old Man River." Caught up in the spirit of the moment, the vocalist added fresh words to the show tune. As if the
original lyrics, "the darkies all work on the Mississippi," weren't problematic enough, he embellished them with "niggers all work while the
white folks play."

How such a modulation fell on one's ear, or whether one even noticed it at all, depended on which side of the city one lived on, and

which side of the looking glass. If you did hear it, the absurdity of "I Am an American Day" must have been impressive. Suddenly the season was ripe for those who, like Chester Himes, had a soft spot for paradox.

The paradoxes of Avenue life had turned Himes into a literary surrealist. He was beginning to sense the limits of protest fiction: "It had accomplished as much as it could during the life of Richard Wright and I felt a new approach was needed," he explained to an interviewer. Where once he wrote about Negro subjects fighting back against bigotry, now he was writing about "the absurdity of racism," and he didn't criticize absurdity—he let it run its course and then laughed at its audacity. Himes turned away from characters he identified with and moved toward social satire, blunt sensory impact and sarcasm that made a reader see stars.

Some folks become cynical under the weight of absurdity. Cynicism is for white people; it belongs to those who think the system is just and that some correctible harm has corrupted its smooth-running ways. Nihilism comes from seeing that the corrupted system is running the way it is supposed to; in the 1940s, nihilism bubbled up from the Avenue. Headline in the *California Eagle*: EVERYONE A SUSPECT IN HUNT FOR PAIR WHO SHOT OFFICERS.

Himes came to L.A. a realist:

> I turned on the radio. One of Erskine Hawkins' old platters, "I'm in a Lowdown Groove," was playing. Alice and I had discovered it together shortly after we'd met at the Memo on the Avenue. I welled up inside, turned it off. But the words kept on in my mind. I got a hard, grinding nonchalance. To hell with everybody, I thought. To hell with the world; if there were any more little worlds, to hell with them too. (*If He Hollers*)

He exited a nihilist. In the handful of years he had spent in L.A. (with a side trip to the Bay Area), Himes witnessed an impressive number of racial crises. He'd watched the zoot suit riots and the roundup of Japanese Americans, seen living standards decline for those who lived in the ghetto and observed the tensions in the shipyards. No stranger to cops, he became a connoisseur of the bland, easy-going brutality of L.A.'s gendarmes. He watched and he wrote it, and the experience transformed him. Despite his gangster mask, Himes was no tough guy. Flooded with strangers, black L.A. was a lonely crowd even for a gregarious newcomer. For a mistrustful, isolated ex-con like Himes, the city was unbearable.

His fiction starts with exactitude and balance and ends, decades later, untethered and extreme, all sensation and artifice. It ends in a tradition he founded, or one that found him: the school of black noir. It took a while. By the mid-1950s Himes had written several more protest-novels, brooding, clamorous works, none of which sold worth a damn. He left the United States and was living in Paris by 1956, part of a rich expatriate scene that included Richard Wright, James Baldwin, and jazz musician Bud Powell. Around then Marcel Duhamel, editor of Gallimard's *Serie Noire*, a popular line of thrillers, dangled a proposition. He gave Himes a fat advance and said, "Get an idea. Start with action. Give me 220 typed pages." Two months later Himes turned in his first crime book. In his inaugural detective novel, *For the Love of Imabelle* (published in the United States as *A Rage in Harlem*), Himes situated his two cops, Grave Digger Jones and Coffin Ed Johnson, in a world few black writers chose to look at, and he tangibly delights in what they see—a world of chartreuse hair and zipgun dialogue, a ghetto culture that was unexplored territory. Freed by his decision to no longer tear at social conditions in order to make a change, he now reveled in the perversity of things as they were and viewed such things through the distortions of a shot glass. He enjoyed the view.

> Grave Digger and Coffin Ed weren't crooked detectives, but they were tough. They had to be tough to work in Harlem. Colored folks didn't respect colored cops. But they respected big shiny pistols and sudden death. It was said in Harlem that Coffin Ed's pistol would kill a rock and that Grave Digger's would bury it. (*For the Love of Imabelle*)

Born in the early 1920s, Grave Digger and Coffin Ed were World War II vets who had stalled out at the detective level. They looked like anybody else among the crowd, just a pair of scarred working stiffs. But they had the guns, and the guns—far more than their badges—gave them respect from the rest of the crowd. Across nine books they tailed sociopathic teen gangs, cult messiahs and gutter-level scam artists, a rogue's gallery of those who profit off false hope. Established pulp fiction conventions—the cops ever closer to the bad guys with each page turned—let Himes speed through a narrative, and by the time he careens to the end those conventions have been rolled for change and tossed to the rain-slick curb.

Crime fiction broods on freedom. If we are all able to do as we please, are we able to do whatever we please? What happens when enjoying liberty becomes taking liberties, and freedom to act breaks the laws of society? Back in the days of Sherlock Holmes, detective fiction took society's side and assumed it was a civic virtue for a protagonist to bring those who crossed the line back to the fold. Somewhere after that, though, crime fiction came of age, and with it the idea that pursuing crooks at any cost turned good guys into bad guys. With lines blurred, novelists like Raymond Chandler and Jim Thompson suggested that notions like justice and honor were as much personal, nontransferable constructions as they were shared public property. Sometimes the bad guys have more fun, while the good guys are the biggest hoods of all.

Crime fiction begins with the notion that "we" built this society and then asks what we should do about it when some of us get selfish. But Himes started from a different place. His Harlem—really a stand-in for all of black America—was a patently unfree place where folks were anything but allowed to do what they please. The L.A. that scalded him was a separate-but-unequal township where living standards for the underclass were going south just as the South seemed to be coming west. Society was unfair and the law was a gun upside the head: the innovation in Himes's crime novels is that the folks on the other side of morality, of the law, aren't the criminals—they are black folks. In that absurd setting, what is the job of the black cop? Besides impossible, that is.

Coffin Ed and Grave Digger are getting grief from their white superior down at the station in *Cotton Comes to Harlem:*

> He then looked from one detective to the other. "What the hell's going on today? It's only ten o'clock in the evening and judging from the reports it's been going on like this since morning." He leafed through the reports, reading charges: "Man kills his wife with an axe for burning his breakfast pork chop. . . . man shoots another man demonstrating a recent shooting he had witnessed. . . . man stabs another man for spilling beer on his new suit. . . . man kills self in a bar playing Russian roulette with a .32 revolver. . . . woman stabs man in stomach fourteen times, no reason given. . . . woman scalds neighboring woman with pot of boiling water for speaking to her husband. . . . man arrested for threatening to blow up subway train because he entered wrong station and couldn't get his token back—"
>
> "All colored citizens," Coffin Ed interrupted.
>
> Anderson ignored it. "Man dressed as Cherokee Indian splits white bartender's skull with homemade tomahawk. . . . man arrested on Seventh Avenue for hunting cats with hound dog and shotgun. . . . twenty-five men arrested for trying to chase all the white people out of Harlem—"
>
> "It's Independence Day," Grave Digger interrupted.
>
> "Independence Day!" Lieutenant Anderson echoed, taking a long, deep breath. He pushed away the reports and pulled a memo from the corner clip of the blotter. "Well, here's your assignment. . . . "

Tom Ripley in *The Talented Mr. Ripley* finds it convenient not to correct a stranger who mistakes him for someone else. . . . Fred Mac-Murray in *Double Indemnity* slips and falls for a gorgeous married woman. . . . In white noir the hero blinks for a moment, gives in to a single weak impulse, and his life is over. Order shatters round his ankles and we are supposed to realize how much darkness lurks beneath the surface of things when good intentions make way for bad. The moral universe of black noir is different; it's about realizing good intentions don't matter any more than bad ones in a world run by white folks. All intentions are equal and equally pointless. All choices in the end amount to one, have the same value—a value determined by people who think you are less than human. It was just as E. V. Blackwell, the Boilermakers' leader, said to the protesting black unionists: "You can't win. We got all the damn money."

Himes's crime novels were at once dazzling and formulaic, set in a Harlem he barely bothers to describe or understand. There is a good reason for that: what animates the books is not Harlem but Los Angeles. As he acknowledged in more than one interview, Coffin Ed and Grave Digger were derived from a pair of cruel Negro cops he had encountered while on the West Coast. "The two cops," he said in a *Publishers Weekly* interview, "are roughly based on a black lieutenant and his sergeant partner who worked the Central Avenue ghetto back in the 1940s. My cops are just as tough, but somewhat more humane. The original pair were pitiless bastards."

In another interview Himes called them "more or less the lords of the Los Angeles ghetto in the late 1930s, just before the war. They were the most brutal cops I ever heard of."

He might have been telling tales, and he was writing *fiction*, but assuming Himes drew on his L.A. experience here as elsewhere, one notorious pair of Avenue cops loom suggestively large as the inspiration for his most popular characters. Charles Broady had been with the force since 1914, and several generations knew better than to give him lip. In 1916 Broady beat a black woman so badly that seven weeks later she was still in the hospital and unable to testify against him. A few years later he beat a 14-year-old white boy who had argued with his son. In 1935 he was implicated as a witness in the mysterious prison hanging of a 19-year-old black murder suspect.

"There can be no justification for the recent harassing of Eastside citizens by patrolman Charles A. Broady," said a brave 1941 *Sentinel* editorial. It was probably the only time in the whole decade that a Negro newspaper took on a Negro cop. "There are many cases in which a police officer must resort to hard-boiled tactics in order to enforce the law, but there can be no reason why respectable citizens and taxpayers should be placed in the same category with thugs and criminals."

Partnering with detective Broady was the burly Carl D. Kimbro. A jury found Kimbro had justifiable reasons for killing a black, 18-year-old, alleged car thief in 1943 with a shot in the back. A few years later, however, Kimbro pled guilty to attempted extortion, in a case involving allegations he was shaking down bars in Little Tokyo. By then Broady had left the force and was tending bar himself in Little Tokyo.

Himes was hardly alone in taking inspiration from police and crooks who explored the limits of acceptable behavior. Some of the best writing of the era was found in terse, unsigned crime reports that ran in two of the three largest black newspapers in L.A. The prose has a common hostile wit and storytelling smarts that strongly suggest the same person wrote them all, though nobody I've spoken to seems to know who the author might have been.

SATURDAY IS A HEADACHE

Saturday, traditionally, has been pay day in many parts of the country for generations. Wives look forward to it, and husbands usually respond by bringing home the old paycheck, or its equivalent in cash. It's a good custom, one calculated to build peace and security on the home front. When it is broken, the consequences are sometimes very painful.

Take the case of the Bronsons, f'rinstance. Last Saturday, Edward Bronson arrived at the domicile at 4066 S. Central loaded down with folding money. His wife, Barbara, awaited him and her pro rata share of the cash, but Edward was not of a mind to part with his hard-earned gold, and he said so. Naturally, words followed, sharp and fast.

In most circumstances, men are not equal to the sharpness of an angry woman's tongue. It was decidedly so in this case. Edward Bronson, finding himself on the losing end of the verbal battle, seized a coffee pot and applied it effectively to his wife's head. Having thus asserted himself, he departed hastily for parts unknown.

When the police and an ambulance arrived on the scene, Mrs. Bronson was holding her head and moaning incessantly. Edward, as we hinted before, had left. After treatment, Mrs. Bronson was permitted to remain at home to bemuse, perhaps, over the eventful turn which changed Saturday from its traditional meaning to become one big headache.

—*California Eagle*, October 5, 1944

Call him the Creeper: I do. He had access to the police blotter at Newton Station and, poring over it for piquant detail and tabloid sensationalism, he turned the police report into a self-renewing source of ghetto reality.

No TV dinner really makes its own sauce, and no story really tells itself. But a great writer makes you *think* events are unfolding without assistance. What the Creeper did better than most was to pry open the narrative, shoot a camera up in there and present it in a pinballing cinematic style.

FRYING PAN SENDS WIFE TO HOSPITAL

This is a story of where an argument over pork chops can lead. It also indicates to what lengths people will go defending the honor of their ration points.

Mrs. Ella Mae Gibson of 1438 East 50th Street may not live following an altercation with her husband over what Sunday's dinner should have been. Mr. Gibson wanted pork chops. Mrs. Gibson didn't.

Gibson, a shipyard worker, told police that his wife forced him to do it. He said she attacked him with a fork; in the face, too.

He said the necessities of self-preservation led him inevitably to cracking Mrs. G. across the head with the family frying pan. She had him in a corner, he said. She had him in a corner with the fork.

What could he do but belt her one with the frying pan?

In support of his contention of self-defense, Mr. G. offers the following vital statistics:

His weight: 140 lbs.

Her weight: 200 lbs.

According to police, Gibson stands a good chance of beating the rap.

—*California Eagle*, September 23, 1943

Long before black-on-black crime would be documented as tragedy, the Creeper reported it as farce. Both Himes and the Creeper made an elemental deduction: since the citizens of the ghetto have so little control over their lives, they were exonerated for behavior that would be frowned upon elsewhere.

LIQUOR STORE OBJECTS TO HAVING CHURCH NEAR IT

Officers of a new Church of God in Pasadena ran into some unexpected opposition last week when they asked the Pasadena Planning Commission for a permit to build a church at 980 Lincoln Ave.

From Sherman L. Over, Negro homeowner and businessman of 917 Lincoln, came opposition on grounds that "We don't need any more churches. There are 12 Negro churches in town now and none of them full. . . . "

—*Los Angeles Tribune*, October 8, 1949

A street-corner preacher in a toga bullwhips passersby. . . . The lone peacemaker is killed in a sidewalk brawl involving 300 to 400 rioters hurling beer bottles and furniture. . . . A man shoots up his house because a radio program made him mad. . . . A man is stabbed in the neck for refusing to buy a stranger a drink. . . .

Boiled down almost to a rebus, the everyday became uncanny. In a neighborhood where the everyday seemed surreal, the oddest detail could be highlighted and thus give the action a baffling power.

HE SHOWED THE RABBITS AND SHOT HIS GUN

James Price can produce a rabbit when he says he will, and he can also produce a gun—a process, he learned to his unhappiness, that can result in a charge of assault with a deadly weapon.

Saturday night Price, just a wee bit under the weather, went into a beer parlor at Wilmington and Imperial and got into a scattered sort of conversation with the manager, Benson Johnson of 11648 Croesus. Price also lavished some of his flavored conversation on Cornelious Outley, who sat at the bar imbibing in solitude.

As inspired conversation will on an occasion such as this, Price's became a bit bothersome, and the manager asked him to leave. Price regis-
tered a reaction that is a cross between indignation and chagrin. He
invited the manager outside—to see his rabbits.

The manager accompanied him outside, and sure enough there
were the rabbits. The manager looked, then returned to his duties.
Price followed him inside, and instead of rabbits this time he produced
a revolver.

His response to Johnson's remonstrations was a single shot that hit
Johnson in the right chest and emerged under the armpit, lodging in
the leg of Outley. Price is being held for assault with a deadly weapon.

—*California Eagle*, November 11, 1948

Such writing was beneath, or beyond, contempt at the time when it
appeared. The Creeper didn't even deserve a byline, his editors
deemed, and however he paid the bills, it wasn't from filing 300 words
a week.

Himes's books were popular in France and only slowly became
marketable in the United States, where they first reached a readership
more or less identical with the figures that populated the books: ghetto
dwellers, those who haunted the pulp racks at corner pharmacies and
subway newsstands.

Yet the sensibility of such work saturated a market and a culture all
the same and has influenced a modern aesthetic of ghetto-centricity.
This work points the way for blaxploitation cinema, for racial themes
in the work of directors like Quentin Tarantino and John Singleton.
The fiction of the L.A.-born novelist Walter Mosley builds on and
transforms the tradition of black noir. As did Himes, Mosley plays with
the formulas of a familiar genre—the detective novel—to critique race
relations. The finder of facts—Mosley's accidental detective Easy
Rawlins, no less than the Creeper—enjoys no legal authority and has
to use his wits and trickery to play one side against the other and make
moral judgments on a morally ambiguous world. Rawlins rejects the
method used by detectives in classic detective novels, for he knows
that deductive logic and an oversized magnifying lens won't save his

skin nearly as well as knowing the nature of his people. The influence of the Central Avenue crime blotter reaches from the era of Himes and the Creeper through Easy Rawlins and Eazy-E—still one more L.A. product. From the Creeper to gangsta rap, one finds an aesthetic formed by the intertwined voices of reporter and parodist. Those dual voices flow through hip-hop music today; hip-hop reinvents the world as black noir.

But before black noir came with beat and flow, it came as pulp and tabloid; before it reinvented the world, it restructured Central Avenue. You couldn't make it up, and you didn't need to.

> A young Watts mother was allegedly stabbed to death in broad daylight last Thursday noon by another woman because she had kidded her about her big feet, her out-size clothes and her preference for eating "greens."

The Creeper left the pulp crime field some time in the 1950s.

> Hurt by local press accusations that he is "trigger-happy," [white police officer] Owen H. Tucker, a World War I marine, said he had killed only one Negro previous to Oliver Gilmore Jr. who he shot last Dec. 8. . . .

Chester Himes left Los Angeles in 1944, eventually settling in Europe. Perhaps they both wound up on the Left Bank, where they shared an espresso while listening to Bud Powell and swapped stories of the rugged cops they had once known on the Avenue.

CHAPTER 7

Sweet Papa Pigmeat

THE JAUNTY EMCEE MADE THE INTRODUCTIONS. "I'M NOT GOING TO tell jokes that you heard 30 years ago," he said, "but I'll introduce you to my partner Pigmeat, who will."

Then the headliner came out and the two quickly had them laughing. "Jack, I'm living," said Pigmeat Markham, his thickly knotted tie straining at his throat, his eyes protruding.

"You living?"

"I'm living between the sky and the earth and ain't touching dirt nowhere!"

"Aw, you must mean a airplane—"

"Ridin' in on the Pullman porter."

"Porter."

"Ridin' in on the train."

"Right here in Los Angeles, California."

"Sure enough."

When Chester Himes called for a new realism in the arts of Central Avenue, the arts as performed by Pigmeat Markham were most definitely not what he had in mind.

But what the hell: Pigmeat Markham most definitely did not play to the likes of Chester Himes. He performed for the domestics out on their night off, and for the old folks and kids and those whose thoughts were on subjects other than the state of the Negro arts.

He performed, for instance, for the young Alvin Ailey who, growing up on the Avenue after a boyhood in Rogers, Texas, would catch Pigmeat's show at the Lincoln Theater and fondly recalled it decades later in his autobiography. For Ailey and other youths at the Lincoln, Markham was quite possibly the funniest man alive, certainly the funniest man on the street.

"Yes it's me and I'm drunk again," Markham said with a voice that required no microphone, a bawl like Satan with a trombone. "Now go and tell THAT to the pastor!"

He'd sit down with a pretty girl on the stage, sharing a taste of King Kong Liquor ("ten cents a dipper"). The drink brought a poem to Pigmeat's lips, one he promised would "knock you dead on your ash can":

"The woodpecker pecked on the school house door/he pecked and he pecked till he couldn't peck no more."

"Why?" the woman asks.

"Because his pecker was sore!"

Groan all you want; in 1942, Pigmeat was living large. He was coming off a job writing and playing characters on the Andrews Sisters radio show and making low-budget black motion pictures. Meanwhile, he owned the stage at the Lincoln with a down and dirty sense of humor, summoning chitlins and nagging wives, dice games and knife fights. He was bonding with unpretentious people who felt he was just like them. Kids on the street picked up his lines: "Don't start no mess," they'd say.

"Whatever situation that arose, his facial expressions and body language would meet it," said Sonny Craver, onetime emcee at the Regal Theater in Chicago. Craver performed as a straight man to Markham.

He wore the baggy pants and the turn-around shoes—shoes on the wrong foot. Coats that were too long, pants that were too long, he reminded you of a black Chaplin—just twice Charlie Chaplin's size.

He *walked* funny. He *talked* funny. He had a rhythm when he talked—a roll in his voice that suggested "I want to talk to you, but let's don't be serious." And he moved with that shuffle walk of his, the kids call it hip now but then it was just his natural strut. He was just a funny man, period.

Markham did not face an audience and tell jokes; no Negro funny-man would, not even into the mid-1940s. The fact is, even though there were Negro clowns and comic performers, there were no blacks doing anything like standup comedy. A man who meets a customer's eyes and makes fun of his world wields power, the kind of power whites weren't about to grant.

Black show business was a world Leonard Reed knew better than most. He was on the Avenue in the 1940s, producing a revue at Shepp's Playhouse, and he remembered even earlier days of Negro comedians. "My partner Willie Bryant, I've seen him eat up white comics. But they wouldn't let black comics work in white clubs. They might let in a black dancer, but they didn't want any black comedians standing there trying to make white people laugh. These were the times." Sharing a joke with somebody is sharing your humanity; that undermined the notion of blacks being not quite human.

Instead, Pigmeat, Reed and countless others worked with sidekicks and in sketches, drawing humor from situations rather than commentary. Pigmeat had another layer of protection, too, another way of declaring he didn't belong to his audience's world. Like many earlier clowns, Markham performed in blackface, with the residue of burnt cork smeared over his already dark skin, white makeup applied around his mouth to make his lips seem enormous. The effect was to exaggerate his expressions and to caricature his blackness.

"It was the white man's idea to make the Negro comic put on cork," explained Reed; he owned the theaters, controlled the booking and wrote laws that no blacks could watch white performers in public theaters. The original minstrel shows, featuring a roster of blackface Caucasians joking, singing and dancing, were the most popular theatrical form for most of the nineteenth century. Minstrelsy *was* the pop culture of the era. Then, in the years after the Civil War, blacks began putting on the cork and entering the theatrical profession, performing for those with the money and liberty to buy a seat in a theater. Many of the most famous Negro entertainers of the turn of the twentieth century had worked in minstrel troupes—Bessie Smith, W. C. Handy, Ethel Waters, Eubie Blake, Ma Rainey.

From the antebellum era down to the Depression, black showfolk made the most of minstrelsy. Reed was both the rule and exception: born in Oklahoma to a white father and a mother with Indian and Negro blood, he was extremely light-skinned. Drawn to performance, he traveled in both white and black minstrel troupes during the early decades of the twentieth century. "Early in my career I worked white shows. Never worked blackface," he claimed. "No sir, I never was a Negro. I was white until I got ready to be a Negro, and when I got ready to be a Negro then I became one." He could afford to laugh; Reed confused people on both sides of the racial line and did it so deftly as to make a good living.

Reed knew better than to share his thoughts on segregation when he played to black audiences in the Deep South. Criticism of race relations in Duke Ellington's *Jump for Joy* had brought bomb threats; in the South it might have gotten him lynched. But beneath the surface of what was said and from behind the blackface mask, there was the possibility that authority could be mocked and hung out to dry.

That's how Pigmeat came to be called "the Judge" by his peers. The Judge was a character he came up with one night in some godforsaken dressing room, but it was more than a lark—it was a way of dealing with the world that the audience instantly cottoned to. The Judge was Markham's most famous role, a thunderously stupid barrister who showed up drunk and smacked the unfortunates called before him with an inflated steer's bladder. Now *that* was comedy.

The steer's bladder, Markham always felt, was the secret to his success. "They used to have fresh meat markets in the old days, where you could go and get a pig slaughtered or have a chicken's head cut off," recalled Markham's daughter Kathy Maldonado. He would bring several bladders home, soak them in water overnight, grease them up with Vaseline. Pigmeat had a pump contraption that inflated the prepared bladder.

"These are my brains," he said with satisfaction. "They feel right."

Bailiff: "Hear ye, hear ye! Court's in session. All rise cause here come de judge—Judge Pigmeat!"

Pigmeat: "Awww, the judge is high as a Georgia pine today; everybody gonna do time this morning!"

He wore a robe and a tasseled mortarboard hat, carried a telephone directory doubling as a code of law.

Pigmeat: "Now you respect me—you see this black robe and hat. You know I'm something up here!"

Prisoner: "All I want is some justice."

Pigmeat: "You gotta get justice; you're a citizen, aren't you?"

Prisoner: "I know my rights and I want my rights."

Pigmeat: "You mess around here, I'll give you a darned good left!"

Like Pigmeat himself, his Avenue base the Lincoln Theater presented a daunting façade. Hanging over its stairwells were portraits of Abraham Lincoln, as well as of Bilo and Ashes, two blackface entertainers Markham had outlasted by decades. Booking shows and leading the house band at the Lincoln was a man of Caribbean descent and thuggish manner named Bardu Ali. He had recently been stabbed backstage in his backside by comic Dusty Fletcher, which led to Fletcher leaving town abruptly, which led to less competition for Pigmeat. The comic made the most of it. In no time his catchphrases were barked in homes east and west of Central, and teenagers were consternating their parents as they emulated his low ways.

White performers found that by putting on the mask they were freed to offer political and social commentary—along with their racial stereotypes. It worked a little like that for blacks in blackface, too. Burnt cork was a distancing device essential to Pigmeat's routine. It gave him license to act up; it declared that what was said onstage was exaggeration, play. Sonny Craver called it "That invisible screen. With the blackface, the way I understood it, you wasn't white or you wasn't black. When a black comedian wore blackface, he wasn't a black comedian any more! He was a *comic*."

An assortment of mentors helped steer Pigmeat to the top. One was Bob Russell, an elderly trouper at the end of his career when a young Pigmeat joined the Florida Blossoms Minstrels. They roomed together on the road, and Russell made the kid memorize comedic routines and listen to his stories about the showman's life. From Russell Pigmeat learned the fundamentals of clowning.

Further education came from an encounter with a performer bearing a most unlikely name. "Joe Doakes was a comedian and a very funny man," Markham told an interviewer in 1959. "I was just a boy then. He'd do a little dance in which he'd shake his head and his lips until his lips would dot each of his ears with makeup, and he didn't have such big lips either." It was an exceptional act, but not an unusual one; popping eyes and smacking lips were tools of the trade. But Joe Doakes's act may have been the ultimate in the art of mining the Negro face for laughs, combining grotesquerie, caricature, and humiliation in one unforgettable profile. Pigmeat remembered the routine decades after Doakes had disappeared, perhaps because it expressed something basic about entertainment in those early decades of the twentieth century: black features added up to more than just a face. The minstrel's façade was a carnival all by itself. So it seemed at the time.

Joe Doakes showed Pigmeat the lifeblood of the black showman. But the primary lesson, the tutorial that brought Pigmeat fully into the world, came from someone known only as Mr. Booker. Mr. Booker gave Pigmeat a face. In his autobiography *Here Come the Judge!*, published in 1969, Markham recalled running away from home at the age of 14 and joining a local carnival run by a small-time concessionaire. "Mr. Booker come over to us before the show, with a can of Stein's burnt-cork and showed us how to put it on in front of the mirror. He also had some pink and some white lip make-up. You may wonder why a Negro had to do that, and all I can tell you is that's the way it was. Just about every Negro entertainer in those days worked in burnt-cork and lip make-up."

These were the theatrical conventions Pigmeat inherited as a youth. They were the conventions that he had used to his advantage, becoming a star in the process. And they were conventions that by World War II had caused him to seem almost freakish, mummified. By 1943, Pigmeat Markham was many things: the ranking funny man on the Avenue, a hero to young fans, the Judge. He was also a curious anomaly, the last great black comic to perform in burnt cork.

You could draw a line, one snaking like a wagon train, from Pigmeat Markham back to Bert Williams. Markham called him "the idol I've never met"; if not for the blackface comedy Williams had dragged into the twentieth century, Markham himself might never have run away from home. Bert Williams worked in burnt cork and white lips. He was certainly the most famous black minstrel of them all, and some who saw him claimed he was the greatest comic of his time.

Williams transcended the mask, conveying a sense of shared humanity that white audiences took to heart. "Bert Williams makes us glad that the slaves were freed," opined one theater critic. "He is a man of another race who can lampoon us and cartoon us in our own foibles and weaknesses and make us like it." An international star, he eclipsed the mask. But he never took it off. Which is why W. C. Fields may have said the most astute thing anyone ever uttered about him. "Bert Williams was the funniest man I ever saw and the saddest man I ever knew."

Born in Antigua in 1874 and raised in Riverside, 60 miles east of Los Angeles, Williams headed to L.A. and launched his career. In a written reminiscence Booker T. Washington recalled visiting L.A. and seeing the young Williams working as a bellboy in the Hollenbeck Hotel. "Bert Williams has done more for the race than I have," Washington said. "He has smiled his way into peoples' hearts. I have been obliged to *fight* my way."

A theatrical column in the *Los Angeles Times* from 1915 recalls Williams's stay in town: "It was right here among us, in this land of sunshine, fruit and flowers, that Mr. Williams led a highly picturesque and variegated career as a showman, and indeed got the foundation that has put him at the top in comedy land." As an adolescent, the article says,

Williams was staging Shakespeare productions during school hours and performing with the Samuels and Trice minstrels after class.

Williams joined a performing troupe to earn tuition for Stanford University. But life as an entertainer soon dispelled thoughts of higher education. He played banjo in Barbary Coast cafés and lumber camps between San Francisco and Eureka, earning twelve dollars a week and all the pie he could eat.

In 1894 Williams and his comic partner George Walker were hired to perform at the Mid-Winter Fair in San Francisco. "Exotic savages" had been billed as part of the exhibition, but when they failed to arrive by opening day, Williams and Walker were exhibited as African natives. How they felt about this masquerade went unrecorded; however, a few days later, after the Africans had arrived, Williams and Walker roamed through the fair. "We were permitted to visit the natives from Africa," Williams later told an interviewer.

> It was there, for the first time, that we were brought into close touch with native Africans, and the study of those natives interested us very much. We were not long in deciding that if we ever reach the point of having a show of our own, we would delineate and feature native African characters and still remain American, and make our acting interesting and entertaining to American audiences.

This encounter turned Williams into an avid student of African culture, and commenced a lifelong interest in its history and anthropology. Once while addressing a visitor, he pulled out a copy of John Ogilby's *Africa* and started to teach. "I suppose that with this volume, I could prove that every Pullman porter is the descendant of a king."

Facing a paucity of job opportunities and with a storehouse of mixed feelings, he reluctantly began honing a comic persona that refined and transformed the stereotypical "darkie" figure of stage lore. The crude babble meant to represent slave speech "to me was just as much a foreign dialect as that of the Italian," said the comic. He accepted—

loathed, yet accepted—the characteristics of minstrelsy, while bringing to the stage a talent and compassion that rose above his setting.

Williams corked up for a while, put it aside and pursued a singing career. Then one night, he experimented once more. "At Moore's Wonderland in Detroit, just for a lark, I blacked my face and tried the song, 'Oh, I Don't Know, You're Not So Warm.' Nobody was more surprised than I was when it went like a house on fire," he told an interviewer. "Then I began to find myself. It was not until I was able to see myself as another person that my sense of humor developed."

Blackface launched a maddening doubleness, for if it turned a poor man into a well-paid celebrity, it ritually evoked his low status in the world. Williams was hired to entertain and mingle at society parties; here was a man who read *The New Republic* and quoted Ralph Waldo Emerson who felt it necessary to put New York elites at ease by showing up in full costume and bellowing in his rich baritone, "Is we all good niggers here?"

Among a segment of educated African Americans, the burnt cork became an embarrassing symbol of backwardness. A college professor from Kansas wrote Williams and Walker:

> May I ask this question? Is it not possible that while at the same time you hold the old plantation Negro, the ludicrous darkey, and the scheming "grafter" up to entertain people, that you could likewise have a permanent character representative of [Alain] Locke, the Negro student at Oxford, England, having an American Rhodes scholarship by reason of his superior ability, mentality, morally and physically?
>
> Such would tend to lift the young Negro mind up to imitate and emulate these heroes. . . . *You* have the opportunity.

But in truth, black entertainers had no opportunity to portray black life at its best. White producers and promoters, not to mention white audiences, would not have permitted it. The most that could be hoped for was a stereotype that had, enfolded within it, sharp slivers of self-possession and social commentary. The performers who dreamed of presenting African culture as it really was knew this as well as anyone alive. But Williams and Walker found steady work in the stereotype business, and that meant seeing themselves not as they were, but as others saw them. It must have been lonely work. "I am *what* I am not *because of*, but *in spite of* who I am," was how Williams once put it.

"Nobody in America knows my real name," he said on another occasion. "And if I can prevent it, nobody ever will." "Nobody," as it happens, was the title of Williams' signature tune.

When George Walker died in 1911, Williams went solo and reinvented his act. He broadened his ragged bumpkin character, crafting elaborate "lies" (his term)—wooly stories rooted in folk tales—in which he performed multiple parts, much as Richard Pryor would do decades later. It's in this period that Williams achieved his greatest fame, leaving the world of all-black productions to become the first and only Negro entertainer featured with the Ziegfeld Follies. On Broadway his poker playing routine became a standout everywhere the Follies traveled. Williams would mime five men playing cards around a table; it was said you could tell each gambler's hand simply by watching his expression. In another era he might well have excelled as a dramatic actor; in another skin, he might have been a great silent comedy star. As it was, he spent his last years drinking heavily and lugging around the manuscript of a drama he had written and hoped some day to star in.

"The burnt cork weighed him down," wrote theater critic Heywood Broun. "It smothered what may have been genius."

"People ask me if I would not give anything to be white," Williams once reflected.

I answer . . . most emphatically, "No!" How do I know what I might be if I were a white man. I might be a sand-hog, burrowing away and losing my health for $8 a day. I might be a streetcar conductor at $12 or $15 a week. There is many a white man less fortunate and less well equipped than I am. In truth, I have never been able to discover that there was anything disgraceful in being a colored man. But I have often found it inconvenient—in America.

Williams and Walker were Broadway stars on a tour of American theaters in 1904. That same year, in Durham, North Carolina, Dewey Markham was born. After leaving home at the age of 14, Markham joined a carnival and stayed on the road for much of the rest of his life. Conditions were rugged, especially in the Dixie that was his home base. Once when his troupe was coming into a Southern town, Markham thought they were pulling up on a festive cookout. When they arrived, however, the truth became clear: a white lynch mob was barbecuing a black man.

Negro showmen had to tread carefully in the South; when you performed for white audiences, you watched what you said when patrons came up to chat. Getting too friendly with a white person, especially a white woman, could be a fatal mistake; it could be dangerous to give one the brush-off, as well. Black minstrels cultivated a deft, defensive backstage manner, a diplomatic apartness that was a kind of mask in its own right.

In the early 1920s Markham joined Gonzell White's traveling show and changed his first name to something more suggestive than Dewey. "I'm Sweet Papa Pigmeat," he'd roar to audiences, "I've got the River Jordan in my hips and all the women is rarin' to be baptized." Pigmeat was slang for young stuff. He hooked up with gillies—small carnivals—along with minstrel and medicine shows. Markham was also a gifted dancer who invented Truckin'—a craze in the 1930s—and steps named Skrontch, Suzy-Q, and Pimp's Walk. Indeed, Jackie Gleason's agile glide likely owes a debt to the creator of the Pimp's Walk.

The booming voice, the nimble movement, the sense of timing: though essential to his art, none were half as important as Pigmeat's face. His countenance gave itself to masquerade: it was expressive and huge, a face like a large rock balanced atop a mountain ("Black Rock" was an early nickname). Obscured beneath his judicial robes, Markham gave the viewer no choice but to focus on that head, huge jowls flying with every swing of the steer's bladder. Deeply lined, molten, his mien was a perfect alias, twisted into an infinite grimace. It was bigger than life and apart from life, a face itself a mask.

"The Fish" by Marianne Moore
All
external
. . . marks of abuse are present on
. . . this
. . . defiant edifice.

• • •

IN A 1949 ESSAY, the writer Bernard Wolfe marveled at the omnipresence of the black minstrel's face. With the voice of a tour guide narrating the American landscape, Wolfe pointed out the roadside diner whose entrance was a Negro's smile, the billboards and magazines here, the beaming dark faces on grocery store products there, the Hollywood darkies everywhere. He lamented their existence in no uncertain terms, but Wolfe seemed awed by it too, by how the smile worked as an invitation, absolving one race of guilt, denying another humanity.

"We like to picture the Negro as grinning to us, and always the image of the Negro—as we create it—signifies some bounty for us," Wolfe wrote. "Eternally the Negro gives—but (as they say in the theater) really gives—grinning from ear to ear."

Pigmeat *really gave*. The term "ham actor" is rooted in minstrelsy; blackface performers used ham fat to remove the burnt cork. Pigmeat was the consummate ham. "I am an African American Negro comedian," Markham wrote in his autobiography. "And I'm proud to be all three. It's what I've been—nothing more and nothing less—since that day in 1918 when I ran away from home in Durham, North Carolina."

After a long career on the circuit, he had earned the right to be proud, the right to believe that he knew things about audiences that critics did not. So when he took Bardu Ali's offer and came to the Lincoln Theater, he could not have been less prepared for the response he got: a volley of hostile criticism hitting him like a steer bladder upside the head. He was doing basically the same blackface act he'd performed for years, but the young activists of the Avenue were not amused. Local columnists, the NAACP, church leaders were all turning up the criticism, calling him a sorry anachronism from the Southern past. One newspaper said he was "a marked man, wanted by the NAACP, the Urban League and any and all Negro advancement societies wishing sudden death to Uncle Tom." What did he do? Nothing new, nothing he hadn't been doing for decades on end. Putting on the burnt cork was all.

Markham couldn't understand the response he received. To him the equation was remarkably simple: people laughed. They filled the seats at the Lincoln and they howled when he scrunched up his big face and leered at a comely lass. He wasn't a politician; he was on whatever side of an issue got the most laughs.

Decades later, the criticism still bothered him. "A lot of people have pointed out that my comedy is not exactly high-class. It comes from Tobacco Road, not from Sugar Hill. Well, I won't argue with that," said Pigmeat.

And a lot of others say my characters like the Judge who's always whopping people over the head, do not represent the modern Negro; that they are caricatures. Well, I won't argue with that, either, long as we admit they're funny.

But when these people tell me I gotta change my act—well, that's where I *will* argue. If I dig them right, they want me to start off with some sort of an introduction that'll tell the audience that [I am] doing what Negroes *had* to do in order to get ahead in the white man's world—that my act is a kind of a historical thing that has no reaction to what's going on in the drive for Negro rights today.

Now many of these "critics" are my friends—some are even in show business and have offered me lots of money, more than once, to work in shows with them. And I think that right there is the answer to their own arguments.

They offered me that money because I added something to the show—I was *funny*. Not historical—funny.

And how did I get to be funny? I was born and raised black. I learned my comedy from black comedians. The earliest skits and bits I did on stage or under a tent were invented by black men. The audiences I learned to please, all those years in small towns and in big cities, they were mostly black too.

He had a point. But in 1943, many loud young voices *were* asking him to change his act, and for the most confounding of reasons—not on humorous grounds at all, but because they felt the very fundament of his act—blackface—was bad for Negroes. It was a generational dispute, and maybe a class conflict too. The young activists felt Pigmeat had no class, that he was setting a bad example for all the kids who looked up to him.

The ham fat was already in the frying pan before he staged a parody of "Uncle Tom's Cabin." In February 1944, the John Kinloch–led Youth Council of the NAACP had played a key role in swatting down a new Hollywood production of Uncle Tom's Cabin. What good could come of gnawing again on that old cracker? they asked. Kinloch lobbied U.S. vice president Henry Wallace at the Ambassador Hotel and came out with a statement from Wallace criticizing the production. Kinloch was focusing attention on black images on the stage and screen, and then he heard about Pigmeat's send-up of Uncle Tom in his very backyard. Hollywood stereotypes were bad enough, but they were nothing compared to the foolishness Markham could cook up.

He had set Uncle Tom's Cabin in Watts, a Watts peopled with caricatured mammies and Toms wearing bandannas and Old South costumes. It was painfully anachronistic and even worse, it was hilarious: "funny and disgusting," a critic from the Junior Council averred. Worst of all was the rumor that *Life* magazine had photographed the production for an upcoming photo essay. "Unless some miracle is performed to check publishing of the pictures, in a week or two what happened on the stage of the Lincoln theatre will be heralded as the Negro's interpretation of artistic achievement."

Rumors of the imminent *Life* article increased pressure on Markham to temper his act. There were backstage visits and ardent discussions. An arrangement was made; Kinloch's Junior Council would critique his performances and Pigmeat would make changes per their wishes. "If this plan works, the shows at the Lincoln will be greatly improved, and parents would need have no fear in allowing their children to attend the theater," a council member announced.

Pigmeat's act drove people crazy; it had the ability to make Kinloch and his fellow young activists sound as judgmental and censorious as their parents. For the council, putting him in the stockade was one more triumph; for Markham, it was something like a knife to the heart. Running his skits past them wasn't the worst of it from Pigmeat's perspective. His career was over. He described a meeting with activists in his autobiography:

> We had a real friendly talk and it turned out they wanted me to stop this blackface makeup thing. They said things was beginnin' to change with us, and me comin' out there in blackface caused a lot of unhappy memories, and it would be more dignified if I was to just go out there the way I was, in my own skin, instead of coverin' it up like I was ashamed of it.

They felt that the mask obscured his humanity; Pigmeat thought the mask was his humanity. And when politics forced him to leave the mask behind, he thought it spelled the end of his career. "To tell you the truth," Markham wrote,

> I'd been working in blackface for so many years that I was scared to go on without it! . . .
> As I say, we talked quite a while. I pointed out to them that it wasn't my blackface makeup the people was laughin' at, so I wasn't holding the Negro people up to no ridicule. I showed 'em how it was the way I guilt up a joke, and the fact that the joke was *funny*, that made the people laugh.
> "You're just answering your own argument," they finally said. "If it isn't the blackface that's getting the laughs, why can't you go on without it?"

Unconvinced, Markham was certain he was about to flop. According to Lincoln Theater bandleader Bardu Ali, word spread backstage that Markham was revising his act. "That first time he went onstage without his makeup, everyone was expecting something to happen," he said. What they expected was a wreck of massive proportions.

Leonard Reed thought he never recovered from losing the mask. "It broke his heart," said Reed.

> He went downhill when he stopped doing cork. He didn't feel that his mugging and his facial expressions would show up and they didn't, you know. Because he wasn't positive enough about them without the cork. He felt hurt—I think it killed him, and I think he died of a broken heart.
>
> His expressions lost something. You see, when he had the white mark around his lips and around his eyes he could bug his eyes and move his lips and people in the audience could see it. But with him normal, it's like having a brown wall and painting brown on it—you can't see nothing.

The burnt cork weighed him down. The mask of the minstrel had hardened into something like a shell, until that was all he thought he was. To twist an old blues lyric he could have sung all night long, if it wasn't for blackface, he wouldn't have had any face at all.

In the aftermath of his public humiliation, Pigmeat went on hiatus. He left the Lincoln in 1944, fading from view while hanging out among the hustlers and lowlife characters of Bronzeville, a bustling community at the north end of the Avenue.

The tradition of black minstrelsy came to an end when Markham left the Lincoln Theater. In his wake, the owners of the Lincoln pondered their own future. Business was good: they had instituted a 1 a.m. swing-shift show because so many workers were buying tickets. There were raucous talent shows and noisy crowds, and soon the staff had to hire a guard and initiate a policy of escorting out those who talked too loud at movies. A critic sniffed at the Lincoln scene:

> the audience is quite as noble as the entertainment. It put me in mind of a dog on a hot afternoon, somnolent at times, but spurred intermittently to action that would put a buzz saw to shame. . . . How anyone

properly entering into the spirit of things . . . could have an inhibition left or any portion either of body or psyche unexercised is beyond me.

An audience that had formerly been handed its entertainment by whites who meant them no good was speaking more directly to its entertainers, and the entertainers were drawing material from the people in the seats. You could say it was dangerous stuff for the white folks to see, because they'd get the wrong ideas about the nature of black folks. You could also say what was dangerous was the solidarity expressed by young black audiences. Either way, you were right.

In the aftermath of Pigmeat's fall, the Lincoln's owners felt honor-bound to clean things up and announced a new booking policy. Burlesque-style shows were out, high-toned productions were in. The Lincoln promised "stirring drama, portraying the problems and victories of the Negro people." It tanked. By the end of the year, Pigmeat was back, minus the blackface, presiding over revues starring T-Bone Walker "and his human-toned guitar," escape artist "The Human Icicle," and a film titled "The Falcon Coeds." People *did* find him funny. Old habits were hard to break.

CHAPTER 8

Bronzeville Balls

Our heart somehow goes out for the poor lil, quiet and nice Jap nabors of ours who seem so sad and almost embarrassed that a lotta them keep their eyes to the ground. Thass all right folks, we brownskins know how ya feel—we're behind the 8-ball too.

—*Bill Smallwood, California Eagle, December 18, 1941*

IN THE MIDDLE OF THE DECADE, WHILE HE WAS COLLECTING HIS thoughts and pondering career options, Pigmeat Markham spent a large amount of time in one particular part of town. It was called Bronzeville, and he spent so much time there he bragged it was only fair he be appointed to public office. There was much for a man with change jingling in his pockets to do in Bronzeville. Pigmeat was buying, and he was far from the only one.

The area was one of Los Angeles's oldest neighborhoods, a 66-square-block district only a moment before called Little Tokyo. On the map this downtown community was concentrated between San Pedro Street and Central Avenue, overlapping Skid Row and stretching north all the way to the shadow of City Hall. The neighborhood was well established; a small group of Japanese immigrants had gathered here around the turn of the twentieth century, recruited to work in the rail yards. In 1908 it was called Little Tokyo for the first time, and by the early 1920s the area had a flourishing ethnic identity, with grocery stores, banks, boarding houses and hotels.

Little Tokyo continued its growth—until Pearl Harbor. It's unclear how many Japanese Americans were shipped off from Little Tokyo after General John L. DeWitt's proclamation of March 1, 1942, authorizing removal of all Japanese Americans living on the West Coast; one historian places the figure at just shy of 8,000. They were first taken to the recommissioned Santa Anita horse racetrack facilities and eventually to a camp at Manzanar, California. By early May 1942, Manzanar was known as the "Little Tokyo of the Mountains."

After internment, Little Tokyo became a staggering anomaly at the center of the city: while the rest of Los Angeles was stuffed with newcomers, here was a ghost town featuring everything but tumbleweeds. Signs advertising closeout sales in Japanese and English still hung in many of the 300 vacant stores. Decorations and paper lanterns hanging from shop awnings became torn in the breeze. Still, a ghost presence of Japanese culture clung to the precinct: calligraphy marked storefronts, huge signs for Japanese American businesses towered above the streets, a Buddhist temple's wood carvings perched above doors now padlocked. Without commerce or people, the streets took on the odd countenance of a sight familiar elsewhere in the city: the movie set.

The crowded denizens of Central Avenue saw the possibilities. Many Japanese Americans had hastily handed over buildings, businesses and churches to black friends and neighbors as they were taken to Manzanar. Blacks and Japanese had lived in close proximity in several neighborhoods, and a political alliance seemed just beginning to hatch in the late 1930s. That was on hold now, while other schemes hatched. Most of the structures in Little Tokyo were owned by white absentee landlords; by one account Japanese Americans never owned more than 20 percent of Little Tokyo's stores and 10 percent of its hotels and apartments. White owners saw little downside in renting out space—for how long was anybody's guess—to black Angelenos. Many abandoned buildings were simply taken over by Negro squatters desperate for a roof over their heads.

By the fall of 1943, African Americans had reanimated the district, starting with its name. Signs appeared in windows throughout the neighborhood: THIS IS BRONZEVILLE. WATCH US GROW! Black entrepreneurs opened the Bronzeville Chamber of Commerce, and that October the chamber threw a coming-out party for the thriving new community, electing a Miss Bronzeville in a beauty contest. A headline in the *Eagle* telegraphed the excitement: "Little Tokyo No More, Bronzeville Balls!"

Its contents under pressure, a vacuum at its north end, Central gushed like a shaken pop bottle. Yet the making of Bronzeville was never a passive act, never simply a matter of contents under pressure seeking relief. "Bronzeville Balls" is a yelp of self-declaration. Black businesses, nightclubs, restaurants and churches had scarcely had such a chance to flourish in years. Here was a black space carved out in the heart of the city, and it was created not from segregation but from black entrepreneurialism. By luck, speed and the drive of those with few options, a new village briefly willed itself into existence.

The layering of Bronzeville upon Little Tokyo spotlighted a complicated shared history of black and Japanese Americans. Blacks vocally empathized with local Japanese Americans after Pearl Harbor; as a wave of racial hostility swept across the white media, many expressed sympathy with their nonwhite neighbors who were now bearing the brunt of rage.

It would be grotesquely inaccurate, however, to describe the sum total of black feeling for the departing Japanese Americans as sympathetic. There had been, perhaps equally, a noticeable sense of rivalry—given that one minority had been pitted against another, it was no surprise. Now that one minority was being dispatched to camps, however, a new feeling tinged the established rivalry—optimism. Many had their eye fixed on the windfall of a storefront, a restaurant, a sofa put out on the street. Black leaders saw the internment as a golden opportunity for entrepreneurs. In the *Eagle* a local wag set the tone for all those lined up at the starting gate: "Flash: why don't some of you 'hep cats' in the music profession try and take over some of these fine businesses that the Japanese are selling because of their going to concentration camps? Probably you would get a better break than the many Jews who are 'Johnnies on the spot.' I'm speaking about Central Avenue. Catch on?" The hep cats hardly needed the nudge.

There was frenzy in the way the Avenue broke north, as if gold had been discovered. Indeed, there was something of the Wild West to the whole scene, as tinhorns, rustlers and sooners poured in, grabbing for what they could, seizing advantage of a amid confusion. Who was in charge? Whom would you like to be in charge? Federal decree had wiped a choice center square of the map clean; who was responsible for what and who was footing the bill was a judgment call. Bronzeville was a place where looking the other way became almost a physical tic. Nobody around knew who owned a given building. Nobody knew who was responsible for controlling the streets—the mayor consulted with the police, the provost marshal of the Army and the Navy's Shore Patrol, and he still couldn't figure it out. Born of morally mixed impulses, Bronzeville pushed notions of probity and law well past prevailing civic standards, maybe even past the breaking point. Bronzeville *was* the Wild West. It was thrilling, it was dangerous, and it was somebody else's land. Bronzeville was Negro L.A.'s 40 acres and a mule. The appropriation wasn't fair, but given the housing situation, it was hardly a surprise.

Within a year of the evacuation, businessmen on the make had painted the place black. The Miyako Hotel was renamed the Civic. Buddhist temples became Baptist churches. Barber schools opened, grocery stores popped up. Charles Broady, the ranking brute on the Avenue police force, had been drummed off the beat and was now running a cocktail lounge in Bronzeville. Bronzeville was the home of second acts. "This tiny spot in the center of this city of the angels is a thriving minute metropolis," cheered one booster. "It boasts newspapers, churches, restaurants, taverns, Shepp's Playhouse, hotels. All of your earthly needs can be supplied in this area. Also takes care of the check cashing and bill paying and Dr. Kaufman watches over the health."

Musicians and night people seemed especially attuned to the place. Liquor store owner and reputed underworld figure Al Trice opened the Samba Club; with its huge horseshoe bar, the Samba was billed as "Skid Row's most sophisticated rendezvous." Owned by an old hoofer, tap star Foster Johnson, the Finale was a showcase for great dancers. A given bill included exotic dancer Princess Starletta, tap man Prince Spencer, and Roy Milton's hard-swinging band.

Bronzeville was the Wild West with horseshoe bars instead of blacksmiths, and among the first places a stranger would be directed to was Shepp's Playhouse, because Shepp's was the boldest spot in Bronzeville. It was owned by Gordon "Shepp" Sheppard, a pool hall proprietor and cameraman for black motion pictures. To enter Shepp's was to leave behind not just Little Tokyo but even Bronzeville, for Shepp's was a figment of the imagination. Walking up the first set of stairs, you emerged in a room decorated in pale green sateen and scarves hanging from the walls, and dominated by the "Three Star Five Circle Bar," a gleaming marvel mirrored and decorated with drawings of sepia odalisques reposing in champagne glasses. Above that was a floor for live jazz and stage shows. Upstairs from that was a suite of private dining rooms furnished with mission-style furniture, an aerie where high rollers could party away from prying eyes. Music from the bandstand was piped throughout Shepp's inner chambers, and five nights a week the club had a live radio broadcast that gave the city a taste of some of the earliest bebop played on the coast, with Charlie Parker, Miles Davis, Teddy Edwards and Coleman Hawkins all regulars (bop trumpeter Howard McGhee was a financial backer). All of Bronzeville amounted to a scrap heap for big band musicians, its hotels and hot-sheet rooms the final resting spot for players left in the lurch when war proclivities—gas and tire rationing, the cost of keeping a large crew on the road—forced big bands to pack it in. Shepp's retooled these anachronisms for the bebop age.

Judy Garland, Howard Hughes and Gene Kelly were seen at the club and no doubt marveled at Shepp's chorus dancers, long lines of leggy gals dressed in revealing togas. Dwarfing those dancers and bringing them together with its graphic energy was a starburst backdrop of black and yellow stripes. Everything about Shepp's was mirrored and over-sized and evocative of some other lavish era, whether it was a time of Roman orgies or, as one witness suggested, "like several pages from the Arabian Nights or the luscious settings of the harem of the Caliph of Baghdad." The cocktail lounge opened at 11 a.m. There was no cover, no minimum, and no door.

Yet if Bronzeville was a multicultural Wild West, it was short on room to roam. Where once lived 8,000 or so Japanese Americans, now were 30,000 black homesteaders, one newspaper reported. A social welfare organization estimated 175 Negroes were arriving per day in the fall of 1943. On one night alone, 153 people were counted sleeping in front of a last-resort hotel—no vacancy. There was zero incentive for Bronzeville's absentee landlords to fix up the existing stock, let alone build new housing, given the confusion about who would be living there after the war. The former Little Tokyo, according to City Housing Authority chairman Nichola Giulli, "has long since become a black ghetto through overcrowding and lack of proper sanitary facilities."

By the fall of 1943, a frantic Mayor Fletcher Bowron was urging federal officials to act on the need for emergency war housing. In a telegram to President Franklin D. Roosevelt, Bowron noted that some 30,000 to 50,000 minorities had arrived in the city over the past two years and were forced "to live not only in overcrowded, substandard quarters, but in unhealthy if not indecent conditions, which increase juvenile delinquencies and other social problems." City health official Dr. George Uhl described the warrens of this shantytown: "Animals in the zoo have better housing than some of L.A.'s human residents, and the general picture here has begun to smell in more ways than one." Uhl visited a three-story rooming house "with a dungeon-like appearance" that contained 65 rooms renting to workers at about $4 a week. The average space was 9 by 8 feet square, and the entire house had three toilets.

Another rooming house sheltered 22 families. Broken plumbing leaked onto the main floor; a cracked sewer pipe caused waste to bubble up in a sink where a ground floor restaurant washed its dishes. The building manager told Uhl, "The owner of the house tells the restaurant proprietor and me that if we report the conditions here the city might close down our business and we will be the losers, not him. And there are no more houses to rent." In Bronzeville, display windows that had once featured Japanese merchandise were now sleeping spaces, garages housed families, and tents were pitched in vacant lots and alleys.

Federal officials dispatched to monitor local war production began to see conditions in Bronzeville as a threat to national defense. The interviews with residents and reports they sent to Washington document in capital letters the racial tensions and slum conditions. One interviewee described his shock upon arriving. "I was born in the country and I did better than this. Things were cleaner. I can't get used to eating in these dirty restaurants." A resident of the Pacific Hotel painted a vivid picture of life in his building.

The house lady gets drunk with all these little 17-18 year old slick heads who do nothing but drink and smoke that stuff all day long. Her husband who manages the place beats her all the time but soon as he goes out to work (he also acts as bartender at a neighboring saloon) she starts and carries on all day.

Government observers reported on a storefront church where orange crates and soapboxes served as seats. "Sitting through a highly spiritual meeting for two hours, I counted three rats run from one side of the room to the other," an eyewitness said. At one barbershop, all the barbers shared the same single filthy towel.

More housing was the main solution proposed by the city. But there were other, more sweeping plots to tackle problems in Bronzeville, and city figures were charging headfirst at them. City Park Commissioner Luke Wood proposed creating a Negro-only subdivision with distinct boundaries within city limits. The area would arise by purchasing property from white owners and then restricting residence to Negroes. That might work in the short term, but what to do about all the people who kept coming off the trains? In the fall of 1943, Deputy Mayor Orville Caldwell suggested to a House subcommittee: "In-migration of Negroes from the deep south must be stopped until such time as these people can be properly absorbed into the community." Citing the rising tensions in Bronzeville, Caldwell warned "unless the influx is stopped dire results will ensue."

When the news hit the Avenue, the notion of a black homeland district was ridiculed as wildly contrary to the war—trying to beat Hitler at his own game. In the aftermath of his remarks, Deputy Mayor Caldwell declared he was taken out of context, and Bowron never acted on Caldwell's advice. But if these schemes floundered, so did all efforts to build public housing for residents stacked up in Bronzeville and elsewhere. The result was that for the next few years, Bronzeville grew, and everybody continued looking the other way.

A big part of the problem was the area's traditional role as entryway for many of the poorest newcomers to the city. According to one social welfare agent, "The better adjusted in-migrant usually goes to the south or western areas of Los Angeles, and only the friendless and helpless come into Little Tokyo." Anecdotal data collected by federal investigators suggested only half facetiously that whole Louisiana towns were moving in. Newcomers were poor, friendless outsiders who clung to those qualities as marks of self-definition. They were glad to be out of the Jim Crow South, and now that they had a few extra dollars in their pocket, they weren't about to be treated like before. They let people know it, too, and thus rubbed older blacks the wrong way. Bronzeville was viewed as the home of déclassé, Deep South rude boys and girls. It was the place where things got a little out of control.

John Kinloch empathized with the newcomers and mocked the patronizing criticism emanating from the establishment. He asked: "Shall we stand on the corner of First and San Pedro offering the motley throng free copies of Emily Post? Shall we hoist ourselves aboard a soap box at Vernon and Central and expound upon the horrors of profanity and red shoes?" But he didn't know what to do with the new folks, either. They presented a great potential for change, because they weren't attached to the way things had always been done. But they were numerous and unattached to the city, and their restlessness was plain.

Private John Kinloch, circa 1943.

(Photo courtesy of the Southern California
Library for Social Studies and Research.)

The popular band leader Lionel Hampton is celebrated on Central Avenue with a nighttime parade.

(Shades of L.A. collection, Los Angeles Public Library)

The Dunbar Hotel, the landmark where W. E. B. Du Bois, Duke Ellington, Paul Robeson and more stayed, as it looked in 1928 shortly after opening.

(Security Pacific collection, Los Angeles Public Library)

The Lounge and Grill at the Dunbar Hotel was the meeting place of prize fighters and jazz musicians actors, and domestic worke celebrating their night off. It was ground zero.

(Courtesy of the Walter L. Gordon, Jr./William C. Beverly, J Collection, University of Souther California)

852—Home of Eddie "Rochester" Anderson, Los Angeles, California

NBC Comedian and Screen Star

Home of Eddie Rochester Anderson, comic actor and onetime mayor of Central Avenue. His palatial digs were located in the "Sugar Hill" neighborhood a little east of the Avenue.

(Author's collection)

The Lincoln Theater, where Pigmeat Markham bawled all night.

(Security Pacific collection, Los Angeles Public Library)

Ice Water, 1943, a guitar player who once rocked a house.

(Courtesy of the Walter L. Gordon, Jr./ William C. Beverly, Jr. Collection, University of Southern California)

(Below) William Seymour, shepherd of the Azusa Street Revival: "his voice is like the roaring of a cannon."

(Flower Pentecostal Heritage Center)

(Above) Clayton Donovan Russell, civil rights paladin of African American L.A. in the 1940s.

(Author's collection)

Meetings are held in a tumble down shack on Azusa Street, the home of the revival.

(Flower Pentecostal Heritage Center)

The view from the stage at the Club Alabam, circa 1945. That's Black Dot McGee, second from the right.

(Shades of L.A. collection, Los Angeles Public Library)

(Above) "This is the most representative group of men in bookmaking, gambling, and narcotic activity that I have seen in one photograph. This is the cream of the crop."— written by attorney Walter Gordon on back of photo. Dated 1945.

(Courtesy of the Walter L. Gordon, Jr./William C. Beverly, Jr. Collection, University of Southern California)

Korla Pandit, organist, healer, international man of mystery.

(Author's collection)

Welcome to Brother's, the after-hours den where everything was available. On the left, in tunic, is Henry "Brother" Williams, next to him is Almena Davis, editor of the Los Angeles Tribune. On the right is Brother's companion, Aristide Chapman.

(Courtesy of the Walter L. Gordon, Jr./William C. Beverly, Jr. Collection, University of Southern California)

Throughout the 1940s, drag balls were an annual rite at big venues like the Elks Temple and the Club Alabam.

(Courtesy of the Walter L. Gordon, Jr./ William C. Beverly, Jr. Collection, University of Southern California)

Floor shows and "chorine cuties" were a staple entertainment on the Avenue and at the Club Alabam, where Patsy Hunter choreographed.

(Courtesy of the Walter L. Gordon, Jr., William C. Beverly, Jr. Collection, University of Southern California)

Dancer, journalist, and civil rights activist Alyce Key, striking a seductive pose.

(Courtesy of the Walter L. Gordon, Jr./ William C. Beverly, Jr. Collection, University of Southern California)

A new residential development goes up.

(Photo courtesy of the Southern California Library for Social Studies and Research.)

Loren Miller in his law office in 1948, the year he knocked down restrictive covenants.

(Ed Miller collection)

Jack "Open the Door, Richard" McVea in a moment of quiet reflection.

(Author's collection)

Police raid on Café Zombie, Avenue haunt, during the post-Black Dahlia crackdown of 1947.

(Herald Examiner collection, Los Angeles Public Library)

Those who wore red shoes, like those in zoot suits, seemed to hold society in hostile judgment. New, ostracized, these detached critics had zero investment in the tattered power structure. Bronzeville was a strange free space, and they had come to put down their marker. A crazy commerce flourished—you could make money, you just couldn't find a place to live. In the gyroscopic heart of Bronzeville straight businessmen were winging it, while on the other side of the moral line hustlers seized the moment. Bronzeville was picking up underground status as a place not just afflicted, but proudly afflicted; what some saw as dangerous miscreants others celebrated as the roughest, scrappingest newcomers to Los Angeles. If the city saw the district as some version of hell, even many of its black citizens kept a wary distance. "In all the discussions of Little Tokyo or Bronzeville or what have you, the principals have been afraid to admit that a goodly portion of the flotsam and jetsam of the race clutters up the area," Almena Lomax wrote in the *Los Angeles Tribune*. "Admittedly there are many sober, industrious, God-fearing people there; there is also scum, which contributes to drunkenness, prostitution, murder, brawls and whatnot." Lomax wisely left the definition of "whatnot" to the reader's imagination.

Where long-settled blacks saw an abundance of vice, those of the demimonde saw simply abundance. As alto saxophonist Norwood Poindexter said of Bronzeville, "It was a notorious section of Los Angeles, Mack-men with their Cads and girls. Skag [heroin] was everywhere. Seemed like half of L.A. was strung out."

Acts of defiance flourished. In 1943 there were heated battles between whites and blacks at 5th and San Pedro streets. When the white owner of the Paramount Café on the north end of the Avenue refused service to a group of blacks, he probably gave it no thought at all, for it was something he had likely done many times before. But when they rose up and tore the place apart, perhaps he gave it a second thought. They then proceeded down the street, walking into other cafés and demanding service, accosting white patrons, stopping others on the street. A white cop on the scene expressed sympathy with the gang, noting that they had finally gotten "sick of that stuff."

The streetcars—"moving theaters" in Robin Kelly's great phrase—became favored spots for anonymous acts of revolt. Those citizens of Shreveport, Louisiana, who flocked by the dozens to Bronzeville brought with them their memories of how black masculinity and autonomy were policed in public transit. In Los Angeles seats were slashed, motormen were heckled, and riders acted the fool. Early in 1944 there were assaults on conductors and motormen running in black areas on an almost daily basis. As historian Kevin Leonard has noted, federal observers were becoming ever more alarmed. Rumors flowed that blacks would riot on January 1, 1944, and that "Negroes were reputedly organizing a group known as the Obnoxious Society, with a subgroup of Bumpers, who were to go about bumping shoppers." Crime, rumors, random acts of incivility, graffiti, jokes, goldbricking: such things have gone on since the days of slavery, anonymous acts of protest at a time when such acts were all that was possible. But in mid-century Bronzeville, they took on a critical mass. They became subjects one talked about openly, badges of honor signifying status. As Chester Himes wrote of Bronzeville's citizens in *If He Hollers Let Him Go*, "those spooks down there were some really rugged cats; the saying was they wouldn't drink a white cow's milk." He said it with pride.

Nobody knew what to do with Bronzeville, or how long it would exist. Were the Japanese Americans going to be allowed back? For the moment—and the moment was all Bronzeville had—the influx of defense workers ensured that there was money to be spent. Opportunists set up to help them spend it: in one four-block area, Bronzeville featured some 47 liquor stores. Gambling was almost as common. By the fall of 1944, gangsters from other parts of the country were eyeing the district. Three times a week starting in September, a Bronzeville-based radio crusader harangued against playing the numbers—a form of lottery—that was establishing itself nicely in his neighborhood.

The numbers games and bookmaking were as much a part of the local enterprise as the Bronzeville Chamber of Commerce. Gamblers funded Little League teams and bankrolled legitimate businesses;

with most financial institutions firmly in white hands, the economic clout of gamblers made them role models and important employers. The Dunbar Hotel was rumored to be owned by numbers players, and gambler Lucius Lomax not only bankrolled the fledgling *Los Angeles Tribune* but also bought a printing press for the *California Eagle*. "He was the chief financier on the Avenue," said attorney Walter Gordon. "A handsome man, straight black hair, very dignified. He looked just like a duke." His wife, Almena Lomax, the editor of the *Tribune*, explained, "He had the ambition of a lot of people in the underworld, to see Negro business flourish."

Wherever numbers were played in Bronzeville, chances were good that Elihu "Black Dot" McGee was in the thick of it. Black Dot—the nickname described how he looked—was a dark-skinned, handsome man with a pretty moustache who was beloved by nearly all. Officially, he was a former boxing manager who had retired to become a dog breeder, a gentleman sport who loved little more than to see his Doberman pinscher Fedor Von Trail do well at a Los Angeles Kennel Club competition. A little less officially, he had been implicated in truck hijacking, bookmaking and prostitution. Black Dot also managed two terrific jazz clubs on the Avenue, the Downbeat (next to the Dunbar Hotel) and the Casablanca, an after-hours spot that was a jam session favorite. They were musicians' hangouts, places where people went to listen. They were also places owned quietly by white gangster Mickey Cohen, and McGee was said by some to be Cohen's trusted soldier on the Avenue.

"I was involved in gambling in other days in the black community," Cohen admitted in his autobiography *Mickey Cohen, in My Own Words*. "I have a lot of friends there that love me and that I love dearly." Among them was the man who kept a tight leash on Fedor Von Trail.

Taking the long view in an age when many sportsmen thought no further than tomorrow, Black Dot relied on charisma, charm and the big stick of Cohen's gambling empire to make his point. Black Dot was known to lecture the young hoods hanging out in front of the Dunbar, reminding them to honor their mom's on Mother's Day. Even when he was involved in a gunfight in front of the Casablanca—the one in which he shot a burglar with whom he had done jobs in the past—even then folks thought McGee was a swell guy. "He was the unofficial mayor of Central Avenue," saxophonist Teddy Edwards recalled. "He was the best-known guy on the street."

His patron Mickey Cohen kept his eye on the Avenue. A Jewish hoodlum raised on the streets of Boyle Heights, Cohen had hustled and provided protection on downtown corners bordering Little Tokyo early in the Depression. Cohen rose through the ranks of organized crime—grad school was in Chicago, New York and assorted jail cells in the East—and he returned to L.A. in 1939, focusing on establishing a uniformity among the numbers played in the city. His proposal was that everybody play the game he ran. Cohen was a regular on Central, the rare white man whose sense of style was in tune with the curbstone cowboys gathered outside the Dunbar Hotel. "*Oh*, he used to come out a lot," said Sugar Tit, a onetime shoeshine boy and chauffeur on the Avenue. "That guy's shoes looked like glass. I think he had a guy who stayed at his home who took care of all of his clothes, cause this guy used to *dress*. He always had a Dobbs 20 hat on and he used to break it down. You know, the pimps used to wear it with the brim up, rolled all the way around. But he used to break his down. That was a sharp little dude."

The whites who made their way down to Central after dark were of a few categories. There were jazz fans and players, who did all right as long as they didn't expect special treatment. There were slumming Hollywood folk like the actor Sonny Tufts, who chased that dark stuff and spent weeks on the case. But Cohen was a category unto himself. A homeboy. "He was a big, big spender, but he was a nice man," said Sugar Tit. "He was a murderer but, you know what I'm saying, he was a *nice man*." A marker of Cohen's acceptance was how he addressed his peers.

See, blacks in those days, we were "colored" or "Negro." But he was the only guy that—I heard him talking to some of the black guys. "Nigga" he'd say,—not nigger, he'd say "nigga." And they wouldn't, it would just be like he was one of the guys! *We* called each other "nigga." And the white redneck would call you "nigger"—there was a big difference. Mickey was that kind of person, that's how he came off to me. What he did on the other side of town, you didn't give a rat's ass. Who cares?

Gambling was hardly the extent of the local diversions. On the scene, particularly along 5th Street, observers noted the appearance of a passing parade of flamboyantly attired men accompanied by scantily clad women. Very quickly Bronzeville became known as a place where men of all races with a wallet in their pocket could "date" black women. East 5th Street probably symbolized everything that the black leadership thought was wrong with Bronzeville. Not just that there was criminality going on there, but that it was so pridefully going on there. "The high esteem in which the pimp is held on E. 5th street must be destroyed," a letter writer complained to the *Tribune*. Another writer ventured a statistical assessment, positing "at least 90 percent of all the women on E. 5th St. are prostitutes. About 50 percent are bold ones."

The mid-1940s Central Avenue pimps wore well-shined Peters Brothers shoes with white stitching around the soles. They donned Dobbs hats and suits called 3-Ds that they purchased downtown. They drove the Eastside (preferably in a 1942 model Lincoln Continental, with the wheel in back) with little bottles of Noxzema in their cars, which kept the shine off their faces and left a strikingly smooth affect; some even brandished a powder puff to the same end. Hair—well hair, of course, was crucial. But the most important aspect of the hair was the razor cut around the ear. That clean line defined a sense of style and order crucial to the persona.

In Bronzeville, living on the street was a desperate necessity. Pimps turned the notion of living on the streets into a performance, and they assembled a fashion sense, verbal style and philosophy to deal with the harsh conditions they faced. They were powerful figures along the Avenue, symbolizing a mastery of the system—make that "the system," for they turned life into a game and boasted of their facility at winning.

For some working hard to get by, pimps were regarded with a slightly cosmic affection. They knew how the wheels turned. "Overwork killed my father, and I promised it would never kill me. And it never has!" bragged sportsman Artie Graves.

Pimping had a long-established style and history on the Avenue, but in Bronzeville, which didn't believe in history, pimps spoke in harsher tones. The hustlers there were quicker, more broke; they didn't care about sinking money into the community. Central Avenue pimps were fabulists; 5th Street pimps were thugs. Sugar Tit said:

> It was a different proposition than Central, because [in Bronzeville] all the dirtbags hung around. Artie Graves used to say "a good pimp don't need to follow his women around." Down on 5th street there was a bunch of 'em used to follow their women; good pimps don't have to do that, women find them. They were the bad pimps, the ones that beat up their women and went out and did their second story stuff and lived in gambling joints. Most of them were using drugs. No class.

That is how divided black L.A. was: even the pimps waged class war.

Paradoxically it was this disregard for social standing that made them icons to some. Up in Bronzeville, a pimp style that signified class (as it did on Central Avenue) was switched out for a new style that signified not giving a good goddamn. A new kind of pimp caught the attention of black bohemians in revolt, among them the young Charles Mingus. He was a jazz bassist from Watts, one of the most important composers and bandleaders in jazz history, and in the late 1940s Mingus seemingly gave pimping a whirl. He boasted of it in his autobiography *Beneath the Underdog*, but that book features a streak of tall tales. Others, however, concur that Mingus was a pimp.

"Well, he probably thought he was," said his mentor and friend saxophonist Buddy Collette. "Yeah, maybe he was able to find some girl along the way that was willing to hear his story; yeah, I think that's not too difficult. You find one that's heading in that direction and you just went in encouraging that. 'I can set that up.' He probably tried all that."

Pimping's allure also affected another young entertainer, a promising singer and dancer who was staying in a Bronzeville hotel while his act conquered Hollywood clubs and downtown theaters. Sammy Davis Jr. was smitten with the 5th Street sheikhs. "Sammy Davis Jr. liked that element better than he liked the Central Avenue element," says Sugar Tit.

He was a wannabe. He wanted to hang around all the whores and pimps. Sammy was all the time gambling and hanging around and talking loud. He was famous but he was still Sammy Davis Jr., and he liked going with the whores and he used to do it a lot, a lot, a lot. His uncles got all upset with him but he used to do it. When he went to fucking around he stayed out of Hollywood and he came out on 5th Street.

In the end, here is what Bronzeville had become by 1945: the Wild West with Mack men, their Cads and their girls. That's what Davis liked about it. A devotee of Western movies as well as of Bronzeville, Davis loved a good shoot-em-up. Dressed as a cowboy, he would strap six shooters to his hip and dare strangers to beat him—just try it, just once!—in a classic high noon duel. As far as symbols of the spirit of Bronzeville, you could do far worse than this: a devotee of 5th Street pimps and their poontang, striding the lawless street and challenging strangers with an achingly wide-open grin to draw.

CHAPTER 9

Tongues

Oh honey sock me on the nose yama yama yama yama root de voot de voot ... oh honey so sock sock sock sock sock cymbal sock cymbal rymbal dymbal a nimble nimble nimble ... so sock me on the nose ... ose gose goose goose goose goose mose gavoose bablow your nose ... hello rose how's your toes put some papowder on your nose ah rosettah are you feeling bettah ... ah rose nose nose rose me lamble damble damble roozy voot mop mop broom broom sweep sweep so honey sock my nose.

—*Leo Watson, "Honeysuckle Rose"*

BY THE FALL OF 1945, WITHIN WEEKS OF THE ATOM BOMB FALLING ON Hiroshima and then Nagasaki, the always-looking-for-an-angle club owners of Bronzeville were on the case. Pianist Eddie Heywood was promptly billed as "atomic action manifest" for his stint at Shepp's Playhouse. The band of Sammy Franklin had abruptly changed its name to the Atomics, there was a spot called the Atomic Café, and you could get your laundry done at the Atomic Cleaners. At the Samba Club, patrons could hear a singer named Francis "The Atomic Bomb" Gray and drink something called an atomic cocktail.

The terrible explosions over Japan were felt distantly all around black Los Angeles. Perhaps it was especially so of Bronzeville, for Bronzeville had its own history of apocalypse and fury. To understand what was going on at the Samba Club and in the private rooms upstairs at Shepp's, we must examine the birth of fire in Bronzeville and walk into the frenzy of an earlier time, back before Bronzeville had a name, before Little Tokyo had a name, back to the first years of the twentieth century, when the area was in a primal stage. Then, a small group of blacks called this place—if it had a proper name, nobody remembers it—home. It was a quiet place, until it got loud.

How loud? On the front page of the April 18, 1906, *Los Angeles Daily Times*, a panic-inspiring report described nocturnal howls and bizarre behavior rising from this downtown sector.

> Breathing strange utterances and mouthing a creed which it would seem no sane mortal could understand, the newest religious sect has started in Los Angeles. Meetings are held in a tumble-down shack on Azusa Street, near San Pedro Street, and devotees of the weird doctrine practice the most fanatical rites, preach the wildest theories and work themselves into a state of mad excitement in their peculiar zeal. Colored people and a sprinkling of whites compose the congregation, and night is made hideous in the neighborhood by the howlings of the worshippers who spend hours swaying forth and back in a nerve-racking attitude of prayer and supplication.

The alarmist, patronizing tone aside, this story covers a lot of ground without coming close to understanding—how could one, in 1906?—what was happening at this shack on Azusa Street. It was a tumultuous moment. Los Angeles in 1906 was witnessing the birth of modern-day Pentecostalism. Today, by one estimate, there are some 10 million Pentecostals in the United States, and one in four Christians on earth is said to be of the faith. The tradition that was born in the area eventually to be Bronzeville is the tradition of Oral Roberts and Aimee Semple McPherson, a tradition of both political powerhouses and faith-healing televangelists. All have L.A. roots, though all might not own up to them.

Upon moving into that shack, a minister named William Joseph Seymour triggered a spiritual outpouring of an intensity barely fathomable today to believers and nonbelievers alike. The congregation declared that the day of Pentecost, the biblical moment when the Holy Ghost came to earth and signaled the end of time, was upon the land. Seymour believed that the Holy Ghost was appearing in Los Angeles. And whether they bought that or not, eyewitnesses had to admit strange things were happening every day. An eleven-year-old girl had a vision on Saturday, November 24, 1906, a local church newsletter reported: after reading the Bible for an hour, she saw a huge black ball crossing the night sky. As it moved through the heavens, upon this sphere came a gray light, on which was written: PACIFIC OCEAN. The black ball kept rolling, there was a dazzlingly bright light, and on that brightness new words appeared: LOS ANGELES. In 1906 it was as if a sign was hanging over the city, advertising the bizarre events below to those free enough to see them.

Seymour's mission newsletter, the *Apostolic Faith*, kept track of the wonderworks unfolding. The publication reported that a little girl with tuberculosis had dropped her crutches and been healed. That a sleeping car porter had a night vision of a man dripping blood nailed to a cross. "I am glad I received my Pentecost, for it is the best thing I ever had," another witness testified. "I have not been bothered with opium any more [and] I have no desire to go back. I have squared the $10 with that man, and by paying it, the Lord has blest me."

Miracles of healing flourished on Azusa Street, but the signal blessing, the one that came before all others, was a miracle of sound. People began speaking in strange languages they did not know: Hebrew, Latin, Chippewa, Eskimo, Zulu, even signing in the deaf-mute language, as well as tongues nobody in town—nobody on earth—could identify. They spoke in a noise that haunted and rocked the shack, a noise that split the night in two.

It was as if some huge and potent celestial force had borne down on a single Los Angeles neighborhood. "The power of God now has this city agitated as never before," trumpeted the *Apostolic Faith*. The force drew newcomers to Azusa Street with an eerie pull. "One brother stated that even before his train entered the city, he felt the power of the revival."

Can a neighborhood, let alone a neighborhood as ragtag and unassuming as this not-yet-Little Tokyo was in 1906, really be inhabited by such an unearthly power? At the very least it's clear that in the mid-1940s many—first on scattered blocks and eventually around the world-believed a powerful force was flowing from Bronzeville, a force that bore a striking similarity and tantalizing connection to what was happening on the same spot some 40 years before. In 1906, even the hostile newspaper reporters sounded impressed, or confused, by what was going on. Things would only get more confusing.

The man most responsible for what came to be called the Azusa Street Revival, William J. Seymour, remains a cipher. Those who have retraced his steps have mostly been fellow Pentecostals, and the picture they paint is incomplete but riveting. Seymour was a child of slaves, a self-taught minister who was blind in one eye after a bout with smallpox. He came to Los Angeles at the invitation of a black Holiness congregation. The Holiness movement is rooted in Methodism and believes in the blessing known as sanctification—originally the moment when the Holy Spirit made his presence felt, sanctification became understood as a flooding of holy power that leads to an immense sensation of spiritual cleansing, purity and light. Sanctification became an article of faith among a fringe within Protestantism during the nineteenth century; it also became known as the "second blessing." (It followed the initial blessing of religious conversion.) Belief in sanctification was controversial, so incendiary that the group inviting Seymour to Los Angeles had already been thrown out of their Baptist church for espousing the second blessing.

He arrived in Los Angeles on February 22, 1906, and though he was a mild, somewhat fumbling man, he quickly stirred up trouble. Seymour turned out to be too radical for a church that was itself far outside the mainstream. His unorthodox teachings—his belief that in order to receive the Holy Ghost's blessing, one first needed to speak in

tongues—got Seymour evicted from the Holiness circle that only a little while before had themselves been tossed out. A revolution was
afoot, and worse things than evictions happen in revolutions. Seymour
slogged on, adrift and without a ticket home, taking shelter in a house
on Bonnie Brae Street in a black neighborhood.

It's important to emphasize the African American-ness of these
events: black Holiness followers bringing a black minister to L.A. to
live and preach in a black neighborhood. The events that followed
were among the most earth-shaking, life-changing and uncanny of the
twentieth century, as well as the least understood. For a twentieth-
century mass movement, not to mention a movement born of a scientif-
ically inexplicable eruption of speaking in tongues, the Azusa Street
Revival has received surprisingly little research. We know more about
millennial movements in medieval England than we do about the most
important millennial upheaval of twentieth-century America. Among
the insufficiently understood aspects is the role black culture played in
the initial outpouring of Pentecostalism.

In his Bonnie Brae Street exile, Seymour formed a prayer group and
continued preaching the primacy of tongues. He had yet to receive the
Holy Ghost baptism himself; that is, he had yet to burst into an unknown language, which he taught was the one true proof that the Holy
Ghost had touched a believer. But on April 9, 1906, seven of his followers fell to the floor, and over the course of a prayer service, one after another began speaking in tongues. A crowd gathered, and just one more
strange thing happened: one of the seven, a woman with no musical
training, is said to have played a standup piano with great accomplishment and sung in what was taken to be Hebrew.

Even in 1906 Los Angeles had a firmly established reputation for
harboring fringe religions; already the citizenry were amused by the
parade of fakirs and messiahs. Yet something about the outburst of
tongues began connecting with a portion of the public. A crowd gathered around the house and services continued, people filling the porch
and yard. From the very start what was happening here was understood as a social force, as a cascade that no house, no inner space could
contain. As one witness explained of the scene, "The porch became

the pulpit and the street became the pews." Seymour soon moved to a larger building (the shack on Azusa Street), but once the streets had become his pews, his mission would never really withdraw indoors again. The outburst of babble quickly outgrew its first address, as it would soon outgrow the city.

At the onset of the twentieth century, Azusa Street was an unpaved byway, basically an alley, which dead-ended into the Los Angeles River. It was also said to be the first all-black street in L.A. The building Seymour secured for his mission had long before been the city's first African Methodist Episcopal church, resting on land once owned by former slave Biddy Mason. After the AME moved elsewhere, the address was a tombstone shop and most recently stables, and the trash-strewn rooms testified to the degraded condition of the flat-roofed, whitewashed, two-story, clapboard structure. In no way did the structure distinguish itself from the rugged, industrial spirit of the surrounding neighborhood. Seymour cleaned up the trash, scattered sawdust on the floor and then placed redwood planks across nail kegs for seating.

His vision of the mission's layout bears comment. Upstairs was a small tarrying room, its walls lined with canes and crutches tossed off by the healed, pipes left by smokers who were cured. The walls downstairs were lined with tin mailboxes where visitors inserted donations. Churches, then as now, typically featured an elevated pulpit at one end, facing a long row of pews below. Seymour built a small platform in the center of the room and nailed together two wooden crates as his lectern. He was collapsing the space between pulpit and pew, cleric and layperson. Seymour used no prayer books, programs or prepared sermons. Spontaneity ruled. Services happened whenever they happened: they might start at ten in the morning and run beyond midnight. His mission had no name, no pretense. He simply opened the doors, invited everyone in and started preaching. What followed was nothing so mundane: for three and a half years there flourished a ceremony that was the distillation of something purely democratic, or maybe purely anarchic. There was no "right way" to behave in the mission; in the back of the room people debated and heckled what was going on, while at the altar people were swooning with the power of God. (At first there were occultists, spiritualists and magicians on the periphery.) Near the beginning of one service, a member promised: "We have no planned program, nor are we afraid of anarchy or crooked spirits. God the Holy Spirit is able to control and protect his work. . . . God can use any member of the body, and He often gives the more abundant honor to the weaker members." The mission had a name for those supposedly "weaker" members: Saints. The name suggests the value Pentecostals gave even the poorest among them. Lay people as well as clergy could stand and preach. Power was being radically decentralized, scattered among the seats like sawdust.

Healing was a crucial part of the services, but what gathered the most attention from outsiders and probably even insiders was the flare-up of foreign and unknown languages. You prayed for it and waited, for there was no way to schedule the arrival of the Holy Spirit. His coming could take excruciating days, weeks. When it hit, members spontaneously broke into ancient languages and sang in choirs of tongues.

Azusa Street was not the first place where people had spoken in tongues. In the nineteenth century, such groups as Irvingites and Shakers experienced bouts of tongues, as did Mormon leader Brigham Young. Most significant, perhaps, was an outbreak of evangelical fervor at Cane Ridge, Kentucky, in 1801. During services lasting five days and nights, perhaps 20,000 people reached a fever pitch, and hundreds were said to fall and convulse, breaking into "holy barking." Cane Ridge has sometimes been called the start of the Second Great Awakening of American Protestantism. But tongues were an unexpected— and not entirely welcome—byproduct of the Cane Ridge revival. They seem to have been understood as a manifestation of the group's intensity rather than as an expression of the presence of the Holy Ghost. At Azusa Street tongues were essential to the experience, for they distinguished those who received the baptism from all others.

The teachings of Charles Parham, a Topeka-based Holiness adherent and healer, had greatly influenced Seymour's thinking. In Houston, Texas, in 1905, Seymour enrolled in a Bible class taught by Parham. Given that this was Texas and that Parham's other students were white, the instructor took care to have his pupil stand in the hallway outside the classroom. Local custom, and Parham's personal inclination, brooked no integration of black and white. Parham did, however, crack the door open for Seymour's benefit.

Through that door came Parham's description of sanctification, his passion for the baptism of the Holy Spirit. Elaborating on this established Holiness belief, though, Parham taught that the only true evidence of this baptism was speaking in tongues. (He based his teaching on a passage of the New Testament's book of Acts, the first place in which the Bible mentions speaking in tongues. According to Acts, the Holy Spirit swept down "like a mighty wind" on early Christians during the feast of the Pentecost and caused them to speak in a mystery language.) Seymour brought this radical doctrine with him when he arrived in Los Angeles a year later and in the process turned a subculture into a worldwide movement.

Seymour was a humble man with no natural eloquence; his sermons were more notable for the impact they had on believers than as rhetorical jewels unto themselves. The man himself remains maddeningly out of focus. A century ago a reporter described his affect:

> This founder of the sect stands full six feet in height. He wears a rubber collar, decorated by no sign of a necktie. Adorning his mouth is one massive gold tooth, ranked by rows of other teeth, perfectly straight and white. The beard that he wears could be called a flowing one if it was longer. It flows—what there is of it. His voice is like the roaring of a cannon, and of all his most striking characteristics, he has but one eye.

Seymour made a vivid impression on those around Azusa Street, yet he retreated from the attention of strangers. He had by various accounts zero charisma. Arthur Osterberg, a pioneering member of the mission, described him as "meek and plain spoken and no orator. He might preach for three-quarters of an hour with no more emotionalism than that there post." Often Seymour could be found bent over in the pulpit, his head inserted into one of the two boxes that, cobbled together, served as his lectern. Even he seemed overwhelmed by the torrent of voices at Azusa Street, by the cacophony of tongues.

What did speaking in tongues feel like? Glen A. Cook, a newspaperman and part-time minister, recalled the moment the spirit came to him.

I had been seeking about five weeks, and on a Saturday morning I awoke and stretched my arms toward heaven and asked God to fill me with the Holy Ghost. My arms began to tremble, and soon I was shaken violently by a great power, and it seemed as though a large pipe was fitted over my neck, my head apparently being off. I was not filled with the Holy Ghost. I cannot describe the power I felt. The nearest description that could be given would be the action of a pump under terrific pressure, filling me with oil. I could feel the filling in my toes and all parts of my body which seemed to me to swell until I thought I would burst. I do not know how long this continued but it seemed to me a long time. The pressure was now removed and my soul and spirit seemed to leave the body and float in the air just above. My body seemed hard and metallic like iron. This was undoubtedly the baptism into the death of Christ.

Having the spirit visit you was an overpowering, violent experience. Corporeally, Holy Ghost baptism might be accompanied by dancing, writhing, twitching. Vocally, it arrived with screams, sobs, laughter, shouts. There was a profound sense of losing control over one's physical self, losing track of one's identity. It must have seemed like an assault. "On Friday evening, March 1, His mighty power came over me, until I jerked and quaked under it for about three hours," wrote a witness.

It was strange and wonderful and yet glorious. He worked my whole body, one section at a time, first my arms, then my limbs, then my body, then my head, then my face, then my chin, and finally at 1 a.m. Saturday, March 2, after being under the power for three hours, He

finished the work on my vocal organs, and spoke through me in unknown tongues.

The Azusa Street evangelicals were expected to travel far and wide
to convert the masses; fortunately for them, they had also been given
xenolalia, the gift of foreign tongues. Their newsletter is full of stories
of missionaries startling immigrants with their fluent Swahili, or
Welsh, or Kree. Thus Seymour felt secure in sending Saints off to save
souls in distant places. As shown by the tale of minister A. G. Garr,
things didn't always go as planned. In 1906 Garr felt the Holy Spirit
had given him the ability to hold forth in Hindustani and Bengali and
had given his wife fluency in Tibetan and Chinese. His mission sent
him to India, where upon arrival, an evangelical already in the field
who had actually studied those languages told Garr his Hindustani
was incomprehensible. Garr refused to believe him and charged out
into the wilderness, addressing baffled crowds of Indians. After what
must have been a difficult stay in the backcountry, Garr and his wife
departed for China where, historian Grant Wacker writes, "they buckled down to the arduous task of learning the language the hard way."
Eventually, the mission dropped the notion of dispatching untrained
missionaries.

In this wild place, in the mania of anonymous strangers springing
up to lay their hands on newcomers and then falling back into the
crowd, there was a political dimension deserving of closer examination. First of all, the mission was exceptionally open to women.
Women were welcome to testify, receive Holy Ghost baptism, be
healed and give witness. One eyewitness account even said that a
group of women—not Seymour, whom they brought in—were the true
instigators of the revival.

Second, since the Holy Spirit infused the individual directly, not
through a mediating clergy, the individual's relationship to God was
paramount—church hierarchy, ritual and bureaucracy were beside the
point. Pentecostalism empowered the meek. Who were the people in
the pews? Overwhelmingly, they were laborers, domestics, cooks, janitors, and the poor—newcomers who had not been assimilated into the

city's social fabric. L.A. was a boomtown in 1906—its population about 228,000 and bursting with strangers, over 30,000 in the previous year. Racially it had the largest black population west of Texas—still quite a small one compared to the South, about 5,000 or 6,000 strong. In this vortex they found a home.

The power of Holy Ghost baptism knocked people to their knees, part of why it was such a great social leveler. A passage from the *Apostolic Faith* captures the class-eradicating aspect of tongues. "There are 50,000 languages in the world. Some of them sound like jabber. The Eskimo can hardly be distinguished from a dog bark. The Lord lets smart people talk in these jabber-like languages. Then He has some child talk in the most beautiful Latin and Greek, just to confound professors and learned people." (This article was signed "Banner of Truth.") Demolishing the high-and-mighty while exalting the lowliest, tongues had signal, secret meanings for African Americans in L.A.

And at this mission founded and maintained by blacks, for a time a radical racial harmony prevailed. Seymour ministered to a congregation that included Negroes, Anglos, Mexicans, Russians. Racial distinctions were explicitly put aside: "the color line," wrote one white participant, "was washed away in the blood." "In the beginning, color meant nothing to us," another member wrote. "There were no blacks and no whites. . . . It was God's Spirit welding us together, and that is a kind of unity that you can't define." "Everybody was just the same," explained another; "it did not matter if you were black, white, green, or grizzly."

Gaston Barnabas Cashwell, a blond-haired, white evangelist from Dunn, North Carolina, witnessed Seymour's integrated service. If the mixing of races wasn't shocking enough to him, a young black man putting his hand on Cashwell's head and praying for him to be baptized certainly was. The Southern gentleman said the experience caused "chills to go down my spine"—not the experience of the second blessing, that is, but being handled so familiarly by a Negro. He recoiled, but having traveled this far and reluctant to leave, Cashwell lingered and—feeling emboldened—eventually asked black congregants to lay their hands on his head in order for him to be filled. Cashwell began speaking in German. A believer now filled with the fire, he took Azusa Street back to North Carolina and attempted to minister to integrated congregations.

Azusa Street looked like integration in action. But to fully understand what was happening there, and to understand Pentecostalism's success and incredible spread around the world, it is necessary to weigh how the revival made contact with West African religion—and how it reached outside Protestantism. Because in this alley of downtown Los Angeles there flourished—accidentally, clandestinely—a sense of divinity brought over in slave ships.

The accounts by whites at Azusa Street form a parable of what happens when Europe unguardedly merges with Africa in the new country. Consider the recollection of Florence Crawford. At her first visit to the mission, Crawford felt nothing, only a frustrating sense of boredom. "I went in and sat down," she wrote.

> They sang a little, but that didn't seem to touch my heart. They went down in prayer; but that didn't move me at all. Pretty soon they got up, and they sang again. Finally a big black man got up on his feet and said, "Hallelujah!" It just went into my soul. He waited a minute and again he said, "Hallelujah! I said, "God, I have heard the voice from Heaven. I have heard it at last." You say, "Is there anything in a Hallelujah?" Yes, there is a lot in it when it has the Spirit back of it.

What is in a hallelujah? Perhaps a store of racial memories from a continent where people spoke in unknown tongues.

During four centuries of bondage, slaves proved adept at nesting African worship within religions that were forced upon them in the New World. In the case of Haitian vaudou (or voodoo), perhaps the most studied example of a process of intermingling called syncretism, it was expedient to embed numerous West African deities within Catholicism, to merge qualities of African spirits with European saints and thus bring across a raft of Yoruban practices, among them spirit possession and a devotional mode that focused on dance and music. As James Baldwin said in *The Devil Finds Work*, this process is part of what defines black religion in America: "The blacks did not so much use Christian symbols as recognize them—recognize them for what they were before Christians came along—and, thus, reinvest these symbols with their original energy."

Parham cracked the door open so that Seymour could eavesdrop in Houston, but in Los Angeles Seymour flung the door open and Africa streamed in. Seymour himself was deeply influenced by slave culture, for his parents were both former slaves, as were his grandparents. Born in Louisiana, he grew up in a downstate parish that had been a slave-owning stronghold. Raised a Baptist, he was in close proximity to slave-era Christianity and Creoles who were steeped in vaudou. Another of the leaders at Azusa Street, Lucy Farrow, was an emancipated slave from Houston who was the niece of the writer Frederick Douglass. In these and other ways the culture of Azusa Street seems to have been energized by the African diaspora, as well as, perhaps, the race consciousness of the era.

What was happening in the nascent Bronzeville was a form of spirit possession—even some white converts at Azusa Street used the term to describe their experience. Spirit possession is a core aspect of numerous African-based religions. Trance states, the examination of dreams and visions, faith healing—all these aspects of the Azusa Street experience were also characteristic of West African religion. The very collective nature of the service seems tied to Africa, for even though participants described the experience of an outside force overwhelming their bodies, there clearly was as well in 1906 an experience of individuals themselves inhabiting a larger force, a sense of the individual's experience transforming the experience of the group. It was a chain reaction of soul. At Azusa Street, a new sense of individual identity was evoked, a sense older than the Republic.

It's hard to derive much inspiration from Seymour's surviving writings; they describe a fire that they themselves never generate. Which seems somehow fitting, for the revival itself couldn't be written down, nor did it exist as a set of sermons or doctrines to be practiced. Pentecostalism came alive in the moment and in the process it destroyed the moment. Like a jam session the Azusa services were off the clock, defiant of any schedule, far more akin to play than to work, and upon occasion they went on so long they achieved their own separate status, their own reality, gaining force from sheer duration, extending from now to never-endingness, services rolling on from morning until past midnight, depending on the proclivities of the "soloists." The clock was smashed. Paradoxically, the service was utterly immediate, a series of flashing moments when bodies broke down and the divine blessing hit in an instant. The Pentecostal experience lived between minds and texts and was found between hearts and God—Pentecostals kicked away all that obstructed the immediate contact with the Holy Ghost.

The music at Azusa Street also reached back to slave culture, incorporating rhythmic singing and collective improvisation in a fashion dating to plantation times. Witnesses from 1906 routinely referred to speaking in tongues as singing, and their accounts suggested that the revival was a kind of mass vocal performance. Standing at the center, conducting with a minimum of agitation and a maximum of contained poise, of cool, was Seymour. All these qualities—collective improvisation (the mass uproar), ad-libbed solos (individuals speaking in tongues), even coolness—have long-observed connections with African cultures that fed the slave trade.

This out-of-bounds blackness, interspersed as it was with an outburst of race mixing, made people nervous. Even Charles Parham, the Holiness man who taught Seymour, recoiled at the integration he had inspired. After news of the mission spread, Azusa Street members prepared for a visit from Parham as if a foreign dignitary was coming. Their zeal, though, masked underlying differences between Seymour and his mentor: Parham was a Ku Klux Klan sympathizer and a believer in the pseudo-scientific white supremacist theory of Anglo-Israelism. When he encountered the mission in October 1906, the visitor was horrified. "Men and women, whites and blacks, knelt together or fell across one another," he noted. "Frequently, a white woman, perhaps of wealth and culture, could be seen thrown back in the arms of a big 'buck nigger,' and held tightly thus as she shivered in freak imitation of Pentecost. Horrible, awful shame." After witnessing the mission in Los Angeles, Parham told Seymour "God is sick at His stomach!" Holding their ground, members asked him to leave.

Civic leaders also fretted over the revival. There was murmuring about kissing between the races—the soul kiss, it was called—and fears of additional physical intimacy. One writer warned that "white people [were] imitating [the] unintelligent, crude negroisms of the Southland, and laying it on the Holy Ghost." A lurid account in the *Los Angeles Times* described a young white female who "engaged in whispered conversation with the black leader and appeared to press her face against his perspiring chops in her eagerness to tell her story. . . . Pandemonium reigned supreme when the meeting was practically turned over to the Negroes at 10 o'clock. Black wenches threw themselves on the floor and cackled and gabbled."

The criticism barely touched Seymour. The divine fire kept falling, and those at Azusa increasingly took their message to the streets of the city. The official response was swift, and it was ironic, too: nonbelievers who were mocking tongues as psychotic babble were also reading into it seditious messages (one account paints it as a full-fledged anarchist rally). Members were arrested for preaching on downtown streets and put on chain gangs and in hospitals for the insane. Police tried to shut the mission down; the child welfare office sought to close it; the health department cited it, too. Pentecostals worried civic leaders because they refused to keep their noise indoors and took not just their message but, more troublingly, their spectacle to the city at large.

Right out in the open, believers broke into tongues: "The porch became the pulpit and the street became the pews." One account in the *Apostolic Faith* suggests the bafflement Saints themselves felt as they circulated:

> I got off [the streetcar] close to our mission and saw two colored police officers with whom I was slightly acquainted, and felt led to speak to them of what the Lord had done for my soul. I commenced speaking in

an unknown language and they said I was crazy and carried me to the station.

The writer, who calls himself simply "a worker," uses a tone that is plain and direct, strikingly affectless. Unable to process what is happening to him, unconcerned, he uses no metaphor, makes no assumptions about what tongues portend—they just happen.

> While waiting for the patrol wagon at the corner, I was enabled to preach to quite a crowd of people. I also preached up at the police headquarters in both English and in [an] unknown language. They put me in among the prisoners. I continued to preach and they quickly took me out of there and carried me into the emergency hospital and kept me in there all night. I preached a good part of the night to them and they listened very attentively. Before morning, they were all my friends. One of the attendants interpreted one of the languages that I spoke as the Kru language, a tribe in Africa that he was acquainted with.
>
> Of course a charge of insanity was filed against me by the officers the day before, and I had to be taken before the superior court judge for commitment. . . .
>
> A couple of weeks ago, they arrested us for disturbing the peace while holding a street meeting. We praised the Lord and the marshal and his deputies put their hands over our mouths and choked us quite severely without avail. One brother was handcuffed. We had trial by jury and took no counsel but the Lord. We pled the case and the Lord was with us. The court was full of people. During the trial, we all broke out in the unknown language and made quite a commotion in the court.

Pentecostalism was an incredibly auditory movement, one that was described by opponents as well as by devotees as uproar. "There has been some unusual noise in the town of Whittier," relates a dispatch in the *Apostolic Faith*. "We are charged," Seymour said with palpable pride, "with using boisterous language, [and making] unusual noise."

Music was crucial to the frenzy, and even the music approximated noise. Seymour encouraged the singing of Negro hymns and spirituals at services. Mostly they were performed a capella, though sometimes with an instrument or two accompanying—there were bones (cows' ribs) and washboards played with thimbles, a piano, sometimes a violin. Perhaps the most awe-inspiring sounds flowed directly from tongues. Forming what were called "heavenly choirs," two to as many as twenty or so members would break into song, harmonizing while singing in a strange language. Sometimes the product was pure sound, noise broken free of syntax: "it would sweep over the congregation, no words, just worshiping, intoning in the Spirit," said Ernest S. Williams.

Harmony such as that was difficult to maintain. The spirit of Azusa Street changed for the worse around 1909; after condemning Seymour's race mixing, Parham opened a nearby mission that siphoned away white members. Soon Parham turned over his mission to a hand-picked minister from Texas whose racial views outdid his own; W. F. Carothers believed that racism was a blessing handed down from the Holy Spirit to keep blacks and whites apart. That racial divide presaged a split among Pentecostals nationally and a split within the Azusa mission as well. Race barriers went up on Azusa Street as they existed outside it, but by then Seymour was out of the picture. He died of heart failure in 1922, and his mission limped into the 1930s, expiring before decade's end.

In some sense, though, Azusa Street continued on as underground fire. A mere five months after the mission opened, 38 missionaries had taken off and had begun spreading the word. Within Los Angeles, kindred missions popped up in various corners of the city. During the first two years of the revival, they spread to over 50 countries. By 1910, there were 50,000—and maybe as many as 100,000—converts in America. A tide was going out and out, both gaining and losing definition as it went.

Meanwhile, people continued moving to Los Angeles, many bringing with them the sanctified, Holiness and Pentecostal beliefs that flowed through Seymour that they had picked up in Florida,

Louisiana, Texas, Georgia and elsewhere. As Pentecostals built churches in all those places, they baited their services with hymns and praise played on an ever-wider variety of instruments, taking musical devotion to regions veterans of Azusa Street could scarcely imagine. There grew in far-flung places a desire to fight fire with fire, to use the devil's music against him. Historian James N. Gregory has detailed the evangelical influence on Dust Bowl refugees in California.

The Pentecostals differed from most other faiths in their emphasis on music and in the range of instruments and arrangements they used in services. Instead of the traditional organ, piano, and slow hymns, they sang rousing up-tempo gospel tunes backed by guitars, banjos, tambourines, sometimes by whole bands.

Central Avenue pianist and teacher Horace Tapscott told journalist Gary Marmorstein he knew where rhythm and blues was born. "Dancing, playing horns and drums in the churches in the 1930s—that's where it all started," he said in 1988. It started with the rhythm and noise of newcomers. Many who came to Los Angeles in the Depression, among the blacks looking for work and all the Okies and Arkies and Dust Bowl refugees (over 200,000 of the latter arriving between 1935 and 1950), were missionaries bringing praise to the mission. A sound was being born.   • • •

CACKLE AND GABBLE: by the mid–1940s, a colossal ruckus would once again wake up the neighborhood. Yet again, as the *Los Angeles Times* had put it, the night was made hideous by the howlings of worshippers.

A music based on the dancing, drumming and singing that poured out of Pentecostal, Holiness and sanctified churches was poised to rip up the streets. Rhythm and blues was hitting the Avenue in a drape shape with red shoes. When it came, the sound of Bronzeville in the 1940s came as it had in the first decade of the century—as vocal noise. The foundational sound of 1940s Bronzeville was established in a flurry of tongues flapping, channeling ancient languages. The band was on the way.

Can a neighborhood, let alone a neighborhood as ragtag and unassuming as Bronzeville in 1946, really be inhabited by such unearthly power? It's a shame Slim Gaillard is no longer around to supply an answer. Slim would know. At the beginning of the 1940s, a quizzical missionary came to wander the Avenue. He was an imposing man—"a skyscraping zooty negro guitarist," *Time* magazine called him—who spoke a language few understood, a language of his own invention called "vout." Though Gaillard professed no allegiance to organized religion, he was by popular acclaim the messiah of a disorganized faith, one that made jive talk resonate with the knowledge of the elders.

Few have so brilliantly grasped the possibilities L.A. offered while confounding its limits. Born in Detroit in 1916, or maybe it was Cuba—his tales contradicted themselves—as a young boy Gaillard went on a trip with his dad, a member of the merchant marine, where he was inadvertently left behind in Greece. When Gaillard found his way back to the States, he launched a musical career that in the late 1930s saw him starring in New York cafés and then conquering the West. An adventurer and clown, jazz improviser and smooth talker, in the mid-1940s he was the toast of the town—appearing in Hedda Hopper's gossip column, serenading Hollywood lovebirds Ronald Reagan and Jane Wyman, performing on the radio with Danny Kaye and Oscar Levant. "Poodle-da-skoodie, poodle-da-skoodie," he averred, and Hollywood nodded at his sagacity.

Vout was a private language that signified coolness and secrecy. In L.A. Gaillard even published a *Vout-O-Reenee Dictionary*, a pocket handbook with which Avenue hepsters would never be at a loss for a word. Under P, one finds:

PICK-UP	learn
PIE-THEE	salt
PI-NI-O	appetite; hungry
PIPE	trumpet
PLATEE	load
POL-EE-TEE	more
POP-EYE-SAY	spinach

Vout was studded with repetitions of a few nonsense syllables (-reet, -oroonie), and every once in a while he dropped in a real word, too. Gaillard spoke Greek, and he threw in some of that. But most of the time vout was a goof meaning nothing when anyone but its inventor used it. Then it spoke volumes.

"He was a clown on the surface, but it was all a cover, a façade—he was a really deep, wonderful musician," recalled singer Frankie Laine, who sang in L.A. clubs in the 1940s.

> We used to use words in the olden days, words like solid, killer, crazy. But I never heard terms like vootie and voutie and roonie that he used. And when he had a hit with "Cement Mixer" and got hot, everybody started talking like that. It was quite the rage.

For a few years, Gaillard sustained an aura of inevitability. He opened a record store off the Avenue, spinning records and broadcasting "live from the heart of Voutville." He entertained thoughts of achieving conventional respectability, for he told the *Los Angeles Times* that classical pianist José Iturbi and violinist Jascha Heifetz were joining his combo. At the height of his fame, he announced that he was retiring to write symphonies and told the *California Eagle* he was hard at work on a play titled "South of the Border."

Underground beat artist Wallace Berman, who frequented the Avenue jazz clubs, drew a portrait of Gaillard circa 1940: there's a dinosaur, a lizard, naked beauties and a hypodermic needle poking Gaillard in the eye. Blood pools beneath his smiling countenance. It's powerful because Berman shows how for all his joshing, there was something scary about Gaillard, too. He was a messenger of a new breed, spokesman for anarchists, hopheads, beatniks and juvenile delinquents. He was even declared a public threat, with local radio station KMPC banning his music. A station DJ told one reporter that such music "tends to make degenerates out of our young listeners" and another reporter that it was "suggestive shouting and mumbling."

So it was.

In the pages of William J. Seymour's the *Apostolic Faith*, a headline jumps out at modern eyes: ELECTRIC MESSAGES FROM THE FIELD. That's what the Azusa Street Pentecostals called the animating force of the Holy Spirit. In the mid-1940s a kind of black jargon flew out of Bronzeville, rising on the wings of Slim Gaillard's suggestive shouting and mumbling. Fueled by vout and gilded by zoot, steeped in the cackle and gabble of dead ancestors, a fresh argot tumbled forth. Some called it rebop, a term that established a brief currency. Dootsie Williams, shipyard worker and a black independent record producer, claimed in an interview that rebop "is where Negro music leaves the sexual and becomes neurotic." Whatever it was, people were speaking it by the nautical mile. Even the song titles coming out of Central Avenue in the mid-1940s speak in tongues: "Be-Baba-Leba," "E-Baba-Le-Ba," "Ee-Bobaliba," "Hey-Ba-Ra-Re-Bop," and "Yep Roc Heresy." Singer Tina Dixon was billed as the E-bop Girl; saxophonist Jim Wynn's band was called the Bobalibans. All of it nothing but messages from the field.

Voo-it! Voo-It! One singer shouted; another ordered a serving of frim fram sauce with chafafa on the side. Soaking it all up was the kid who in a few years would write "Louie Louie."

Zoot . . . voo-it . . . vout—it was a twentieth-century Great Awakening. Currents were crossing, and at their nexus was the zooty Negro mouthing "putti-putti-putti." Meanwhile, playing drums in Gaillard's Los Angeles band and chiming in on back vocals was a lumbering, leering man named Leo Watson. Having Watson back Gaillard was a little like having Albert Einstein chauffeur a really bright high school physics teacher. Gaillard was the star, but Watson was the genius—the secret inspiration for Gaillard's demented vocal style. Born in 1898, Watson was a pure, protean talent with a gift for shambles. He spent much of the 1940s living on the streets of Bronzeville.

Some jazz writers and scholars have described Watson as the greatest scat singer, using the same improvised technique that Ella Fitzgerald would help make famous. Born in Kansas City, Missouri, Watson gained attention in the 1930s singing with the luminous jazz group the

Spirits of Rhythm. It was strange, frivolous music with a huge injection of hokum: Watson banging on a suitcase or playing a ukulele-like pocket guitar called a tiple while singing a swift stream of consciousness. The Spirits stole the air out of a room with their showmanship and seemingly endless ability to control tempo. Writing in *The New Republic*, critic Otis Ferguson celebrated Watson's crew.

> The Spirits live by the thing they started with, which was an American mode of playing and singing and lifting the whole place in defiance of all known laws of gravity. They can play anything they want to, and you may with a shallow enough eye see only the rip and jump that may be caught with the eye. They are now on their way to the Coast and maybe days will be fat for them again, but in general you will not be overimpressed by the surroundings they play in, for this is a white man's world and Negro musicians are taught to know it by a process which is called kicking around. But if you will listen, if you will let the ear carry where the mind's sense of the ludicrous cannot penetrate, you will find music as truly in the center as it was ever found, and the things music was made from, and the people through which and by which it lives.

Letting the ear take you where the mind would not; it was not so different from letting the Holy Spirit take you where the Devil would not.

Ferguson was writing early in 1941, as the Spirits of Rhythm were leaving New York and heading to Hollywood. After they arrived, however, things fell apart. There was a high-profile marijuana bust that made the papers, the band scattered, and Watson took to the bottle. It didn't seem to dent his talents, but it made him less predictable than ever.

Watson haunted Bronzeville, popping in and out of the jazz clubs. The editors of *Esquire* magazine tried hunting him down; they wanted to give him an award for being one of the greatest jazz singers on earth. It took them three months of searching before they found him, loading trucks in a war plant. He didn't settle anywhere for long and rarely kept a recording date. "Leo came to the recording studio, sang some of the most fantastic riffs in the world, then disappeared again into the obscurity of a Main Street beer parlor," a musician told journalist Leonard Feather.

To know him was to forgive him. (Leonard Reed: "He was a little different from somebody else. He was very outgoing, let's put it that way.") For what he did on stage with his whole being somehow excused what his whole being did when he walked down the street. Wherever he went, he truly couldn't help himself. Billie Holiday once broke a stack of 78s on his head—it was the only way she got him to shut up. At the start of the zoot suit riots in 1943, he hailed a cab and sped to 12th Street, strapped on a drum and pounded his way through the conflagration. He liked singing, but he loved the drums: jazz singer Jon Hendricks recalls Watson at a jam session where he pounded out a solo that seemed to have no end. After the cops came, Watson kept right on playing the drums, then the patrons, then the walls, finally beating on the sidewalk—it was where he'd been escorted—long into the night. His was music made by a mind in upheaval, a mind picking up frequencies from either deep within or deep without.

Many saw him in exactly this fashion. In 1944, magazine writer Carlton Brown wrote an autobiographical novel called *Brainstorm* that recounted the author's mental breakdown. A guiding spirit of *Brainstorm* is Leo Watson, fictionalized as Lew the Lion. A word-sound volcano whose performances initiate the reordering of the narrator's psyche, Lew might be a harbinger of spiritual enlightenment or psychoses. Watson seemed possessed, capable of leading his audience over a cognitive brink.

Key to his style was a voice that glided from note to note like a verbal trombone. He used a technique called melisma—the swooping, smearing style so loved of *American Idol* singers and those who attempt "The Star Spangled Banner." This technique is so solidly rooted in religion that gospel scholar Anthony Heilbut describes it as

the byzantine melisma universally identified with a church moan. That moan usually takes the form of a hum, though it can also be an "ooh," "ah," "oh" and "hey," and it can be expressed in guttural tones or high falsetto. When slurred moans are introduced into spoken and sung words, the result is a hallowing of language, a transcendent state. As with the donning of a scarf or a yarmulke, everything becomes solemn, sacred.

Solemn or sacred is nothing you'd ever call Leo Watson, but a transcendent state is what he was.

Watson's singing frequently exhibited a phenomenon called cryptomnesia, which is endemic in many of those who speak in tongues. It is an ability to communicate the texture or impression of a foreign language one has encountered in only a limited way. Watson evoked Yiddish, Arabic, Spanish and more. He had a naturally punning mind, and coupled with a Joycean sense of verbal flow and the cryptomnesia, his performances were massive upwellings that swept away the day, made the sober drunk and the drunk sober.

Watson recorded a handful of towering sessions with clarinetist and bandleader Artie Shaw. "He was a great jazz singer," Shaw said.

> He had a lot of humor and he knew what it was about, he knew what swung and what didn't.
>
> He was a cute guy and he knew what it was all about. Not many singers do. Leo was what he was—very, very good, very bright, a little crazy.

How was Watson spending his time in L.A.? Teddy Bunn, the brilliant guitarist of the Spirits of Rhythm who came to town with him, knew.

> Drinking that wine. And that's what he died of, that wine, laying in them places, and on the streets, you know. He'd be laying down and the guys would pick him up for the night, he'd get some sleep, and then he would—they'd let him out in the morning, and he'd go right back to that wine. God rest his soul.

CHAPTER 10

Honk

Did you ever meet JOE LIGGINS? He's an enterprising young fellow
who did so well with the SINGER SEWING MACHINE CO. that he's
opened up HIS OWN BRANCH STORE at 4059 CA, and Jack,
they've sure made some CHANGES in SEWING MACHINES! Charming MRS. RUTH LIGGINS, her husband's assistant, showed me one in
BLONDE OAK that looks EXACTLY LIKE A STREAMLINED KNEE
DESK and another that SERVES AS A CARD TABLE when not in
use and another which is authentic QUEEN ANNE built as a period
cabinet. And Mrs. Liggins tells me EASY CREDIT TERMS are available, so maybe you had better see if JILL wants one.

—*advertisement*, California Eagle, January 9, 1941

THE SOFAS WERE ON THE INSTALLMENT PLAN AT GOLD FURNITURE ON
the Avenue. That was one innovation that made Gold's a popular store
for working-class shoppers; another was the records they sold along
with the drapery and rocking chairs—Gold's had as up-to-date a collection of jazz and jump music, everything on the "race" charts, as was

to be found in town. In 1946 Gold's tried another innovation, sponsoring a radio show called "Golden Grooves" that was hosted by an ambitious young voice named Joe Adams. A board member at Clayton Russell's church, Adams was also the announcer on Russell's weekly broadcasts. Now he was taking to the air himself with a distinctly more secular content: songs by Billy Eckstine and Joe Turner, Johnny Moore and Hazel Scott.

His show was something of a novelty, because Negro disc jockeys were a rarity in the mid-1940s. The furniture store launched "Golden Grooves" in the hopes of luring more Negro families through Gold's portals with their Negro DJ spinning Negro records. What happened next was astonishing: the sponsor received 700 to 1,000 enthusiastic letters a week from white listeners, 100 to 125 from blacks. Such numbers—who knew white folks liked race music?—were hard to ignore. Gold's took notice. They canned Adams: white shoppers weren't going to come down to Central just because they liked hearing Hadda Brooks sing "Riding the Boogie."

By 1946, L.A.'s black population had more than doubled, from 63,774 in 1940 to 133,082, but that just begins to suggest how much bigger the city was getting. Over the same years the white population increased from 1,504,277 in 1940 to 1,805,687 in 1946. Among them were thousands of black and white Southerners, people who had been raised in Pentecostal, Holiness and sanctified churches. Who knows what these folks, along with so many unclassifiable, unknowable others, thought when they turned on their radio and heard Wynonie Harris, Roy Milton or T-Bone Walker—many of them for the first time in their life. But they were ready.

They were well prepared by the world of the last three decades. After Azusa Street peaked, Pentecostalism in America grew along a widening fault line. On the black side, there was first and foremost Memphis's Church of God in Christ, founded by Bishop Charles Mason. Mason was transformed by a visit to Azusa Street in 1907, and subsequently he turned his own church into a Pentecostal denomination. Ultimately COGIC, as it was called, became the largest black Pentecostal church in the country. As writer Michael Corcoran has recently demonstrated, COGIC was home to an incredible variety of early gospel performers who connected with listeners of blues and pop music. There was Sister Rosetta Tharpe, a pioneer of the electric guitar who blazed a hard-rocking style, and Arizona Dranes, playing boogie-woogie piano for Jesus in a style that sounded like Jerry Lee Lewis decades before Lewis emerged. Influential guitarist Blind Willie Johnson, singers Marion Williams and Andre Crouch also came out of COGIC. Sustained exposure to these and other artists would prepare listeners for what came out of Bronzeville circa 1945.

But white Pentecostals, too, were ready for a connection with the new pop music. Pentecostal and Holiness churches in California embraced Dust Bowl refugees arriving in the 1920s and 1930s; as writer James N. Gregory has shown, while mainstream denominations were loath to reach out to these social outcasts, Pentecostals aggressively courted Okies and Arkies, providing them with a place to worship where they did not feel ashamed of their accents and the way they dressed. White Pentecostal and Holiness churches popped up in the smallest California towns, and these, too, featured raw, upbeat music full of shouted exhortations. Baptized in this sound, their children, no less than the children of black Pentecostals, were ready for the noise in the L.A. night.

As much as it was born in any one place, rhythm and blues music was born on Central Avenue. R&B lived as assorted regional subcultures in a handful of cities, but L.A. launched R&B as American pop culture. The music had to be there, and it was. But if R&B was to thrive, L.A. would have to nurture the talents of a legion of entrepreneurs. Gold's little experiment suggested there was quite a white audience out there; they were steeped in the fire, but still needed were people with sufficient know-how to make it pay, hustlers and artists with the resources and drive to join the middle class. Wanted: a hundred Joe Adamses, guys with the presentation and sales skill necessary to market the music to the people.

Around 1942 a piano player in Sammy Franklin's California Rhythm Rascals (they hadn't yet changed their name to the Atomics) stroked his chin and considered his problem: the Texas Hop was a hot dance along the Avenue, and the Rhythm Rascals didn't have any music to Texas Hop to. The pianist, a moon-faced smoothie named Joe Liggins, tried to rectify the problem, sitting down at his keyboard and pumping out a little riff that seemed to get the dancers going. Liggins himself was in no state to do any Texas Hopping—a baseball injury had put his foot in a cast and left him with plenty of time to play piano. Liggins called his little riff the "Crippled Joe," and if in truth it was more of a doodle than a full-fledged tune, the girls sure seemed to like it all the same. They'd gather around his piano and wiggle to the groove, which the rest of the band noticed. "This is a sweet guy," the drummer for the Rhythm Rascals exclaimed. "Man, you drip a lotta honey."

He offered to sell his boss Sammy Franklin a piece of the song—Liggins needed the cash just so he could pay a studio to record "Crippled Joe"—but Franklin's wife said she wanted a new washing machine and wouldn't spare the dough. This was the recording business, in theory a realm of gold platters and mansions on the hill. But it was as well a place where the price of a washing machine could seriously affect several men's fortunes. Rebuffed by Mrs. Franklin, Joe Liggins set out on his own with a stripped-down five-piece crew. His cast was off and he'd rearranged his piano tune for the combo, renaming it "The Honeydripper."

Liggins released his single in May 1945, and soon thousands of people who didn't know the Texas Hop from the Pimp's Walk were familiar with the man who dripped a lot of honey. If you rode the streetcar from Slauson to 12th Street, you could stick your head out the window and hear the highly communicable piano lick on nearly every block. "The Honeydripper" was a huge hit, reaching number 1 on the R&B charts for a record 18 weeks and creasing the pop charts at number 13. The song might have begun as a transient thought, a vagrant sleeping in a doorway of opportunity, but soon it established residency. Soon it was inspiring a legion of copycat grooves.

It wasn't jazz, and Liggins wasn't concerned with "expressing himself." This was low stuff aimed at the belt-level, and those who heard it knew it. At a moment when jazz musicians were refining the bebop sound that twisted you in knots if you were fool enough to dance to it, here was a guy all about the Texas Hop. Reviewing a Liggins show at the Lincoln Theater in 1946, Almena Lomax declared the group was "only a few months removed from the Eastside greasy-pigs in which they first made their name, and incidentally, looking as unglamorous as a hog's backside." She meant that in the nicest possible way. "He has five pieces, and all five men behind the instruments are the homeliest I've seen in an age, the homeliest and the happiest, if enthusiasm for what they are doing is a fair indicator of that state." This was straight-off-the-train music for straight-off-the-train folks. Take off your work clothes, put on your suit, and shout "hoy, hoy, hoy."

Maybe what's most amazing about "The Honeydripper" is how simple it was. Lomax even thought she heard in its unrelenting beat a tom-tom evocation of American Indian music. "The Honeydripper" has such a basic bass line—actually, it sounds an awful lot like "Shortnin' Bread"—that it starts seeming a little monotonous, until it starts seeming a lot monotonous, until it seems positively hypnotic. Live, Liggins would jam on it for 15 minutes. When the Exclusive label initially released "The Honeydripper," they accidentally left the final groove on the record a closed circle, so that the needle kept repeating the end, making "The Honeydripper" a groove that not only felt like it went on forever, but it actually would until you got up and lifted the needle.

Even in the Eastside greasy-pigs where you kept your blade within reach, even there the Holy Spirit had his say. Liggins came from the Dust Bowl with his religious background intact. Back in Guthrie, Oklahoma, his parents were missionaries in a Holiness church—"the church which has songs that sound like the blues, the slow ones, and sound like rhythm, the fast ones," Joe's brother Jimmy (an important bandleader himself) explained to an interviewer. "My mum was a spiritual songster," he said. "Whenever we went out to sing, we had a singin' good time." The parents ran their church and bought instruments both for its young people's band and for their children to play at home—and mom and dad formed a band, too.

"The Honeydripper" is one of two records cited by musicians, journalists and scholars as the foundation of rhythm and blues. "I Wonder" by Cecil Gant is the other; the two singles were released months apart, and Gant and Liggins, both hanging around the Avenue, couldn't have lived more than a few miles apart. But for all the influence "I Wonder" and "The Honeydripper" had on music, their biggest impact was on commerce. White-owned major labels were powerfully uninterested in Negro artists or listeners, but the twin success of these songs proved that there was money to be made in R&B. These L.A. records inspired the establishment of independent labels at home and across the country, and those labels would soon flood the market. They proved that small-time entrepreneurs, black or white, knew something that the major labels didn't about what would sell. They showed that the major labels weren't the only game in town, because if you had a good tune, you could make it. They proved that Negro listeners spent money too, and that the money all had the same color.

Around the time that Liggins was laid up in a cast, a sleepy-eyed Army GI from Nashville, Cecil Gant, was visiting L.A. While singing at a war bonds rally—or so the legend has it—Gant was discovered by a talent scout and offered a recording contract. Soon after, Gant waxed a languorous piano ballad that sustained a blue note of long-distance distress: "Will you think of me every day, though I may be a million miles away? I wonder." These words touched a nerve among those who were far from family and loved ones back home, particularly soldiers stationed overseas wondering about what their return to civilian life would hold. After "I Wonder" was released on the independent label Gilt-Edge in 1944, it sailed to the top of the black music charts.

A husk of myth and misinformation covers both songs. What has been all but unreported—all but unknown, until a pair of writers published a story in a British music journal in 1996—is that both "I Wonder" and "The Honeydripper" didn't just come out of the same town, but were recorded in the same studio for the same independent black label. The story of these records has long gone misreported, and the effect has been to deny one man, Leroy Hurte, his considerable place in popular music history. Hurte's tiny independent label, Bronze Records, was responsible for first recording the two most important early R&B hits. And then he lost both of them to larger labels that steamrolled him out of the business and out of the history books. His name forgotten today, the inescapable fact remains that without Hurte's entrepreneurship, without his ability to know what would sell, R&B would have come out differently.

The origin myth of "I Wonder" has been particularly obfuscated. The story of Gant's emergence from the bond rally crowd asking if he could sing his song is a winsome one, and it has often been repeated. It served a purpose at the time, when Gant was promoted as "the GI sing-sation," and it was suggested that the song itself was a kind of gift to the war effort. But the awkward fact is that it never happened. "I didn't know too much about the war bond rally," said Hurte.

> He walked in [to the Bronze office] and wanted to know if I would record his song. It was pretty common for my organization, because I was the only black recording company at that time, and people who wanted to make records would come in. They'd sing songs for me and I would decide if I could use them, whether I thought they would sell or not. I had a big room with a piano, a control room off of it with a glass window and everything. So when Gant came in asking to make a record I said, "Okay." He sat down and sang "I Wonder." I liked it. I figured that one would sell.

Hurte was as ready to run an independent label as any self-sufficient businessman, black or white, could be. He had studied arranging at Jefferson High School and had been arranging local records for years. He studied broadcasting at a local trade school, integrating it with the help of the National Urban League. He helped run a small group of record stores called Flash Records. Hurte built his own recording equipment, assembling it during wartime when machinery was hard to come by. "I got pretty good quality out of it, that was the important thing. Because I had to compete with Decca, RCA Victor, Columbia and Vocalion, the records had to be pretty good or else people wouldn't buy them. So they turned out pretty well."

Hurte took a job at Allied Recording, one of the few pressing plants in L.A. Allied showed him how to turn a studio recording made on an acetate disc into a mold that, using pressing equipment, would then stamp out the song. Allied pressed the first copies of "I Wonder," and the song, featuring Hurte's distinctive Bronze label logo, started selling from Bronzeville down to Watts. "All uvasudden some song called 'I Wonder' is the current Avenue jukebox favorite," wrote showbiz columnist J. T. Gipson. "Everyone likes the way Cecil Gant (whoever he is) sings it."

One night Hurte was listening to Gant's mellow voice waft through the radio when the announcer cut in: "That was a Gilt-Edge recording by Cecil Gant." Obviously a mistake, Hurte figured. He meant to say, "a Bronze recording." But the announcer knew something Hurte didn't.

Gilt-Edge was a label out of Hollywood owned by a white businessman named Richard Johnson. It was an independent, too, but Johnson had resources that were far beyond Hurte's means, and those resources were easily apparent to even a GI from Nashville, Tennessee. Johnson had rerecorded basically the same arrangement of "I Wonder" that Hurte had devised; Hurte said he'd copyrighted the music, but since the sheet music of Johnson's copyrighted version featured a different notation for the guitar part, Hurte was told he had lost that argument too. According to Hurte, Johnson got Allied to agree to stop pressing "I Wonder" for Bronze; they wouldn't even print the paper labels anymore that Hurte was putting on his records.

"I should have gotten a lawyer that knew copyright law. But there weren't any black lawyers that knew it because they'd never had the experience of suing anybody under those conditions," said Hurte.

He quietly bought a used record press from an Allied employee—it was like buying contraband matériel, given the wartime economy—purchased a printing press to produce his labels, and made fresh copies of "I Wonder" out of the Bronze office. "There was no place to turn, so I did it myself," he explained. The judge had said Gilt-Edge could continue selling their record; he hadn't said Hurte should stop selling his. Working all night long, he was able to print about 1,000 copies each week. Small-time distributors would line up on Monday morning outside the Bronze office to buy copies. Hurte would sell out a week's worth before the day was over. Gilt-Edge was able to line up nationwide distribution, while Hurte relied on his ability to reach the Avenue market and on a network of Pullman porters who sold "I Wonder" on their routes. "I Wonder" briefly made decent coin for Hurte, but it was Gilt-Edge that put the song on national charts and reaped the real money.

"The Honeydripper" has no origin tale as flashy as that of a bond rally virgin birth. Joe Liggins had his version of what happened. He told writers that Leon Rene, head of Exclusive, another black indie on the Avenue, took an interest in his little tune after hearing the band play one of their deluxe 15-minute live versions. Liggins lured Rene to Bronzeville to hear his group, and once Rene did, he all but signed Liggins on the spot, went the songwriter's version.

Exclusive *did* record "The Honeydripper" and did have a hit with it. Complicating this simple tale, however, is the undisputable fact that Liggins had already gone into Hurte's studio shortly before and recorded a driving, stripped-down version of "The Honeydripper." Bronze never released its "Honeydripper," and eventually Liggins headed to Rene.

Why didn't Hurte put out the version he had ready to go? "Now that's something I don't know myself," he said with amusement some fifty years later. "I don't know why I didn't release that. I think if I had stayed in the business a little longer, I would have, but I was getting into something else." When the song came out on Exclusive, Hurte didn't feel robbed the way he had when Gilt-Edge plundered him. This time his rivals hadn't undermined him—his own instincts had done him in.

Hurte had numerous advantages working for him. He was an exceptionally disciplined man whom people found easy to work with. He had the patience and training to amass a wide variety of technical skills. A nice guy, the right time: Hurte built what should have been an empire. Yet Bronze, too, faltered, undercut by white competition and a vast lack of capital.

After his experiences with "The Honeydripper" and "I Wonder," Hurte was on the verge of what he describes as a nervous breakdown. A religious man, he was feeling increasingly estranged from the R&B culture he played a role in forming; weary, disaffected, Hurte left town in 1948, enrolling at Juilliard to study classical music. Although Bronze lasted only a few years, it changed the way the recording industry—and ultimately American consumers—looked at black pop music. "Leroy's the man who taught us how to press records," Modern Record's Joe Bihari told *Blues and Rhythm* magazine. (Modern had hits with Elmore James, B. B. King, Lightnin' Hopkins and others in the 1940s and early 1950s; like the Swing Time label, it was initially based in Bronzeville.) "Leroy was responsible for the independent record business with his recording of 'I Wonder,'" Bihari said. "His company, Bronze Records, did the test pressings for our first record, 'Swinging the Boogie' by Hadda Brooks, but he was too busy to do our production run because he was still pressing 'I Wonder.'"

There's little more complicated than an ambitious black capitalist. Black sociologists and historians have not always been kind to the race's petit bourgeoisie, the aspiring layer of small-time business folk and merchants working within the community. This caste has been accused of running from race consciousness and chasing after white approval. It's been pointed out that during segregation, black businesspeople had a vested interest in the status quo, as they sustained a lock on the consumer dollars of blacks who were barred from white parts of town.

Angeleno Ralph Bunche underscored this line of thinking in a 1940 essay: "despite his appeal to race pride and loyalty, the Negro businessman is not distinguished by his civic-mindedness, his efforts and sacrifices on behalf of his group." What would Bunche have thought, then, of the black Los Angeles realtors of the 1940s who sought out homes in white areas and recruited black buyers to take on the challenge of integrating neighborhoods? Was that looking out for oneself or for one's people? And what would he have thought of Forrest "War" Perkins? Perkins's biography calls such glib criticism into question, suggesting that sometimes an abundance of racial yearning courses beneath acts of personal advancement. Perkins illustrates how in a segregated city, individual black advancement is rarely just focused on the individual.

Hurte *did* have the opportunity to meet Perkins, first in the early 1930s, when Hurte was singing in the Four Blackbirds (a vocal group in the Ink Spots mold). Perkins became their manager, lining up film and radio appearances. In 1932 Perkins edited the *Achiever*, an Avenue-based Negro cultural magazine; Hurte was his art director. This ambitious journal published a statement of purpose in its first issue:

> The *Achiever* is an independent publication devoted to the interest of the American people, particularly of those who are members of the working class. It believes in a far-sighted program which looks to the welfare of the "common people," the men and women who work. It is not connected with any existing political party. It is against anarchy, poverty, graft and crime, debt slavery and unemployment.

Stories in the *Achiever*'s first issue sketch its phenomenal reach. There is a cover article by Loren Miller, the radical lawyer who the very year the *Achiever* debuted participated in a famous trip to Russia with Langston Hughes and other black intellectuals. There is also an article by businessman George Beavers celebrating the Golden State Mutual Life Insurance Company. Fellow travelers and insurance salesmen found common ground in Perkins's journal, their ideas rubbing against each other, competing yet seen as part of the same cause, each viewed as incomplete without the other. Each held a claim on advancing black Los Angeles, and neither side by itself had the whole story.

Perkins's activism didn't stop with the *Achiever*. He was a pioneer black radio figure whose engineering know-how helped Clayton Russell broadcast his radio program in the late 1930s. In 1941, Perkins had a weekday morning program of his own; he was taken off the air after he criticized the Navy's treatment of black sailors.

So was he a salesman who had his principles, or a race man who had to make a living? Perkins was a damned good salesman who came to California in 1932 and sold perfume, real estate, hot dogs and doubtless much more during the Depression. By one account he established a fledgling independent recording label in the late 1930s, which would make him a pioneer in the field, and he seems to have owned his own pressing machine, a crucial advantage for anyone wanting to make or sell records. Clearly, he knew the distribution hurdles that frustrated Negro labels in the marketplace and sought to circumvent the major labels' lock on distribution. Perkins was a leading local promoter of R&B, traveling through the Deep South and along the Avenue selling bootleg versions of R&B hits out of the trunk of his car that undercut the competition. Perhaps not coincidentally, Perkins abruptly left town in the mid-1940s, reportedly to Alaska and elsewhere until the coast was once again clear, reappearing on the Avenue around 1946, just when the prospects for black pop had never looked brighter. He formed an alliance with popular bandleader Roy Milton, and then Perkins was caught bootlegging Milton. Soon he felt the need to once again leave town and moved for good to the Philippines.

Milton, meanwhile, was taking aim at Liggins. His piano-sodden 1946 hit "RM Blues"—with female keyboardist Camille Howard channeling Arizona Dranes—was a sleepless stroll down dark gin alleys. Both Liggins and Milton were tradesmen who wanted to get paid. Liggins wasn't just a bandleader; he was a merchant of sewing machines who targeted the pool of black domestics sewing for white Angelenos. When Milton wasn't rehearsing his band, he was running a 24-hour grocery store in Bronzeville and sleeping in the back room. Somehow he managed to procure items ordinarily hard to come by during wartime rationing. "He always had sugar, and I sold it. I don't know how he got it, but he got it," said Donna Gentry, a dancer who worked in the grocery. "Roy was a businessman as well as a musician—but I think he was more of a businessman. As a musician he was good but he was truly a businessman."

For a few years in the center of the decade, Bronzeville was one large bazaar where artists and businesspeople careened from stall to stall, a hustler's convention for everyone trying to make two bucks out of one. It was the triumph of the black-market bluesman, the appliance dealer–hep cat, the bootlegging civil rights crusader. Here the informal economy was pretty damned formal.

It was home as well to Ben Waller, who in the mid-1940s ran a hat-cleaning operation in Bronzeville while also running the nightly broadcast from Shepp's Playhouse. By the end of the decade Waller had become what *Ebony* magazine called "the only Negro today owning and operating a major theatrical booking agency," managing Joe Liggins and Roy Milton and booking such Avenue talent as Percy Mayfield, Lloyd Glenn, Floyd Dixon, Peewee Crayton, and Jimmy Witherspoon on cross-country tours. Waller helped establish a level of showmanship that built crowds coast-to-coast, going that extra mile to give audiences a reason to remember a star's name. For the saxophone honker Chuck Higgins, for instance, Waller hired a 250-pound girl to travel with the band as a de-facto professional fan. When the band entered a new town, Higgins would stop at a Salvation Army shop and buy cheap clothes he didn't mind losing. That night at the show, the designated fan would "spontaneously" lose all self-control and rip the clothes off Higgins, dragging him off the stage. "That always got the crowd going," Higgins laughed to journalist Jim Dawson. "Shit, I couldn't play, so I had to do something."

These weren't art-damaged, no-money-having jazz musicians. They were tycoons, people who were aware of how an act was going over with the crowd. Perhaps nobody summed up the scene better than a mumbling former used-car dealer named John Dolphin. Upon arriving from Detroit around 1947, Dolphin bought a record store from War Perkins at 40th Street and Central Avenue (he also did taxes and repaired radios at the shop). He gave it the name "Dolphin's of Hollywood," though the address was a long way from Hollywood. Asked why, Dolphin said "If Negroes can't go to Hollywood, then I'll bring Hollywood to Negroes."

He surely brought Hollywood hustle to Negro L.A. Dolphin signed local artists to his various labels, presciently named Money, Cash and Lucky, and then featured their releases along the walls of his store. At his shop on Central and then after moving to Vernon Avenue, Dolphin put a disc jockey in the window, one who would play the songs Dolphin was selling, the songs recorded by artists Dolphin had signed to his labels.

With DJs like Dick "Huggy Boy" Hugg, Hunter Hancock and Charlie Trammell, Dolphin took it to the streets, his DJs shouting out to their homeboys driving by, dedicating a song by the kid who'd just crossed the street to the girl going the other way. Dolphin would urge his listeners to come down and buy the tune they'd just heard on the air, and many—white and black—did. The city was listening.

Loving John, as he was called, tipped the scale way past 200 pounds, dressed like a gangster and liked to pay people—when he *had* to—from a wad of bills that would choke a jet engine. "He treated everyone like a fool," said singer Gaynel Hodge. Dolphin's slogan was "We'll record you today and have you a hit tonight." The check was coming sometime later. "With John I didn't get nothing and I knew I wasn't gonna get nothing, but I was gonna get airplay. He'd keep me hot," Chuck Higgins said. He kept them hot, too, right up to when a songwriter he had neglected to pay stormed into his office one day in 1958, pulled out a .32 caliber automatic and shot him. After that Dolphin cooled off considerably.

Two forces converged on Bronzeville in the mid-1940s, and together they outlasted Loving John. There was the speaking-in-tongues fervor of Azusa Street from the turn of the century, returning four decades later and twining with a buccaneering capitalism that made sewing machine salesmen heralds of a new day. Pentecostal mingling with moolah equaled global teenage revolt. In the months and years ahead, so many names would gain prominence in Los Angeles rhythm and blues circles: Maxwell Davis, Bullmoose Jackson, Johnnie Otis, Wynonie Harris, Crown Prince Waterford, Jimmy Witherspoon, T-Bone Walker, Johnny Guitar Watson, Von Streeter, Little Esther, PeeWee Crayton, Ray Charles and more. You could string the names of the famous, the important and the unknown from Fifth and San Pedro to Rancho Cucamonga, and still somebody's name would be left out. Insofar as one man can ever truly represent another, perhaps Cecil McNeely can stand in for them all.

As a young boy McNeely walked the streets of South Los Angeles, knocking on doors with a turntable and records. Raised a Christian Scientist, he took religious talks, recorded on discs, to white working-class neighborhoods. Police would stop the child missionary and demand he play his records on the street, proving they were what he claimed them to be. Then they let him go.

As a teenager attending Jefferson High, young Cecil once had a run-in with a teacher. To classes, truthfully he did not give his all. For simultaneous with his attendance McNeely was leading a bebop band on the Avenue that also included the teenagers Sonny Criss on alto sax and Hampton Hawes on piano—the latter two among the finest jazz players of the late 1940s and 1950s anywhere in the country. Together the three were making $60 a week gigging at the Downbeat, a club that wasn't supposed to let them in as patrons, let alone as talent. McNeely was interrogated in class, and he chose to answer, Socratically, with a question.

McNeely: "How much money do you make?"

The teacher named his salary.

McNeely: "Well, I already make more money than you. How do you think you can teach me anything?"

The man wanted to be paid. Upon his high school graduation—somewhat surprisingly, McNeely had one—he continued to be paid. Though he had been noticed in the local press as a rising jazz star, McNeely seemed distinctly underwhelmed. He had been to the jam sessions where two tenor saxophones entered in competition and only one walked away whole. He wanted to be *that* guy.

Scrounging for a new song to play at his first recording session, in 1949, McNeely quickly penned an instrumental called "The Deacon's Hop." After the recording session, two things happened. First, the fat, cigar-chomping owner of the record label decided the name "Cecil" would not do printed on a record label, and renamed him "Big Jay."

The second thing that happened was "The Deacon's Hop" instantly earned notice. The tune starts out with a long swaggering beat made for hand-clapping and shake-it-off-your-shoulder action. It's one cool cat strutting down a corridor of peers. Then "Deacon" explodes in a chorus drenched in shouts and perspiration, in mass affirmation, an acknowledgment that however high you hold your head above others, you are still a member of the group, and the group will call you back, swallow you whole when it wants. Live, when the song could cycle on for what seemed like forever, "The Deacon's Hop" was pure crude individualism transcended, a ritual of losing control—identity—and regaining it and losing it over and over again.

"The Deacon's Hop" was lifted by a column of sax men stomping and humping and squalling. Jim Wynn and James Von Streeter and Wild Bill Moore—he "played a high squeaky horn, sounded like a vampire bat in heat," said Hampton Hawes—all overblowing so urgently their notes curved away from music and toward something distorted, daft and new. What followed in "Deacon's" wake was a pack of squealing saxophones, a progression of hits that stretched into the mid-1950s. Every ambitious Negro combo had to have its sax squealer. "The Deacon's Hop" dragged an underground cult of wailing into the glaring California sun. The beboppers called it showmanship, crass commercialism, and in that they were not wrong. Worst of all, they called it noise, and for all their toxic ire, they were not wrong about that, either. There was something intentionally brutish—ugly—about the honking craze and the repetition of riffs that veered ever more toward atonality, toward squall. Noise.

There's no other word for it. Big Jay and the rest leaned harder and harder into Babel, pushing a listener's endurance and comprehension, finally breaking through to the sublime. Big Jay got hoarser and hoarser, a preacher losing his voice as he exhorted the congregation. What melisma was to Leo Watson, the honk was to Big Jay: an appeal to the reptile brain, preaching past the thinking mind and hitting the soul.

With "The Deacon's Hop," Big Jay McNeely had a name for himself. However measured this Christian Scientist was in person—at way less than 6 feet, he wasn't even that big!—when Big Jay was holding his saxophone, he was a basalt obelisk. In black church services, the deacon was the person who kept things moving and set the emotional tone by shouting out the verses of a hymn the house was singing. He worked the room, dispensing a hand of friendship, a consoling grip.

Big Jay sure liked to wander the floor when he played his saxophone. He'd establish a beat and then storm into the crowd, blowing a riff and leading a procession out the door into the street—sometimes even into a club *across* the street. He wandered. One night he wandered to an after-hours spot by the name of the Nightcap, and there became transfixed by a convulsing painted lady. Literally a painted lady, for she was dappled in fluorescent hues that made her skin glow under the Nightcap's black lights. Who can say when or where inspiration will strike? Thus whetted, Big Jay painted his saxophone in colors never before seen in nature, added strobe lights that made his instrument glow unto the night. He would lie on the stage like baptism was imminent and wail in repose as the crowds—black and white children, together in song—wailed their cryptic imprecations at his feet. They went nuts. He would walk across tables and bars kicking highballs in the laps of strong men, leading a mercenary army into the nocturnal streets. Honking.

In a fine short story titled "The Screamers," LeRoi Jones paid tribute to McNeely.

Jay first turned the mark around, opened the way further for the completely nihilistic act. McNeely, the first Dada coon of the age, jumped and stomped and yowled and finally sensed the only other space that form allowed. He fell first on his knees, never releasing the horn, and walked that way across the stage. We hunched together drowning any sound, relying on Jay's contorted face for evidence that there was still music, though none of us needed it now. And then he fell backwards, flat on his back, with both feet stuck up high in the air, and he kicked and thrashed and the horn spat enraged sociologies.

Inspiration became industry. For a few years raving was a big business and those who raved were something like spokesmen. Earl Bostic, a strong-lunged Midwesterner who looked like an accountant, offered to lead a diplomatic initiative to heal race relations, circulating a nationwide petition among his fellow band leaders calling for a concert to agitate for civil rights. Arnett Cobb, Texan, claimed he invented a secret new reed that could harpoon notes higher than anyone else's and said he'd been offered $5,000 to market it. Cobb also attempted to trademark the gesture of strolling into the crowd—he called it the Arnett Cobb Walk—and told the black press that "with a few minor matters to clear up [he] will have it patented." Illinois Jacquet, who had soloed on "Flying Home" in 1942 and was now a sort of caterwauling emeritus, announced he'd taken out a $100,000 insurance policy on his lungs.

One could not rest. Soon, Big Jay would perform in roller skates and a Ben Hur toga while utilizing a light system he called "lobsterscope." A classic photo from the early 1950s: he's playing one of his legendary shows at the Olympic Auditorium, a gladiatorial cupboard that stank of cigar smoke and beer, the site of boxing and wrestling matches and roller derbies. Big Jay stood in the ring, a heavyweight titlist ready to shoot fire at all comers. In the picture he's on his back at the edge of the stage, fat pearls of sweat inching earthward off his dome. In the audience, t-shirt-wearing, Brylcreemed white and brown kids, heads flailing and eyes rolling back in their heads, say yeah. Fifteen years later, no Beatles crowd would look more frantic.

Joe Houston was a sax honker who came to Los Angeles in the wake of Big Jay's success. In Jim Dawson's biography of Big Jay, Houston interprets the Olympic Auditorium scene. "[It] is direct from the church. Like a spiritual thing. The church's sanctified thing goin'. Why do you think all those white kids were waving their arms and pounding their thighs and having such a carry-on? They went for religion!"

Once again the night was made hideous—not by a church-going working class, but by black, brown and white teenagers brought together by the glowing horn that brayed into darkness made hideous by lobsterscope. As with Azusa Street, the city would retaliate. They harassed McNeely's concert bookers; he was allegedly arrested one night on the charge of "exciting Mexicans"; the city sent mental health experts to document the mass psychosis, and his followers were tarred in the press with the pejorative du jour, "juvenile delinquent."

After those Olympic shows, Big Jay noted the crackdown.

Well, they didn't understand what was going on. It was so rare for them to see kids enjoying themselves like this—and the fact that the whites were admiring this black guy. It was coming too early.

They'd come out and take pictures and try to analyze it, they'd say there were a thousand white kids dancing like Watusis. If you've never seen white kids respond that way, you can imagine—here's a black guy screaming and hollering, kids responding to me the way they would be responding to Elvis, and I'm black. You can't have that.

They used to come by and watch us—cops would be taking pictures, and what they'd do is bar me from playing.

He got watched at the Olympic, at the El Monte Legion Hall and all over the Southland. As a pint-sized Christian Scientist, Cecil McNeely had gotten rousted for taking the word of God pressed on disc to white enclaves. Now here he was, blasting a righteous noise from his horn, the Word made flesh under fluorescent lights. Now the records all had his name on them and they were selling like mad.

Big Jay: "See, you have to try to figure out where you fit into this whole music business. And I always liked the showmanship, you know."

CHAPTER 11

A Reluctant Volunteer

ON A MAY WEDNESDAY EARLY IN THE WAR, JOHN KINLOCH ATE RED beans, lobster thermidor, crepe suzette and Maryland hog maw for dinner. Or so he claimed, in a column in the *California Eagle*. Falling asleep after the unlikely feast, he had a weird nightmare: Hitler launches an air raid on Los Angeles, sending more than 1,000 Luftwaffe planes into the sky over Central Avenue. The air explodes. With bombs dropping and "big buildings and gas mains and billiard balls bouncing around free as butterflies," the community begins melting into the air. He drives to Paul's Liquor Store in Watts and hears rebel voices on the radio calling for Negroes to form guerrilla units to fight the invaders. Loudspeakers order blacks to line up at Hollywood and Vine for an unknown assignment. An interned Little Tokyo curio merchant is installed as governor of California. And then Kinloch describes a near-death experience as Paul's Liquor Store explodes and he is buried beneath the rubble.

The nightmare graphically brought the war home, Kinloch painting a delirious picture of what the conflict ultimately was about. His imagination might have been more active than that of most folks, but few on the Avenue had trouble personalizing the war. Nationally, a body of evidence suggests blacks felt a special connection to the fight. Government officials were scrutinizing citizens' attitudes toward wartime sacrifice, studying the differing explanations Americans gave for why they were fighting. In January 1941 Roosevelt had delivered his "Four Freedoms" speech to Congress, a once-famous enumeration of the values America would defend in conflict (freedom of speech and worship, freedom from want and fear). Two years later a War Department study showed that of more than 3,000 whites polled, only a third had even heard of the speech, and just 13 percent could name one of the values Roosevelt said we were fighting to preserve. Meanwhile, the black press was full of references to the Four Freedoms, and among Negroes there was a healthy debate underway about their meaning and whether they existed for everyone. These freedoms were in some way more alive, and taken more to heart, among Negroes during the war years.

As early as 1942, some were documenting differences among black and white responses to Nazism. A Howard University report on Negro attitudes toward German anti-Semitism showed that blacks regularly drew connections between Germany's treatment of Jews and their own experiences at home. The study made clear that for blacks in World War II, there was a intimate investment in the fight.

Which is why the barber at the Dunbar Hotel had a picture of Hitler on his razor strop. And it's why John Kinloch, after wrestling with his conflicted feelings, packed up and went to war.

Like many other black men his age, Kinloch learned to fear the postman, the bringer of induction notices. True, he'd very publicly spoken out in favor of black military service. At a "Youth Night" event at the 1942 NAACP convention in Los Angeles, the scheduled speaker was E. Frederick Morrow, an NAACP field secretary talking on the eve of his induction into the army. Morrow chose the moment to blast conscription, declaring that institutional racism in the ranks made a farce of America's lofty language. He invoked the Roman gladiator's salute to the emperor, "Ave, Caesar, morituri Te salutant" (Caesar, those who are about to die salute you). Morrow bitterly turned the phrase inside out, declaring, "America, we who are about to die salute you."

Kinloch had put together the evening's program, but he wasn't scheduled to speak. Morrow's sarcasm, however, proved too much for him to ignore. Taking the microphone and extemporizing a rebuttal, Kinloch cautioned against cynicism and said that America had the ability to conquer its racism, declaring that stakes were too high not to join and fight. Coming alive in the moment, he urged that blacks "should enter the fight with the realization that great things for the Negro lay in the future, if we defeat the common enemy—Hitlerism." Then, returning to Morrow's declaration, he ended with his own avowal: "America, we who are about to live salute you!"

It was an inspired speech, remembered vividly years later by at least one who was in the room. Yet it was hardly Kinloch's only word on the subject. In his column he had also declared,

> here's the way I look at the whole war situation, which is as good a conversation starter as anything this side of Holy Writ. I look at the war situation like this:
> "CAN I BE DEFERRED, EXEMPTED OR JUST PLAIN FORGOTTEN SOMEHOW LIKE IF A SECRETARY IN WASHINGTON D.C. COULD DROP MY WHOLE DRAFT RECORD INTO SOME CONVENIENT SWILL PAIL . . . ?"

Was he posturing when he spoke at the convention, or posturing with his Bob Hope–style rank cowardice? Simply, he was young and racked with opposing feelings, reflecting the ambivalence of many young black and white men of his time. His principles led him to champion the war effort, and the sound of the postman's footsteps made him nervous. Both were real.

"Have no idea what my status in connection with military service is or will be," he wrote in a letter to his mother. He sounded a note of hope that his work on the *Eagle* might qualify him for a deferment as it had for other journalists.

> I believe newspapers are considered a "vital industry." I have not registered of course and if I go I'd imagine it will be as a working journalist.

At any rate, I am perfectly willing to render whatever service and take whatever sacrifices are deemed necessary by the authorities. After all, I intend to fight for my constitutional rights the rest of my life. I can't very well back out of earning them.

He was loudly of two minds. To his girlfriend, he wrote that he had received a 1-A classification and then said that whatever happened, "either way, it's OK with me." Fear or glory, hero or cannon fodder, Bronzeville or boot camp. Either way, it was out of his hands. The postman arrived at his parent's Harlem address in the summer of 1943.

Kinloch left L.A. on December 1, 1943, for basic training in Mississippi. If he thought his experience south of the Mason-Dixon line was going to be any different than that of black soldiers before him, the trip down showed him otherwise. Packed in a railroad car with other Negro privates, Kinloch looked out the window and viewed acres of cotton fields as the troop train pulled into a small Southern town. At the station the soldiers were greeted by a little boy who raced along the train yelling "nigger, nigger." As initiations to the South went for black privates, this one was mild. But it didn't end there: the train stopped beside a garage where four or five white men in overalls stared menacingly. The child resumed his heckling, and a crowd of whites assembled. Black inductees new to the South often discounted the things they heard secondhand about Jim Crow's customs. "Why don't you bastards go back to work," a soldier called out to the whites, and a warm day suddenly got hotter. It would have turned worse had not a number of black soldiers taken the opportunity to poke the barrels of their military-issue carbines out the window and in the general direction of the locals. As the train pulled out of the station, a crisis avoided, the officer in charge told the soldiers if they pointed their weapons again he'd close all the windows on the sweltering car.

That was hardly the only lesson Kinloch learned about Southern ways; on furlough and heading to Harlem to visit his parents, he slugged a foul-mouthed white conductor and was ordered off a train. He walked 10 miles to the next station and was lucky he made it.

Having little choice but to enter the military upon request, Los Angeles's black men sought to turn their condition into an advantage, demanding that there be a home front battle as well. They had followed news of riots and racial confrontations on training bases in the Deep South and as close to home as March Field, Fort San Luis Obispo, Port Hueneme, and Vallejo, California, and they had been kept informed by the black press about the heroes of the race and the hardships they endured. But only when they signed on did they realize just how much the battle would be within their own ranks.

Kinloch was part of a company of 225 black men commanded by a loathed white officer. He was denied promotion and responsibilities by a Captain Smith who said he was "too smart for a nigger."

Smith was notorious among his black soldiers. "This guy, he hated Negroes," said Edgar E. Zeno, Kinloch's best buddy. "He'd just tell it to you like it was. He'd say as long as you were there, you would be a private."

Designated a company clerk, Kinloch killed time in London, playing ping-pong and sightseeing until D-Day. The Army disproportionately kept Kinloch and other Negroes as far in the rear as possible, toiling away in service jobs a long way from the battlefield. After the Normandy invasion, Kinloch was sent to France and became an Army war correspondent attached to the Public Relations Section at Cherbourg. Reporting stories was preferable to doing nothing, but perhaps to his surprise, he was growing restless. Something was changing inside him; he began yearning to be sent to the front. Writing and editing for Army publications and for the *Eagle* back home, Kinloch described Negro combat engineers and balloonists at the D-Day invasion and the gutsy black truckers in the Red Ball Express supply unit. Taking note of how some Negroes were contributing to the war, he wanted to do something as well. He was pleading to be sent on a long-term assignment to cover the work of black soldiers. "Negro soldiers in the field can't be covered by an occasional flying visit," he lamented in a letter. "A guy's got to live with a unit to understand it."

In France he and a friend, journalist Trezzvant Anderson, made a pact that should the possibility arise, each would apply for transfers to frontline black units of their choice. For Anderson it was the newly created black tank battalion, but for Kinloch it was the infantry—the soldiers who fought hand-to-hand combat in the foxholes. Whatever reservations he once had, he now yearned for action. "What am I doing, anyway—I am batting away behind a typewriter just as safe and snug as I was back in Los Angeles," he moaned.

Then, in January 1945, a letter to his mother:

Dear Mom:

For awhile I am going to be doing some special work that I'm afraid I can't tell you about for censorship reasons.

At any rate, I can say that it is something I have wanted to do for quite some time.

The urge to take action was certainly stoked by events in late 1944. On December 16, the Germans broke through Allied lines in the Belgian Ardennes section, triggering the Battle of the Bulge. Allied forces were far outnumbered, and American casualties high—81,000 killed, wounded or captured. These losses forced General Dwight D. Eisenhower, supreme Allied commander in Europe, to circulate a declaration that black volunteers were now eligible for infantry duty. An early memo said that blacks would be fighting in fully integrated platoons; when that statement raised concerns among some whites, the order was quickly rescinded and replaced with a follow-up that softened the integration, calling for all-black platoons to be formed for the purpose of fighting alongside white ones.

In the end it amounted to nearly the same thing: there would be shoulder-to-shoulder integration at the point of enemy contact. Thousands of blacks seized the opportunity, and by March 1945 more than 4,000 had volunteered, and 2,800 had been cleared for training. Ultimately, some 2,221 Negroes became combat soldiers.

Bodies were needed, and the order to let blacks fight came of necessity. Pressure was exerted on one side from commanders who were trying to hold the line. On the other side were forces asserting that integrating the Army was a moral imperative—among them Brigadier

General Benjamin O. Davis, the first black general in the army, and First Lady Eleanor Roosevelt. In the end the order to integrate was composed of both inarguable necessity and moral calculus.

The implications were understood instantly. Not for 162 years, not since the American Revolution, had blacks and whites fought on the line as equals. Segregation had nurtured the stereotype that blacks were cowards who made poor soldiers. For black Americans, it was to be the ultimate test. Plenty of them had already died, and Negro valor had already been demonstrated, from Dorie Miller to the Negro tank battalions. But the foxhole was the final taboo, off-limits for what it signified—that race did not matter. If a white depended on a Negro to protect his life, it would send a powerful message to the defenders of Jim Crow. Blacks knew it, from Benjamin O. Davis on down. Davis called the new policy "the greatest [advance] since enactment of the Constitutional amendments following the emancipation." Segregationists knew it too, which is why Mississippi senator James Eastland and others were spreading rumors of Negro treachery and claiming that the Army had so little confidence in its black soldiers it hadn't given them ammunition at Normandy.

These and other comments lead many Negro soldiers to wonder why they should risk their lives at the front. That was the sentiment of Abie Robinson, a newspaperman on the Avenue who got a deferment. "Hitler got to moving and killing so many goddamned white soldiers somebody said 'send them niggers!' And they started sending them," he said.

Robert Kennard was a sergeant from Los Angeles. In an oral history Kennard remembered the moment Eisenhower's memo circulated among his men.

> I called all my guys together—I was a first sergeant—and I said, "Now, you can go if you want, but my suggestion is, when the going gets tough, let the white boys figure it out." . . . I thought it was just so racist. . . . You know, all of a sudden the going gets tough, [and the message is] "You can get out there and kill yourself now." I don't think any of our guys volunteered.

Still, for many black soldiers, here was a way to respond to doubters in the Army and segregationists at home. The Double V movement had been shadow play, a manipulation of words and symbols that had no weight on their own. The movement took the intangible notion of a black soldier's loyalty and sought to use it as a fulcrum to move American intransigence—to force whites to look at black loyalty and assign it a fair value. But as the war in Europe reached its final weeks, America still hadn't accepted the movement's fundamental belief that rights defended were rights earned, not so far as soldiers were concerned. After the Battle of the Bulge, better tools than the Double V movement were suddenly available. The call for volunteers had the effect (only halfway considered by its architects) of sharpening a very dull bludgeon into something that fit into the hand and could scar the conscience. Combat provided a way for Negro soldiers to knock certain words out of white mouths.

Many felt the pull of the moment, Kinloch among them. "The Supreme Commander has issued an order, read this week to all Negro troops in the theater, that Negroes will be accepted as volunteers for combat replacements in white infantry units at the front! NO SEGRE-GATION!," he wrote to Charlotta Bass. "This is the first time since Valley Forge that American troops, white and black, will be in combat in the same units," he said before dropping the other shoe. "Well, I have done the only thing that, in all conscience, I could: I have volunteered. . . . This is one piece of history I am going to examine first . . . me myself, personal." He asked his aunt not to tell his mother what he was doing, for it would only upset her. He would no longer be able to write for the *Eagle*, nor able to write home so often. He was fulfilling the pact he'd made with Trezzvant Anderson in France: the writer was picking up a gun.

Hustled off to a training camp, Kinloch and thousands of other black soldiers were given an accelerated course in warfare. They had made big sacrifices to take on this mission, many accepting pay cuts and demotions in rank, for the Army had insisted these recruits enter the infantry as privates—the Army might accept blacks as equals, but they weren't prepared to have them issuing orders to whites.

All his life Kinloch had been a prodigy, the kind of young man who got by on sparkle and a natural talent he intermittently harnessed. He avoided pressure and waited until the last possible minute to make major decisions, counting on inspiration or panic to bail him out. Most of the time it did, but Kinloch was aware of his great unevenness and began lamenting it, vowing to be more responsible and steady and *present* in his own life upon his return to Los Angeles.

He was all of 23 when he entered the infantry, and the experience was transforming him. He wrote: "You know, sometimes I feel a curious kind of detachment from all this—as though I were standing on a hill somewhere watching myself and all the others crawl across this tortured country.... " A few years before he had buckled under the pressure of the responsibility the *Eagle* put on his shoulders, and he would disappear for days at a time, going to movie after movie and driving into the night. He would run from obligation and then criticize his weaknesses. But that was then; in his letters home from late 1944 and early 1945, Kinloch sounded like a person who had lost the ability to blame anyone else for his own mistakes, like someone who knew what he was and what he wasn't.

By late February Kinloch was designated a radio operator, on the move with Company G of the 39th Infantry Regiment of the Ninth Infantry Division. The Ninth comprised 41 black soldiers and 160 whites and was commanded by a white officer, Captain Klutch. Unlike Smith, Klutch bonded with his black soldiers, even getting them extra rations and sitting with them, letting them know they were a valued part of the division.

During the second half of December, the Ninth held a defensive position along the Belgian-German border and then pressed into Germany, crossing the Rhine River at Remagen after discovering perhaps the single bridge over the river the Germans had neglected to destroy as they retreated. Remagen gave the Army entrée to the heart of the Third Reich. Together the black soldiers learned to control their fear—at the front it might take three days to get to sleep, soldier Edgar Zeno recalled, because you knew the Nazis were in the woods. Near Aachen, 69 German soldiers crept up on them in ambush. Nothing could be taken for granted; abandoned farmhouses were booby-trapped, and tree stumps in the woods, inviting seats to tired foot soldiers, had mines hidden within.

The Ninth moved from the south toward the industrial heartland of the Ruhr Valley as part of the Ruhr pocket operation Eisenhower had unleashed at the beginning of April. What was left of a decimated German Army, more than 300,000 troops, was concentrated in the Ruhr Valley, an area covering more than 5,000 square miles and including the cities of Düsseldorf, Essen and Dortmund.

Realizing the noose was tightening, the remains of the German force fought fiercely, a mix of SS, panzer, parachute and infantry troops, children and elderly who were pressed into service.

The Army had taken Winterberg on April 3; the next day the Germans tried to snatch it back. According to one account, Kinloch was planted on a hillside relaying enemy positions on a walkie-talkie when German shells ripped through him. His bloody clothing was torn away as black and white soldiers rushed him to a camp hospital, but there was nothing to be done.

Not even 100 days had passed since he volunteered for the assignment. Victory in Europe was a little more than a month away. Kinloch was one of the first blacks to fight in mixed ranks and one of the first to die defending his right to fight for his country. It took several years for a government reinterment program to bring Kinloch home. He was buried with military services at the Farmingdale National Cemetery in Long Island, New York, on January 25, 1949.

In an essay titled "Democracy Is for the Unafraid," Chester Himes angrily declared the terms by which the war had to be won. In one passage, he evokes the mission of Kinloch and the other soldiers who volunteered for the infantry service.

War is teaching [the] lesson of equality to many of our youths in uniform. Coming upon the bodies of two soldiers lying face downward in the muck of a distant battlefield, both having died for the preservation of the same ideal, under the same flag, in the same uniform, they are learning the ridiculousness of thinking: "This man, being white, is superior to that man, who is black." They have learned that in a week's time the color which made one "better" than the other will have gone from both.

In Los Angeles young activists formed a John Kinloch Club, with loose talk about keeping his ideals alive. But how, really, to keep them intact? Forming a club with the backing of the Communist Party that issued dogmatic statements regarding labor politics, that was one possibility. Another was to speak freely and colorfully in the public square, to invest every ounce of energy you had into explaining yourself and understanding those who jostled you on the street. And to wear loud green suits with an unassailable sense of the moment.

Trezzvant Anderson wrote an article eulogizing his friend at the end of the decade. "Perhaps no marble statue will adorn the resting place of John Kinloch's body, but he rates one. For he was one of the very few Negro correspondents who was willing to go 'all the way' in the carrying out of the ideals that inspired him to his great sacrifice."

Decades later, an interviewer asked journalist Almena Lomax about Kinloch. They'd dated briefly and worked together at the *Eagle*. She remembered him like he was present in the room. "John was probably one of the most brilliant boys I've ever known," she said. "I think it was a great tragedy that he got killed. He was brilliant and he was wicked and I never believed he was dead, I always figured that he must have gotten a way to get out of it somehow."

In a nondescript building in South Los Angeles, there is a library that has survived the fires of 1965 and 1992, a place full of old books about class warfare and newer books about reproductive rights. In a dusty cardboard box, packed with fading letters and short stories and radio scripts and hundreds of other scraps of paper from a life, one finds a Christmas card sent from France in 1944. It reads:

Paris is lovely
It is beautiful
It is lush and
Wonderful

I would gladly
Trade it
All
For a corner
At
41st Street & Central Ave

—John

CHAPTER 12

Exotica

And the night shall be filled
With fragrant smoke
With the smell of baked ham and caviar
No I'm not day-dreaming, babe
I'm just thinking of "after the war."

—Sepia Sage, April 12, 1945

THOSE ANTICIPATING "AFTER THE WAR" HAD REASON FOR OPTIMISM. Much had been fought for and gained between 1940 and 1945. The Fair Employment Practices Commission had ushered thousands of Negroes into skilled positions. Young leaders like Clayton Russell won important battles regarding education, job training, mass transit, public housing and black empowerment. City officials were put on notice that a restive young population had arrived, one impatient with the city's quietly suffocating segregation. Blacks had demonstrated their patriotism and bravery on the battlefield and weren't about to turn the clock back when they came home.

There were big fights ahead to hold onto what had been gained. White workers returning from the front displaced Negro workers with less tenure, and defense industries were laying off people as they converted to a postwar production cycle. A Los Angeles County commission predicted half a million workers, or one-third of the local labor force, would have to find new jobs. In a single week of September 1945, some 37,000 were laid off. A disproportionate number of them were blacks and women, with the least seniority. At war's end, California had an unemployment rate higher than the national average.

Roles were shifting; the unemployed wandered the streets, while the economy converted to a peacetime footing. There was great expectation and muffled anguish, drift and ambivalence holding the highest cards. While the war was on, a sense of mission prevailed, but that time was gone. Now things seemed a little up in the air.

The transition was most difficult for black women, who had gladly exchanged domestic work for well-paying jobs that produced a new sense of self-potential. As one black Rosie the Riveter put it, "The war made me live better, it really did. . . . Hitler was the one that got us out of the white folks' kitchen." During the war some black male commentators noted with displeasure the women in overalls and welder's caps who were lining up to buy mink stoles; who did they think they were? Now that Hitler was no longer a threat, it was black women who were threatening by their presence in the workplace. Among black men who were facing uncertain job prospects, working women struck at their manhood. The postwar years featured the rise of black female dignity and the slow burn of black male anxiety. As an R&B song of the era put it:

"SHIPYARD WOMAN" BY JIM WYNN

> They said the war is over
> And peace is here again to stay
> You shipyard-working women
> Sure did have your way
> But it's all over baby
> Now you girls have got to pay

Something had been paid for: on the surface, it seemed to be a matter of money. In the mid-1930s, Negro picketers on the Avenue participated in a national movement, one that demonstrated against white-owned businesses in the community that refused to hire black workers. Using the slogan "Don't Buy Where You Can't Work," a movement coalesced around the notion that consumers could build a social movement, that spending power was an avenue for social change. A late-1930s boycott of movie theaters that would not show black films (organized by John Kinloch and others) furthered the idea of targeted spending as protest. Such notions flowered during the war years, when a consensus formed on the Avenue that blacks had bartered their loyalty, their time, their safety, and what most tangibly came in return was purchasing power. During and after the war Negroes bought cars and clothes, spent in clubs and restaurants. Money seemed to provide access to a world of choices.

But what were the choices, exactly, and which options were still off-limits? The war had ended the Depression and turned a generation of blacks into something they'd never been before: consumers. They were a long way off from enjoying the economic clout whites took for granted, but nonetheless, something fundamental had changed.

As the economy switched from ships, aircraft and munitions to producing consumer goods, material abundance became its foundation, and consumerism came to symbolize America's primacy in the world. To actively engage with democracy meant accumulating stuff. If Roosevelt hadn't died in April 1945, he would have had to add to his list of Four Freedoms the freedom to spend. In postwar America, to own was to belong. And when blacks became American consumers and still did not belong, fresh dimensions of confusion settled in. Drift and ambivalence were as real as dollars and cents in postwar Los Angeles.

Chester Himes wrote in *If He Hollers Let Him Go:*

In the three years in L.A. I'd worked up to a good job in a shipyard, bought a new Buick car, and cornered off the finest coloured chick west of Chicago—to my way of thinking. . . . but I knew I'd wake up someday and say to hell with it, I didn't want to be the biggest Negro who ever lived, neither Toussaint L'Ouverture nor Walter White. Because deep inside of me, where the white folks couldn't see, it didn't mean a thing. If you couldn't swing down Hollywood Boulevard and know that you belonged; if you couldn't make a polite pass at Lana Turner at Ciro's without having the gendarmes beating the black off you for getting out of your place; if you couldn't eat a thirty dollar dinner at a hotel without choking on the insults, being a great big "Mister" nigger didn't mean a thing.

Himes was laying down an existential, postwar blues, and many were those who worked their variations upon the mood. You couldn't hear it played at Ciro's or the Mocambo. You had to go a little east of Central, where Charles Brown was the headline entertainment, playing the existential postwar blues nightly on the piano at an elegant joint on Vernon Avenue.

When he arrived from the Bay Area in 1943, Brown brought a high-toned manner with him. He told an acquaintance his goal was to meet William Grant Still, the venerated black classical music composer. When he entered the regular amateur night contest at the Lincoln Theater, Brown played a boogie-woogie version of "St. Louis Blues" and then *Warsaw Concerto* and "Clair de Lune." He won. That night Marques Neal, husband of Duke Ellington band singer Ivie Anderson, hired the young newcomer to perform at the restaurant he and his wife had launched, Ivie's Chicken Shack.

It was no shack. Elegance and artifice prevailed there, with a red-and-blue color scheme and stenciled ivy climbing the walls. Clayton Russell, Ethel Waters, Bobby Short, and black film stars all dined there, and Hollywood stars came too; on one memorable night, the feuding gossip columnists Hedda Hopper and Louella Parsons both showed up and flamboyantly ignored each other. They came for the food and to hear Brown deftly weave light classics ("June Barcarolle," "Liebestraume") with pop tunes of the day. The manager ordered him never to play the blues, for Ivie's was a class establishment; but when the manager wasn't in the room, Brown played them anyway and the audience especially seemed to like his gentle, weary style. In part they responded because his weren't the down-low country blues, but nocturnes of insinuation and artifice, blues that summoned beneath their skin all manner of nuanced and furtive feeling. Desire was in there somewhere, and so was loss. One thing led to another; soon Brown had crossed over and was bewitching crowds at top Sunset Strip establishments. A wealthy Hollywood druggist even paid him five hundred dollars a night—laying the bills out on his dresser—to have Brown come to his residence and sing him to sleep. He did it, too.

Brown himself was a man of artifice and nuance. Born in Texas City, Texas, in 1922, he was six when his mother died and after that lived with his maternal grandmother. "She took me away from my father's side of people because they were cotton pickers," he explained to an interviewer. Brown said with some heat that if he played the blues, it wasn't the "porch-sitting, cotton-picking" sort. His blues was a choice, not an ancestral inheritance.

His grandparents managed to send him to Prairie View A&M University, where he was voted most popular student. Brown earned a bachelor of science degree and found work as a junior chemist and a high school teacher. But he was playing music on the side, and music seemed more inviting than chemistry.

His slowed-down, intimate style pulled you in close; his voice made every syllable clear as he seemed to be singing only to you. It might have been the blues, but its gentle worry, its words seeming to unfurl from a nimbus of blue smoke, emerged out of a new, unfamiliar space: the postwar lounge, a million miles from jook joints and tar paper shacks. The well-off people who came to Ivie's didn't fancy themselves sophisticates; they simply were. Negotiating their way through a moment when economic power promised so much and delivered mostly riddles, they were the success stories, and their success made them as cosmopolitan and polished as anybody at the Cocoanut Grove.

Brown had the night. In the afternoon Ivie's was a showcase for the electric organ, an early harbinger of what was soon to be *the* cocktail lounge instrument. Richie Dell Archia, who had known

Brown back at Prairie View, played elegant variations on the Hammond Solovox keyboard for the daytime crowd. Eventually, she'd play more elaborate organs, but even with the Solovox's uncertain oscillations she brought a special alchemy to Ivie's, one that stoked the imagination of urban sophisticates.

"It was about class," said John Collins, who bought Ivie's from Anderson, kept the name and added a formal cocktail lounge. "People came from downtown, from the court buildings, city hall, because of the music—it went on until three o'clock in the afternoon." One night Collins was arriving at work in his old roadster when he spotted two ragged drunks stumbling up the street. "They were 'motherfuckin' this' and 'motherfuckin' that' and cursing up a storm. I was appalled, because they were heading for the front door," he said. "They turned the corner and I couldn't see them anymore but I'm afraid, see, afraid because they're going to go into the restaurant. They were 'motherfuckin'' right up to the door and then I couldn't tell after that." Collins parked his car and hurried in.

"You know, I've never put anybody out in my life, but I thought this was going to be the first time. You can't have people talking like that." He found the two at the bar. "They were not saying a word to each other, sitting up straight, ordering food, they ate in silence, and when they were done they left. Never seen anything like that in my life." Ivie's demanded respect.

Meanwhile, Charles Brown had joined a group known as Johnny Moore's Three Blazers. His playing got simpler, even more direct—he went from neon light to candlelight—and cultivated a forlorn, steady drag that suggested the pace of somebody walking home after they've missed the last bus of the night. Time and again, the songs he recorded in Los Angeles in the 1940s—first with the Three Blazers and then as a solo artist—evoke meaningless wanderings. These were the songs that defined him as an artist and established him as a hit maker. His "Trouble Blues" and "Black Night" both topped the R&B charts, and in 1949 alone he had seven songs on the list.

Brown communicated with a saloon singer's conviction that he was at the center of a very small solar system:

Well I'm drifting and drifting
like a ship out on the sea
well I ain't got nobody
in this world to care for me

If Los Angeles was democracy's arsenal, Negro Los Angeles was democracy's keyboard lounge. The Avenue, with its small rooms and its spinet pianos, was perfectly situated. You could follow a trail from the witty late-1930s sets that Cleo Brown played in the Hollywood boîtes all the way to the ascendance of Nat King Cole in the mid-1940s Central Avenue scene. Along the way, you could hear Princess Bell and Lady Will Carr, a beloved, hard-swinging pianist who played with Charles Mingus and Gerald Wilson; Nellie Lutcher crooning her crowd pleaser, "The Princess Pa-Poo-Lia Has a Plenty Papaya (She Loves to Give It Away)"; Hadda Brooks, Dorothy Donegan and more, working in the space between jazz and pop. Perhaps the gaudiest star of this cocktail circuit was the flamboyantly out-of-the-closet singer Gladys Bentley. A sensation in Harlem in the 1920s, dressed in tuxedo and top hat and celebrated in memoirs and fiction of the era for her crude, bawdy songs, Bentley drove the literary lights of the Harlem Renaissance out of their skulls. By the late 1930s she had moved to the West Coast and was sharing a bungalow with her mother. Bentley performed in the lesbian bars that flourished in Los Angeles during the war years and recorded music for both Leroy Hurte's Bronze label and Excelsior, the label run by Leon Rene. She claimed to have written some 400 songs in Los Angeles.

The most famous piano player on the scene was Nat King Cole, though he is far better known today as a singer than an instrumentalist. But Cole got his first fame as a fleet, lightly swinging charmer with a combo as tight as a pimento plugging an olive. Then, at the peak of his instrumental artistry, in late 1947 Cole started pushing the piano stool back, dramatically stepped to the edge of the stage and sang. The song the audience begged for was a hit born in the exotic vibe of the cocktail lounge that came to fruition in the mass market: "Nature Boy." The melody was slow and beguiling, tinged with chords that evoked Middle Eastern tonalities. The lyrics were written by a bearded Los Angeles vagabond who called himself Eden Ahbez and spoke a message of universal love. "The greatest thing you'll ever learn is just to love and be loved in return," Cole sang. The record was a smash; "Nature Boy" took him out of the lounges, out of the black neighborhoods, away from the piano—and made him black L.A.'s greatest pop star.

He was a figure carefully scrutinized—obsessed over—by the masses, and to deal with the attention Cole established a transparent manner. No secrets here, was the message, my agenda is yours. But all the Avenue places that Cole left behind, the lounges and beer gardens and breakfast clubs, lived on as subculture, as a network of private agendas. They were places where secrets were shared and lines openly crossed, where nothing was transparent and nobody was what she seemed. Gladys Bentley must have been alluding to this world in an article she wrote for *Ebony* magazine in 1950. She said: "Throughout the world there are thousands of us furtive humans who have created for ourselves a fantasy as old as civilization itself; a fantasy which enables us, if only temporarily, to turn our backs on the hard realism of life."

Charles Brown belonged to this scene as much as anyone could. By the end of the war he was a star of the Avenue and he lived like a star, buying three Cadillacs, wearing a mink tie. His career was built on songs that made disenchantment seem a life sentence. Over and over he summoned darkness, even in the titles he chose: "Black Night," "In the Evening When the Sun Goes Down," "Evening Shadows." This was furtive music, and Brown was a furtive man.

He was married in 1949 to yet another piano-playing club performer, Mabel Scott. The wedding was one of the biggest social events of the year, with over 400 in attendance to celebrate the union. The mid-winter color scheme featured palm leaf green, yellow and orchid; ushers included the R&B act the Trenier Twins, T-Bone Walker and singer Jimmy Witherspoon. In the wedding pictures, Brown looks like a young Denzel Washington.

It was a show business wedding, the kind carried out for public relations' sake. For by various accounts, starting with Scott's, Brown was a gay man. He had matinee idol looks and an easy charm that made him the object of countless romantic fantasies, fantasies that might be dashed should his sexuality become a public matter. Sugar Tit, a shoeshine boy on the Avenue, was hired by Brown to drive him to his late-night assignations. "He was a wonderful man," he remembered. "It was funny. When he sang to a room full of people, all the women thought he was singing to them and all the guys thought he was singing to *them*."

Before he was married Brown would take women out in public to the racetrack and drop a thousand dollars on a horse. Up close, though, his secret was out. "He was the great love of my life," said Mabel Scott. "I never loved anyone else. But I wouldn't marry him again, that's for sure.

"He was a homosexual. And the men drove me crazy—he'd be out 'til one or two in the morning, and on the road he'd have our suite—and another suite over there, for his male friends." They were divorced in 1951.

Brown was friends with T-Bone Walker, the ranking bluesman on the Avenue, but Brown was not like Walker—a spokesman for King Konk hair straightener who tucked a pistol in his belt when he took the stage (one night it even tumbled out in the middle of a performance). When Walker went out on tour, his road manager was Harry Bigelow, one of the Avenue's biggest pimps.

Walker embodied the iconic bluesman; Brown embodied a new image of manhood, and there probably was only so far the issue could be pushed. That was, as far as wearing a mink tie would take him. "When he made 'Drifting Blues,' the birthrate shot up ninety percent," said Clifford Solomon, who played tenor in Brown's band. "He made make out music." Brown was selling a fantasy, and that meant keeping the fantasy viable.

Furtively, gay men and lesbians were forming a crowd. *California Eagle* society writer Bill Smallwood noticed it early on, watched a subculture pushing its way into the open.

> What do we care if people stare,
> Or care what people say?

> The golden dogs we're going to
> Are handsome dogs and gay!

His rhyme came long after the word "gay" had first been used as a synonym for homosexual. Smallwood went on:

I've recently acquired a few acquaintances who are true individualists. Of a sudden, now, it comes to there are many such acquaintances in the world—more than the world is aware of. They are to be seen on Sugar Hill, Piccadilly, on the Promenade des Anglais and on the Lido, but wherever else they may roam, they find occasional way to Los Angeles.

These new friends, to be precise, belong to that class of mankind known variously as men of the world, epicures, and even rascals. Most of their acquaintances are occupied with the conscientious evasion of responsibility. My friends, after the fashion of their kind, present a flawless exterior to the world they live in. There is no gap in their armor of savoir-faire. Their manners, in the most critical periods, are as impeccable as their attire. Their dissipations are conducted as the debauchery of gentlemen should be conducted. They are contemplated with reverent awe by the aspiring young men about town. Their life here is complete and self-contained. It bears no relationship to the progress of the world. They go from bar to bar, party to party, from spot to spot, and they face every problem of life with a suave negation which makes their position impregnable.

They face every problem of life with a suave negation which makes their position impregnable: no more concise description of the postwar ambivalence and drift is possible. That suave negation is present in Charles Brown's singing and up and down the Avenue, wherever money was to be made and people still weren't free.

For urban drifters, a place called Brother's was a natural point of rest. An after-hours lounge run by a large, amiable gay man, Brother's was a secret temple of exotica. You entered an alley just off Central, crossed a boardwalk that led up to a home, and you arrived at some other place. Ottomans and cushions lay low on the ground, and in every room people reclined in shadows. "If you've never spent a night in Sudan, then by all means spend an evening at Brother's Rendezvous," enthused a nightclub critic. "Cosmopolitan to the nth degree, your lawyer, doctor, grocer or banker may be seen relaxing here almost any morning."

"You could get anything you wanted there," remembered entertainment columnist Gertrude Gipson. "Anything."

Inevitably, Chester Himes found his way to Brother's. In his short story "A Night of New Roses," Himes describes an after-hours spot he refers to as "Cousin's":

> The whole place was deeply carpeted, overly decorated, lush as an opium den. There seemed to be a hundred fantastic different colored lights in the three rooms, and mirrors stuck at odd angles all over the walls that made them seem like a thousand; but the lights were so dim you could hardly recognize a person across the room. The air was thick with cigarette smoke, perfume and incense.

Henry "Brother" Williams greeted people at the door dressed in a Chinese silk robe; on his arm was his lover, Aristide Chapman. Charles Brown regularly dropped by and performed, as did piano player Art Tatum, Mabel Scott, Gladys Bentley, singer Ernie Andrews and many others.

In 1948 the city council cracked down on local nightlife, ruling that cocktail lounges had to adopt a minimum standard for lighting: low wattage, they seemed to believe, lead to low morals. A secret club, Brother's ignored the mandate; here people saw better in the dark. At Brother's you might spot someone you knew from the outside world, someone you thought you recognized. Doctors, grocers and bankers, as well as piano players, pimps and heroin sellers, came together in a place where all could spend freely the money they earned. Here people with no shortage of disposable income could practice a freedom that Los Angeles had promised them and then abandoned. It was a place where some discovered who they really were.

. . .

OTHERS, WITHOUT THE BENEFIT of a smooth voice or a mink tie, found fresh routes to freedom. One such person was Korla Pandit. He was a drifter who roamed the byways of Los Angeles in the 1940s, a smile on his face suggesting he knew things others did not. People—interesting, glamorous, bizarre people—came to Korla hoping he'd show them how to experience his peace.

He came to the city, he explained the many times we talked, from halfway around the world. He had a privileged childhood in New Delhi, where his father, a Hindu Brahman, was a government bureaucrat and friend of Mohandas Gandhi and his mother was a French opera singer. Korla was playing the piano at the age of two, and by five he was able to perform difficult pieces after hearing them a single time. He studied in Europe and then came to the United States when he was 12, later attending the University of Chicago.

As Korla prepared to leave his family behind and begin the life of a professional musician in America, his father gave him a warning: "Son, get your education first. Show business is a dangerous world. You're a hero today and a bum tomorrow." In recounting the story, Korla took a pause and then added, "Well, he sure knew what he was talking about."

Korla came anyway and conquered the West, or at least the West Coast. His television show, *Korla Pandit's Adventures in Music*, was the first all-music program on television, and Korla was one of the first stars of the medium. He played the organ live five days a week, performing some 900 shows, which makes him one of the most prolific television stars in history.

To have seen him on television—his show began in 1948 and ran in syndication in many cities into the 1960s—was to inhabit a perfumed realm. Fan Michael Copner recalls watching the program as a child:

> All I knew was I associated the church organ with heaven. And I started watching Korla Pandit and thought that somehow the television cameras were getting into heaven, and on rainy afternoons in heaven God must sit around and play the organ. Once I told Korla that when I was a

kid I saw him on television and thought that he was God. And he said, "You know, you could be right."

There was a joke made about Korla, passed along by many who spent time with him. Everyone who told it seemed to think he was the first to come up with it. The thing about Korla, people said, was that he never spoke on his television show, but in person he would never shut up. Korla loved to talk, about India and his past and the meaning of life and how geeky men could pick up beautiful women if they would practice his methods. But for all the talking he did, he kept a secret, one that remained protected all his life. Korla Pandit wasn't his real name, and he wasn't Indian at all. He was African American.

Korla Pandit was one of the very first blacks to have his own TV show, certainly the first in Los Angeles. The bargain that he made, with the station and with himself, was that nobody could know. Where better to live this way than in Los Angeles, where people are richly rewarded for conjuring fresh identities from a dash of half-truth and a pound of hype? He cultivated the public's curiosity, and he fended it off. His wife Beryl was instrumental in the invention of a TV swami. Together they created a dazzling fable about an oracular master musician with talent, charm and supernatural powers. Perhaps he had all these qualities; he just wasn't Indian.

"I have a Native American friend who says he was definitely Mexican American," said Timothy Taylor, an assistant music professor at Columbia University who has written on Pandit.

"I've heard he was Hawaiian. I've heard that he was Filipino," said Michael Copner. "You heard so many stories that they just cancelled each other out."

"He was very Americanized," said humorist Stan Freberg, who worked with Korla in the early 1950s at TV station KTLA. "He was light-skinned, about the color of General Colin Powell. To tell you the truth, I think Korla Pandit invented himself."

• • •

THE STEWART BRIDGE stood on the periphery of Columbia, Missouri, a leafy college town in the center of the state. Elderly African Americans point to the spot where a rope was tied to the latticework above the railroad tracks, and the other end fashioned into a noose placed around the neck of James T. Scott. Protesting his innocence to the lynch mob that had gathered one day in 1923, Scott was hung from the span of the Stewart Bridge.

Scott held what was, for a black man in Missouri in the early 1920s, a good job: he incinerated the dogs and cats killed in University of Missouri experiments. One day the 14-year-old daughter of a university German professor claimed a Negro had attacked her near the railroad tracks. Community groups offered a reward, and the local press made a crusade of catching the rapist. An anonymous tipster claimed it was Scott, and after his arrest, one local paper demanded he "feel the 'halter draw' in vindication of the law."

A white mob burst into the Boone County Jail, dragging the beaten and bloody prisoner through the city until they came to the place over the tracks. Their rope was not long enough for the job; the party sent out for a longer cut, and when the girl's father pleaded for Scott's life, they threatened to lynch him, too.

An invisible line stretches from the world of James T. Scott to that of Korla Pandit. I only learned of it through the idlest of encounters. In the late 1990s I began to frequent an Italian restaurant in West Los Angeles named Carmine's II. There was a big picture of Dean Martin on the brick wall, and the food was nothing special. But what brought me to Carmine's was Sir Charles Thompson. Five decades ago Sir Charles was one of the most talented bebop pianists going; he recorded with Charlie Parker and Lucky Thompson and jammed in the Avenue clubs. Styles change, people forget; and there he was, an 81-year-old master playing in a fashion straight out of an airport piano bar for whatever got tossed into a tip jar. If he knew you were listening, Sir Charles would sometimes improvise a little something on top.

One evening we started talking between sets, mostly about his early days. He said he had grown up in Columbia, Missouri. Truth was, he couldn't recall much: you spend a lifetime improvising, and then in your last days you hold on tight to a handful of riffs learned early.

Still, Sir Charles had two memories of Columbia: one was of another lynching, a murder that led him to flee his home for good and join a New Deal work camp. The other was about a kid in town, an even better piano player, who attended the same segregated school as Thompson. The kid's name was John Roland Redd, and for a while they were close. Then Sir Charles moved away and lost touch. "Later he went to Hollywood and became a famous organist on television," he said. "He used another name, some Turkish title, I guess."

In 1921 a boy named John Roland Redd was born, according to his birth certificate, in St. Louis. Ernest Redd, John's father, was black, as was his mother, Doshia O'Nina Redd. Their three boys and four girls were light-skinned and grew up in Hannibal and Columbia. Ernestine Tapp, a friend of the family in Columbia, recalled going to a movie show with one of the Redd girls: "They tried to make her sit where the white people sat. She had to explain to them that she wasn't white."

The pastor of Second Baptist Church, the largest Negro Baptist church in town, Ernest exerted a huge influence on his children. But right next door to Second Baptist was McKinney Hall, a second-floor dance hall that featured traveling jazz bands. As the Redd children grew up, McKinney began to exert the greater pull. Perhaps it was at McKinney that John first heard Art Tatum play. A legendary piano virtuoso, Tatum became one of his heroes.

"John Roland was so small, he had to get a little boy's shirt to graduate from high school," said George Brooks, a classmate at Fred Douglass School.

He was a fun-loving person. We were all part of the jitterbug generation. One year we went up to play basketball against one of the other high schools. And it was pretty much the whole Douglass school went up there. Afterwards, we were in somebody's house, and there was a piano. And of course, John was attracted to a piano like certain insects are to flowers. He started playing, and it wasn't very long before he had a crowd. And that front-room floor where we were dancing—it broke there in the center. Too much weight! That upright piano was against the wall, and the break was near the center of the room. It was just lucky that the piano didn't turn over. If it had, we wouldn't have had a John Roland.

Several of John Redd's sisters had already moved to Southern California by the time he arrived, in 1938 or early 1939. He initially stayed with his sister, Frances Redd, an actress then filming *Midnight Shadow*. He too sought a career in show business. But while Frances saw black-made motion pictures as a stepping-stone to something larger, John had other ideas.

He began getting work as a pianist, but a more or less unusual type of pianist. One day he casually donned a prop from one of his sister's movies, the turban actor John Criner had worn in *Midnight Shadow*. Perhaps he noticed a mysterious, unplaceable visage when he looked in the mirror; perhaps he thought a turban would hide kinky hair. In any case he must have liked what he saw, for John Redd began performing as a turbaned pianist. Presenting himself not as John Roland Redd, Negro, but Juan Rolondo, Mexican, he was an organist at radio station KMPC and played live dates at everything from Hollywood supper clubs to Balboa Beach to the Pomona public library.

It must have felt secretly thrilling, pulling a scam on the Caucasians at Balboa, then a segregated beachfront. But there were also practical considerations to his decision to go Mexican. You had to join the musician's union to play on a stage in Los Angeles, and through the 1940s the union was segregated, with a local in Hollywood steering the lucrative film and club gigs to whites while the black guys hung out at a separate local on Central. Being Mexican meant being somewhere in between, and probably meant better performing opportunities. But being Mexican had its own problems in 1940s Los Angeles, as the zoot suit riots had demonstrated. Being a Mexican musician might diversify your opportunities, but it still pretty firmly limited them.

In 1943 Redd met Beryl DeBeeson, an attractive, tough-minded blonde who was an airbrusher at Disney's animation studios. She was indispensable to the creation of Korla Pandit. The two were introduced by Korla's sister Elizabeth, and Beryl became his confidante and career adviser. They were married in Tijuana in 1944—they had to cross the border because California outlawed interracial marriages.

In 1948 Rolando got a job playing organ on *Chandu the Magician*, a popular radio drama about an exotic detective who solves crimes around the world. By the end of his *Chandu* run, in 1949, the man beneath the turban had changed his name to Korla Pandit. The exact moment he changed and the reasons for it remain unrecorded—a secret carefully protected.

Was this creation a flim-flam meant to last only as long as it took to cash a check? A chance to buy the Taj Mahal? Perhaps Redd saw Juan Rolando as a short con and realized Korla Pandit was for the ages. From one angle, he was playing a dangerous game, risking discovery and retribution. But from another he was simply doing what show folk have always done in Hollywood: reinventing themselves and saying it was ever so. What we do know is that the live performances continued, with Korla playing regularly at Tom Brenaman's restaurant at Hollywood and Vine.

First, though, something had to be done about the way Korla talked. With an "Indian" accent that wasn't all it might have been, Korla cultivated an act in which he said nothing. Men from the East were supposed to be mysterious, were they not? Silence was expedient, but it was strategic as well.

As was the headgear. The turban, strictly speaking, was problematic. Hindus from India, again strictly speaking, do not wear them. Indians who do wear turbans are Sikhs, and they, alas, do not wear jewels in their turbans. Yet to a Hollywood audience desiring an exotic encounter with the Indian "other" but not knowing what that "other" was, showbiz stereotypes were all it expected. Korla, drawing on the same stereotypes, gave the people what they wanted. He had turquoise, maroon, and burgundy turbans, and each was adorned with a glittering, smoky topaz, like an all-seeing eye. The topaz, he told people, protected him from unsavory influences.

Those influences were everywhere. "He had times when people would try to run up on stage and loudly expose him for what he wasn't by snatching his turban off," says nephew Ernest Redd. "He let the hair grow and grow and grow under the turban, so when they snatched it off and thought they were going to find a kinky grade of hair, it just fell out and they were kind of stunned. It actually came down to his shoulders."

From slavery right down to this morning, countless African Americans have passed as white because they were evading the lynch mob or wishing for an equal opportunity. The subject has been taboo: Crossing over meant denying who you were, meant banishing friends and family from your life. You lived in a gray zone, and it was the loneliest of places.

Passing for Asian was a little different, because you did not blend into white society. You remained a category apart in the eyes of whites. The practice went on long before Korla Pandit appeared. In the late 1930s, Harlem's *Amsterdam News* reported that a Syracuse University football star named Wilmeth Sidat-Singh was, as a reporter put it, "about as much Hindu as flat-foot floogie." In the mid-1940s, Babs Gonzalez, a fledgling bebop singer from Newark, was working in Beverly Hills as a turbaned Indian. In 1947, the *Los Angeles Tribune* heralded a stunt pulled by a brown-skinned New York minister. He prepared for a visit through the Deep South by donning a purple turban, affecting "a slightly Swedish accent," and concocting a tale about being a visiting Eastern dignitary. He was doted on and was able to eat at whites-only restaurants. In Mobile, Alabama, the minister puckishly asked a waiter what would happen if a Negro came to eat. The Negro wouldn't be served, he was told. "I just stroked my chin and ordered my dessert," he said.

If the turban was chosen to obscure what was African American beneath, it may have had the opposite effect on those who were in the know. Turbans were favored headgear for a variety of black nationalist organizations of the early decades of the twentieth century. They were also worn by early-twentieth-century African American magicians, who wielded a symbolic power that made them quasi-nationalist figures. There was, most famously, the turbaned illusionist known as Black Herman, an Afrocentric pamphleteer who claimed to be descended from Moses and was an associate of Marcus Garvey and

Booker T. Washington. (Another black organ-playing mystic, Herman Blount, a.k.a. Sun Ra, was named after Black Herman.)

Hinduism itself had resonance in the 1940s to a generation of Negroes fighting for their rights. Indian Hindus were using racial equality as an argument against British imperialism; Indian speakers lecturing on their struggle were guests in black Los Angeles churches throughout the decade. As it happens, one of the more forceful voices for racial equality in India was a woman by the name of Madame Vijaya Lakshmi Pandit. Which suggests that if Korla was doing everything he could to hide his heritage, he was also proclaiming it to the savvy few hipsters who got the message.

Korla Pandit remained nothing more than a fantastic idea, however, until the moment when an émigré from one culture encountered an exile from another. In 1948 Korla was performing at the opening of a local furrier. TV station KTLA was broadcasting the event, and the station's founder, Klaus Landsberg, was supervising the shoot. An engineer at heart, Landsberg had an intrinsic understanding of the Hollywood deal. Liking the organist, he immediately dangled a TV show in front of Korla and then, almost as an afterthought, told him there was just one catch. If he wanted his own program, he'd also have to play for a new puppet show. Landsberg landed a twofer: a new TV star and music for the puppet show, called *Time for Beany*.

Meeting Landsberg was the break that Korla and Beryl had been looking for. The German-born mogul had played a role in the first live television broadcast, Hitler's 1936 Olympics. Just before World War II started in 1939, he fled the Nazis and landed in the United States, when he was hired by the DuMont network to launch a Los Angeles affiliate. Landsberg built a television station in his own image and went on to give the world helicopter chases and roller derby, Lawrence Welk and Gorgeous George.

The entrepreneur created spectacle and then left it up to the audience to sort out the real from the fake, which was fine with his turbaned organist. From his very first televised performance, Korla was a sensation. "Korla Pandit was always immaculately groomed," recalled Stan Freberg.

He was just like Frank Sinatra that way. Imagine, this is a guy sitting in a corner of a small studio at Melrose, just outside the Paramount gate. He'd come sliding in a half hour before airtime in this impeccable double-breasted dark blue pin-striped suit with a white shirt and French cuffs, beautiful cufflinks, three pointed white hankie in the pocket, and this beautiful turban with a jewel. It was such a waste, because cameramen in t-shirts and tennis shoes are pulling cameras around and cables are crossing over the top of his organ. It was a strange time.

The show, *Korla Pandit's Adventures in Music*, always began the same way, with the numinous light of heaven filling the screen. As seconds passed and the camera drew back, only then would you see that this light was emanating from the jewel in Korla's turban. The camera pulled back more, and Korla's face, with its Gnostic half-smile and ancient countenance, came into focus. All the while Korla would play his signature song, "Magnetic Theme," and then a selection of numbers from distant lands as his male dancer, Bupesh Guha, and a troupe of gamines pranced among the fountains and plywood pillars. His small hands would often play two keyboards at once, a piano and an organ, a music made not for dancing but for easy-chair meditation.

Beryl weighed in on production decisions. She helped design the sets. She oversaw his makeup. She argued with directors over the lighting, insisting that shadows not fall upon Korla's face. He was the star, but he was also a team effort.

He never spoke. Everything he communicated came through those slender fingers and the steady gaze. A woman wrote him that she had been planning her suicide when she caught his show and that something in his look stayed her hand. She sent him a piano in gratitude. His eyes spoke for him, and this was the essence of his wit. Born at a time when a black man in the South could get whipped for making eye contact with a white woman, Korla Pandit made dreamy eyes at thousands upon thousands of aproned white homemakers, stole into their dens as they warmed their fondue pots.

Quietly, he remained a seasoned jazz musician. When boyhood idol Art Tatum haunted the after-hours clubs, Korla would sit in on jam sessions. The nearly blind virtuoso might not have been able to see a face very well, but Tatum had fabled ears, and after hearing Korla play just a few bars, Tatum would greet him by name.

But by necessity Korla sublimated his passion for jazz, erased from his public performances obvious traces of a music that connoted lowdown good times, not to mention black culture. The arrival of a new instrument with almost no jazz associations helped him greatly. It was his good fortune to have emerged a decade after the invention of the Hammond organ, which generated sounds never heard before. By its very strangeness, the Hammond was a tool of the exotic. The soul of the Hammond was its tone wheels, which whirled at controlled rates. The shape and speed of the spinning wheels produced a new electronic music and in their whirring created a simulation the manufacturer called "vox humana": the human voice. The warmth of its sound gave the Hammond an uncanny intimacy and gave Korla one less reason to speak.

Most others approached it as if it was a pipe organ or piano, but Korla turned the Hammond into a one-man rhythm orchestra, slapping the keys and spanking percussive drum blasts that harmonized with the melody, coaxing outlandish vibrato from the two rows of keys, a tremble of air that stretched from the Los Angeles stage to Persian markets and Moroccan harems.

"His music is so much more creative than any other organist's I've ever heard," said Korla's friend Verne Langdon. "Korla created chords and harmonics that I call purple chords—just rich and deep and beautiful. It would not be unusual to see people crying when he was playing. I was one of them."

Here were the first stirrings of the music that became known as exotica. The genre started with big band veterans hoping to hold onto listeners who were dropping swing music in droves. Bandleader Tommy Dorsey had luck with tunes like "Katie Went to Haiti," "Hawaiian War Chant," "Hungarian Rhapsody" and "The Song of India," a piece that became one of Korla's staples. Korla told friends that Dorsey would show up at his concerts and pretend to be asleep in the back, then a week later play Korla's tunes for his Hollywood Bowl audience.

Korla implicitly understood the yearnings of a postwar public full of restless soldiers returning from the Pacific and other faraway places. They sought in backyard luaus, tiki bars and the music of distant shores a sexuality they denied themselves in their daily lives. Think of Carmen Miranda shaking her fruit with a knowing leer; Korla's music embodied that look and the sweet perfumed passion fruit lurking beneath the everyday. It was Brother's for the masses, minus the vice.

In the years to come, Korla would associate with an astonishing variety of real and imaginary spiritual leaders and travel up and down the West Coast, performing on TV, in concert halls, at drive-in movie theaters. He lived a not always easy nomadic life, sleeping on people's couches, playing for small crowds. In the 1990s, when a wave of young L.A. hipsters were rediscovering lounge culture, a cult following gathered around him, watching him play shows at a tiki bar on its last legs.

He died in 1998. Never did he tell his two boys, Shari and Koram, the secret of his past. In the end, to everybody who knew him and to himself, he was Korla—John Redd had died long ago. It was Korla's luck to appear at a time when so much was up in the air and so many were drifting on through. It was his luck to make it in a city—Hollywood or the Avenue, take your pick—where you could run with a good cover story, as long as you ran fast enough.

I saw him once without his turban. It was at his last recording date. The Federal Building in Oklahoma City had just been bombed, and the public was in an anti-Arab mood. Korla, not taking the chance of having someone mistake him for a Middle Easterner, had left the head wrap at home.

He entered the tiny Hollywood studio wearing polyester slacks and Nikes, his lustrous jet-black hair flowing from crown to collar. The session had been hastily assembled; the rented Hammond B3 still on a dolly. He grappled all day with an old Ventures song, "Diamond Head," but the stars were not in his favor. The engineer accidentally erased good takes. Feedback shrieked when Korla just brushed against the organ, and his elaborate toggle-switch tricks were spitting up what sounded like lava erupting out of a volcano. Numerous takes yielded nothing. It was 100 degrees in the small room, and the whole session was going down the drain.

A couple of girls in skirts arrived, and his mood lightened. Then, while we silently waited for an indication that he was ready to record another take, Korla leaned over the keys. There was no erupting lava, no feedback. He stared past the sheet music and summoned a dance tune from 60 years ago. It was a big-band number called "Tuxedo Junction," and Korla played it with a crisp, jaunty touch, swagger that had us imagining dances nobody knows how to do anymore. It wasn't exotica. It was a song he might have heard at a jam session back home in Columbia. It was the sweetest sound he would make all day. The tape was not rolling.

CHAPTER 13

Children of Chaos

We chose the name "Neighborly Endeavors" because we realize that it is only through loving our neighbors that we are going to be able to protect our community. . . . When the Negro realtors start begging you to sell, it will be hard to resist the temptation. Think of your responsibility to your neighbors.

—*Mr. Lund, white Leimert Park homeowner*

LOREN MILLER, ATTORNEY, NEWSPAPER EDITOR, FAMILY MAN, DIDN'T have the time or the inclination to hang out at a place like Brother's. Miller was a public figure, instantly recognizable in the street and downtown. Yet he shared at least one quality with people like Korla Pandit and Charles Brown. It's not that he had secrets, per se, just that he had done things that others, perhaps, had not. Loren Miller was a figure of great experience and he wore that knowledge lightly upon his face. The experience, along with a suspiciously placid smile, would serve him well as he faced the fevered events of 1948.

Loren Miller loved being a newspaperman, but it was his legal work that put food on the table. With a civil rights practice representing people of limited resources, Miller didn't even put that much food on the table. (He once took a case representing a headless chicken; after the health department wanted to slaughter a malformed bird that had no evident head, its owner declared the fowl a miracle and hired Miller to fight the city. Work was work.) Miller built up a practice in the 1940s that became widely known for a particular specialty: the defense of those prosecuted for violating housing covenants. This expertise was just one part of his practice, but it was his work fighting housing restrictions that made him the most important civil rights figure in Los Angeles. Journalist and lawyer Carey McWilliams labeled Miller a likely candidate for the Supreme Court. Today he is more or less forgotten, his greatest victories taken for granted, the sum of his accomplishment barely a footnote in the capital of amnesia.

The construction of the black ghetto in Los Angeles had been achieved through a system of private agreements among property owners, pledges that homes would not be sold to "non-Caucasians." They were written into deeds, and courts declared them legally binding. With the influx of black workers during the war years, these agreements were similarly on the upswing throughout Southern California. They fortified the walled city that was Bronzeville and the Central Avenue corridor, keeping those within from easily moving elsewhere.

Housing restrictions may have been used in many parts of the country, and they were notably popular in the North after World War I, as Negroes moved en masse from the South. But they were all but invented, and then refined, in Southern California. The first court battle over them occurred in San Diego in 1892, when a judge ruled that an attempt to close a Chinese laundry was illegal because it violated the equal protection clause of the Fourteenth Amendment to the U.S. Constitution. Illegal such moves might have been, but in 1919, in a case involving a black Los Angeles police officer who had bought a home in a white neighborhood, a California judge decided Californians could live with such agreements, too. By then, developers were carving whole subdivisions of the city out of miles of dusty lowlands. Subdivisions were being drafted in real estate offices, in a process that provided a fine opportunity to give three-dimensional shape to one's notion of the ideal community. Vast empty spaces had to be filled and developers thought big, imagining themselves as social engineers. Such thinking went unchallenged for decades. "Nobody should undertake to develop less than a neighborhood," suggested Hugh Potter, head of a real estate and builders organization in 1945. "This means not only the home but transportation, churches, schools, parks, recreational areas and . . . shopping centers." It was hard to shape society with a single building, but with a whole tract, the imagination stirred.

From the start subdivisions routinely had language written into individual deeds declaring which people could live there and which could not. In already established neighborhoods, homeowners were adding discriminatory language to their property deeds, ensuring a single address stayed white. The more effective way to influence a neighborhood's complexion, however, was through mutual pacts made by people of an entire block or development who had formed a homeowners association. Like-minded folks could agree among themselves who should live in the area, and protect their vision by signing contracts declaring to whom they would sell their home. Should the agreement be broken, the community association took the violator to court, where precedent was on its side.

Los Angeles was built in enormous tracts, but it was sold to the rest of the country one house at a time—a legion of salesmen, barkers, hype merchants and pitch men promoted Southern California to whites and blacks alike as the place where a family could get a fresh start in a sunny, citrus-scented paradise. Homeownership underpinned what it meant to be an Angeleno; denial of homeownership amounted to a revocation of citizenship rights. In Los Angeles, a sprawling metropolis dependent on the automobile, mobility became essential to existence. Access to the area's expanse equaled liberty in exceptionally brutal ways in Southern California; the shutting off of access was felt in exceedingly personal ways. The more of the map that was rendered off-limits to non-Caucasians, the more non-Caucasians were rendered invisible. It was Miller's genius to apprehend the extent to which in Los Angeles, racism was manifest not through laws but through *geography*.

Talking with mock pride at a Chicago housing conference in 1946, he touted the West Coast's accomplishment.

Speaking as a Californian—and necessarily boasting, for who can mention California, especially Southern California, without boasting?—I am certain that there are Californians who would want me to remind all of you that, due no doubt to our salubrious climate, my state has produced racial restrictive covenants as far superior, if that is the word, to the ordinary run-of-mine racial restrictive covenants as our climate is to the climate of other and less fortunate sections of the nation.

Miller knew better than anyone what Los Angeles could contribute to the national fight for civil rights. Having studied the legal history of covenants and knowing that by the end of the war his home state had more of them than any other state in the country, Miller plotted an assault that began as a block-by-block fight and ended in the Supreme Court.

Among those who knew Miller best, the only surprise about his commitment was how it revealed itself in the courtroom. For law was never a huge part of Miller's sense of himself. He much preferred being a journalist and had struggled to write a novel for years.

"He didn't really like going to court," said Stanley Malone, a former law partner. "The whole court scene—the deference to the judge, the courtesy to the other side—he saw as a shortcoming to practicing law. Especially when you are superior in your thinking."

"Tall, thin slightly sardonic Loren Miller," the *Tribune* called him, and pictures from newspaper stories and journals of assorted eras all seem to feature an astringent sparkle in his eye—one sees a sense of play and a sense of judgment. That sardonic streak helped him cope with the whimsy of Los Angeles segregation. Although black ownership of property was legal everywhere, black *habitation* of a restricted home was illegal. Thus arose a genre of sarcastic headlines in the black press like the one declaring "Negro Wins Fight to Live in Own Home"; thus rulings like the 1946 edict in which a judge declared a white woman could live in her house, but her black husband would have to go.

An Urban League official estimated that by the mid-1940s, some 80 percent of the city was blanketed by restrictions. "We [are] well on our way toward the creation of little islands of super-paradise in that Paradise of the Pacific," Miller joked. "Communities in which none could dwell but blond-haired, blue-eyed Aryans, certified 99.44% pure for at least seven generations, all of them five feet 10 7/8 inches tall, addicts of Little Orphan Annie and lifetime subscribers to, perhaps, *The Cross and The Flag.*"

The real estate interests kept pace with the wartime migration, their efforts to extend a cloak of restrictions across the city turning into something ardent and comic. In Culver City, southwest of Hollywood, citizens congregated at city hall under a banner reading "God Bless America: Life, Liberty and Justice for All," to discuss keeping blacks out. They deputized air raid wardens—the officials watching vigilantly for foreign invaders—to go door-to-door with petitions targeting homegrown invaders. The head of civilian defense urged volunteers to visit areas where deed restrictions had lapsed or were about to and compel homeowners to update their covenants. There was a war on; this was part of the home front struggle.

"You might find some trouble, there may be one person who says 'I don't mind if a Negro lives next door to me, or if I rent to a Negro,'" said the Culver City civil defense chief. "Try to win them over but don't argue too much. Know how you feel if someone talked to you like that. Deep down in my heart I would like to tell them a thing or two, but there is no use arguing too much. Just turn their names over to me and I will send someone else to talk to them. We'll find a way!" It was ominous but it was hilarious, too, this enforced community spirit. The success of property restrictions thrived on block-by-block surveillance, on anxious activists working the street, encouraging everyone to maintain the same standards—property values they said they were upholding, but it was really racial values. Vigilance was essential, for all it took was one quisling to sell out to a black family and there went the neighborhood. Los Angeles is sometimes considered a city of strangers lacking in community spirit, but once upon a time the city positively flowed with spirit, so much of the stuff you could drown in it.

A circular from 1944 shows how restrictive covenants, racial supremacy aside, were also becoming a profitable business. Such flyers were dropped in mail slots and slipped under doors.

Do you know that a JAP OR NEGRO can buy the home next door to the one you own at the above address—and move in with his family and friends—and that you can do nothing about it?

Well that is just what can happen because:
THE RESTRICTIONS ON YOUR PROPERTY ARE VOID . . .

It is in your power to protect your home and your district against invasion by NEGROS, JAPS and WHAT-NOTS. You may accomplish that purpose by entering into a valid agreement prohibiting their use and occupancy by unwanted persons. Such an agreement has been prepared and is in our office awaiting your signature. It has been prepared in such a manner that several copies may be circulated concurrently. If you will undertake to circulate a copy in your immediate vicinity, it will expedite its recording, which may save you from waking up some morning to find that you have dusky neighbors next door.

There are some expenses incident to an agreement of this character. Perhaps the most equitable way to defray such expenses is to make a flat charge of $.15 per front foot, plus 10 cents for each signer. The agreement should be signed by husband and wife, mortgagee, trustee and beneficiary. Where five signatures are necessary, the entire cost for a 50 foot lot will be $8.00 which is very cheap insurance. After all, if your building burns, you can rebuild; but, if the wrong kind of people move in next door to you, it is beyond your power to evict them.

Let's all get together and get this contract signed up 100% without delay!

At least one Negro developer also got into the act, advertising his own tract as "the choicest, restricted, all-Negro, subdivision in southern California." Sometimes self-defense was good for business, too.

Miller watched the rise of the housing restriction industry, and noticed how tensions were growing most along the line bordering black and white communities. "Racial restrictive covenants are the chief divisive forces in modern American urban life," he said in 1946.

> Nowhere are racial animosities greater, nowhere are racial tensions higher, than in all-white areas and all-Negro areas lying side by side. There, whites stand eternal guard to keep their Negro fellow Americans "out," and it is precisely there that, for altogether natural reasons, expansion of the Negro community is most apt to occur. We have made ourselves strangers to each other and, because we are strangers, we distrust each other, we fear each other, we even hate each other.

He could read the writing on the wall. There was plenty of it, too, what with gang graffiti blooming in the 1940s, marking territory and pronouncing boundaries. One side pushes on a border and the other side pushes back: the impact of restrictive covenants on the rise of L.A. street gangs is a topic overdue for study. A black gang called the Lightning Aces formed in the 1930s around Ross Snyder Park and thrived well into the 1940s; members included boxers Dynamite Jackson and Chalky Wright. According to *Los Angeles Sentinel* writer Wendell Green, the Lightning Aces "were the fightenest, crapshootenest bunch of guys ever assembled in one group." But they were more than that and were seen at the time as more than just rough characters—the Lightning Aces were defenders of the race.

"They were generally known as a bad gang and they were no angels, but they carried their race high on their shoulders and were ready to do battle over discrimination or a racial epithet at all times," noted Green.

> Their easily affronted attitude is what made it possible for young Negroes to go to such places as the Coliseum, and the various parks, playgrounds, and beaches, without encountering difficulties. I can remember the time when to go to the Coliseum to see the great football stars in action always meant a fight with some smart "paddy," or a

group of them. Of course the Lightning Aces did not do all of this, but they were a sizable factor in letting the white boys know that if they molested a Negro, there would be a fight.

By the mid-1940s a crop of youth gangs rose up in the white working-class communities of South Gate, Bell and Huntington Park in the southeastern part of the city. The most notorious was the Spook Hunters, whose logo on their club jackets expressed whatever their name left out: a caricatured black face with a noose around its neck. A new cycle of violence came into existence, especially among high schools bridging black and white neighborhoods.

Loren Miller grew up along various borders of identity, region and race. He was born in 1904 in Pender, Nebraska, a small town on the Omaha and Winnebago Indian reservation. His father was born a slave in Kansas and after the Civil War had left Kansas for the North. Miller's mother was a white schoolteacher; she was unable to teach in Pender because of the mixed marriage, and the family moved to a farm outside of town. When Miller was a teenager, the family moved to Kansas.

At 16 Miller entered the University of Kansas in Lawrence, but a year later returned home to help his family after his father died. When he went back to college, it was to Howard University in Washington, D.C., where he majored in journalism. He began writing opinionated essays that attracted the attention of writer Langston Hughes, one of the anchoring voices of the Harlem Renaissance; the two became close friends for the rest of their days. Hughes brought Miller onto the staff of the *Crisis*, the esteemed journal published by the NAACP and edited by W. E. B. du Bois, who became a friend and mentor to Miller. He also wrote for the *American Mercury*, the *Nation*, and other publications.

Chafing at the Dixie-style race relations of the nation's capital, Miller moved to New York, where Hughes lived. Ultimately, he didn't like New York all that much more than Washington: imbued with the Harlem Renaissance but not impressed with it, Miller returned to Kansas, earning a law degree at Washburn College of Law in Topeka.

He set up a practice in Topeka in 1929, a big fish in a Kansas swimming hole. By then his mother and younger siblings had left the state for Los Angeles; after a family funeral brought him there, he saw an opportunity and plotted an escape from Topeka. Miller talked his cousin, Leon Washington, into going with him, and together they were hired by the *California Eagle*, Miller as a writer and Washington as a writer and advertising salesman.

The fledgling journalist kept in touch with his East Coast chums, and when Louise Thompson, a political activist and denizen of the literary salons, asked him to join a group of Negro actors and artists traveling to Russia, Miller jumped at the chance. He accompanied Hughes, Thompson and 19 others sailing by steamship in June 1932 on a trip paid for by the Communist International; the plan was to make a movie in Russia about the condition of blacks in the American South. It was a fascinating moment to see postrevolutionary Russia, if not to make a movie; the Soviet agency producing the picture first intended to use Russian performers in blackface to represent American blacks, and after the Americans arrived the production degenerated into bureaucratic fiddling and grumblings from the bohemian Americans. They ate caviar for breakfast. They were shoved to the front of the bus. Much drinking, partying and cultural exchange ensued; the movie, however, did not. About six months later, having seen a good bit of the socialist frontier, Miller sailed back to the United States.

The trip became an international news story and a scandal at home. Upon Miller's return and for the rest of his life, the adventure would haunt him every time a panel convened in search of Communists in high places. Though he was never a member of the party, he straightforwardly acknowledged his attachment to the cause early on. Those early writings in the *Crisis* and elsewhere were full of revolutionary zeal; they, too, would follow him around for the rest of his life.

In the 1930s Miller suggested a name for Negroes of his era, a rubric with all the romance attached to "The Lost Generation": the Children of Chaos. The writers, vamps, artists and soapbox orators he memorialized were young, desperate and hungry to express themselves in ways unbound by the race-consciousness embraced by the

Harlem Renaissance. He sought an aesthetic that was neither as floridly European as some of the Renaissance artists nor as stocked with romantic notions of Africa. He called for a literature more class-conscious and upfront angry than what Harlem offered. "I made myself eternally famous and radical in those golden, by-gone days by perorating (after a certain number of drinks of corn likker) that the Harlem literary output . . . was tripe, trash and 100 percent no good," he reminisced in a 1930s letter to Hughes. It was as if, after being embraced by the New York intellectuals, Miller could see his future, and he saw himself being smothered by them, too, in velvet and corn likker.

Back in the States, he moved to New York and became editor of the radical magazine the *New Masses*. He lasted about six months, and whether it was this experience or subsequent events, by 1939 he was on the outs with the party and championing individualism over revolution. He had married a glamorous L.A. sociologist with lefty connections of her own, and with his cousin Leon Washington had started a newspaper, the liberal *Los Angeles Sentinel*. Together they masterminded the *Sentinel*'s successful "Don't Buy Where You Can't Work" campaign, organizing picket lines outside white businesses. Miller had matured, or perhaps he had simply begun to accept his lot as a practitioner of the law. He let Washington march on the line and get arrested. Miller would be the one to bail his cousin out, defend him in court and then compose the editorial the following week.

His first restrictive covenant case came in 1939; as of 1945 he had handled about 15, but by 1947 he was at around 100. The surge showed not just that housing restrictions were on the rise, but that in key ways Negro rights were in retreat.

Soon the police department began drawing lines of their own. An aspiring actress named Elizabeth Short was found murdered on January 15, 1947. Posthumously dubbed the "Black Dahlia" in the press for the clothing she wore and the color of her hair, rumors circulated that Short had been seen drinking in the Negro part of town. A media storm followed the gruesome discovery of her body and the police launched a series of raids on Central Avenue clubs, sending a signal that places where the races congregated—particularly black men and white women—were off-limits. Negro nightclubs were, in the words of assistant police chief Joseph Reed, "breeding places where crimes are planned and carried out. We are going to purify the city of Los Angeles.

"It is the women who frequent these places that are cast along the Black Dahlia lines and all too frequently end up in the same way."

Seizing on the Black Dahlia panic, the police department set up roadblocks around Negro and Latino neighborhoods. They stopped cars by the hundreds and lined drivers up against walls, subjecting them to humiliating searches. It was one more sign of lines hardening.

Then, a few months later, something gave way. For years Miller's strategy in fighting restrictions was to argue that their proponents were in violation of the Fourteenth Amendment, specifically the clause establishing the right to due process and equal protection under the law. He had stuck to this tactic even when it failed him in court; a more effective strategy had been to show that a neighborhood had substantially changed since the restrictive language had been written—that is, to show a Negro was moving into a neighborhood where others already lived. But Miller held on to the constitutional argument, convinced that it struck at the heart of covenants everywhere.

He was a member of the national NAACP brain trust that formulated the organization's long-term legal strategy. Along with Thurgood Marshall, Charles Houston, William Hastie and a handful of others, Miller had been combing the dockets for promising cases that could be bundled together into a petition to the U.S. Supreme Court. Late in 1947 the Supreme Court agreed to hear their case, which included four regional appeals—one in St. Louis, one in Detroit, and two in Washington, D.C. The case was *Shelley v. Kraemer*, and Miller would be one of the attorneys arguing before the court in May 1948. Here was a chance to fight institutional racism across the country, not to mention a chance to rip up the map of Los Angeles. That summer Miller headed to his old stomping grounds of Washington, D.C.

Meanwhile, back on Central Avenue, Jack McVea was also starting to get somewhere. He had just recorded a song called "Open the Door, Richard," and when it hit the streets in late 1946—the same spring that the police's new "crime crusher" barricades were brought out—McVea scarcely knew what he had. He'd find out soon.

A saxophonist from a musical family—his father Isaac led McVea's Howdy Entertainers and had a regular slot on KNX's *The Optimistic Do-Nut* show in the late 1920s—the son fell naturally into the musician's life. In the 1940s he assembled a small band of his own in which he played tenor sax.

McVea got the inspiration for his little tune one night in Oregon. His five-piece combo was touring the West Coast, playing a blend of small-group swing and R&B. In Oregon they fell into a groove and McVea started talking over it, performing an old comedy routine he knew by heart. It hardly seemed special; he was only putting music to words lots of people had heard before, just clowning. That was about as deep as McVea's band got, in their zoot suits and sombreros and pith helmets. They danced onstage, screaming and mugging and barrelhousing. And here was a number perfect for goodtime hats and people-pleasing stagecraft, a riff that sent the crowd home happy.

The band was back in Los Angeles, parked in a Hollywood studio and flat out of inspiration as a recording session for the local Black & White label rolled on. Producer Ralph Bass later claimed recording "Open the Door, Richard" was his idea. "I was doing some blues with [McVea]. I got bored to death because everything sounded alike and suggested that he do 'Richard,' which I had seen him do live."

Others said it was McVea's decision to record "Richard." However it happened, "Open the Door, Richard" changed all kinds of history, and its story illustrates how immensely and unpredictably a song can matter. "Richard" mocks the notion that what means the most is what has the most to say. "Richard" seemed to be saying very little, but it spoke loquaciously to the moment Los Angeles and Loren Miller found themselves tangled up in.

There really was a figure named Richard, living in music and words long before McVea caught up with him. Pigmeat Markham, the star of the Lincoln Theater, knew him earlier than most. Markham performed with a minstrel show called the Florida Blossoms in the early 1920s and there met his mentor and inspiration, Bob Russell. A producer and writer with many stage shows to his name, Russell had a career in minstrelsy dating back to the Civil War. Some thought Markham had come up with the Richard routine, since he'd performed it for decades. Others thought a comic peer who was a little older than Markham named Dusty Fletcher was the creator. But the truth, Markham writes in his autobiography, is "that song was written by my old friend Bob Russell, and he wrote it for a long-ago show called Mr. Rareback in which John Mason sang the song." That's as close as we can get to the origins of "Richard."

From Russell on down, "Richard" passed from one variety show to the next. Dusty Fletcher did as much as anyone to make Richard familiar to black audiences. In Fletcher's version of "Richard," he played a tenement bon vivant at sunrise, staggering home only to find the door to his apartment locked. He hollers up to his roommate Richard to let him in, but Richard seems otherwise occupied; Fletcher can hear the heavy breathing coming from inside. "I know he must be in there because I've got on the suit," Fletcher told his audience. Like a blues guitar lick shot out of the Mississippi Delta, like a slang term for the white man fresh out of New Orleans, Richard's weird fame was absorbed in Negro neighborhoods around the country as communal property.

Among those who probably heard Markham do "Richard" at the Lincoln Theater was Jack McVea. His career was on the upswing, for he'd played on the Lionel Hampton Band's landmark 1942 "Flying Home" recording and recorded with T-Bone Walker, Slim Gaillard and Charlie Parker.

He formed his own group, one based on the swank, air-cushioned R&B of Louis Jordan's Tympani Five. They set music to the version of "Richard" that McVea pulled out of his hat that night in Oregon. "That simple melody just came to me," he told an interviewer. The easygoing banter of McVea and drummer Rabon Tarrant, the bebop shadings the pianist throws in, the ghetto banter they cooked up, all of it slayed them live, and then McVea put it on a record. Released late in 1946, "Open the Door, Richard" quickly became a local jukebox favorite. Later, after the song made him a national star, McVea told me the biggest thrill of all was overhearing a little old lady tell a local street-car conductor, "Open the door, Richard."

"Richard" starts out so casually—a few offhand piano notes, a hint of bass—it's as if the musicians don't even know the recording equipment is on. It has the sound of an off-the-meter rehearsal, guys casually jamming until they find something they all know how to play. One-liners from McVea and Tarrant bump into one another, the loose banter pointing in two directions at once—back to the dozens of street corner rhymes of African American folk culture and forward to Bo Diddley's "say man" records and hip-hop. Steeped in black oral traditions, "Richard" is so easy and unforced, so unplanned and happenstance, it doesn't feel like a conscious effort to *say* or *reflect* anything. It just is.

The tune first hit on the Avenue and then fanned out to Negro neighborhoods coast to coast. By early 1947, demand was outstripping the label's supply. The February 15 *Los Angeles Sentinel* announced that Black & White was sending "one of the largest single order shipments of records ever carried by air"—10,000 copies airlifted to New York City alone—"in a C-54, which has the largest plane doors ever constructed."

An R&B craze had launched; numerous black artists quickly cut cover and answer records, many of which also climbed the "race" music charts. Besides McVea's liftoff (number 3), there were versions by Count Basie (number 1—the biggest hit he ever had), the Three Flames (number 1), the Charioteers (number 6). Dusty Fletcher cashed in (number 3), and McVea's mentor Louis Jordan himself was moved to cover the tune (number 6).

But if by February "Richard" was a smash in the Negro community, the praise was far from universal. A shouting match broke out in the letters sections of Negro newspapers, as Richard became an unwitting lightning rod for tensions between rural and urban, old and young, zoot suits and swallowtails. McVea was scorned as a product of Hollywood, his dap band flossy and glib compared with the old school Southerner Dusty Fletcher. The battle over Richard was about style, and whether one responded to Fletcher's ragged but right suit and top hat or McVea's draped shape said a lot about who one was. Meanwhile, pillars of society viewed *any* rendition of "Richard" as an embarrassment, and one critic acutely summed up his minstrelsy roots as "Uncle Tom-y." They sensed in the frivolity of the McVea band everything that was holding back the race.

Perhaps as well critics dreaded the young listeners who wore zoot suits and reflected their energy back on the band. These fans embraced "Richard" and gave him meanings McVea had never intended, any more than he intended to be a symbol of backwardness. To at least some Negro listeners, "Richard" was a barely secret call for justice's doors to spring open. In 1947 students from seven Georgia colleges marched to the state capital demanding the resignation of segregationist governor Herman Talmadge, carrying banners reading, "Open the Door, Herman."

On the road, McVea found himself thrust into the role of agitator. In May, Indianapolis mayor Robert H. Tyndall nixed McVea's appearance at a Teen-Agers Frolic, declaring there would be no mixed dances in town. The chief of police refused to issue a permit; McVea, his manager, and the CIO sponsors of the show researched local law and found a loophole allowing dances without permits if they were classified as private club events. The dance went on, and "Bandleader McVea expressed himself to the hundreds of teen-agers gathered by working the four-hour dance period without one breathing spell," cheered the *Chicago Defender*.

On Central Avenue, of course, the cramped living conditions and squalor gleaned from the song were flourishing. "Richard" became a mirror in which a ghetto community could view itself and gave that population a voice in the creation of popular culture.

Across the country, Richard became a fair housing messenger. A March 1947 story in New York's *Amsterdam News* reported on a sermon given by Reverend Horton A. White, pastor of Plymouth Congregational Church in Detroit. The sermon was titled "Open the Door, Richard": "This ditty which is sweeping the country on stage, air and records, was made to have deep seated meaning by Rev. White as it dealt with restrictive covenants in this community," reported the paper.

> Rev. White stressed the fact that . . . the doors of equal opportunity for better housing for Negroes must be opened so that he can walk boldly into any house in any neighborhood where he is capable of purchasing or renting. In this case Richard (the courts) is not asleep but is prejudiced and stubborn but sooner or later will be forced to open the door when restrictive covenants are definitely broken.

Other audiences tuned in; white people met Richard. They were hearing the same song, but in an entirely different way. By March 1947, "Open the door, Richard" had become a jovial salute on national radio shows, a catchphrase uttered by Jack Benny, Fred Allen and Phil Harris. Jimmy Durante and Burl Ives recorded versions, as did the milk-and-cookies harmony group the Pied Pipers. Some of these covers took "Richard" in directions not even Bob Russell's fever dreams could have rendered. For a moment, the public thirst for all things Richard was boundless; there were hillbilly versions cut by Hank Penny and Dick Peterson and His Vocal Yokels; there was a calypso cover by Tosh "One String" Well and His Jivesters. "The U.S., which loves screwball songs, last week hit the crackpot jackpot," said *Life* magazine.

"Richard" became a marketing craze, perhaps the first of the postwar era. Dime stores sold Richard hats, dungarees, handkerchiefs, shirts, bracelets and other memorabilia. He was used to sell Ruppert Ale, Franklin Simon perfumes, and Best Yet hair attachments. Bugs Bunny riffed on the song in the cartoon "High Diving Hare." Opera star Lauritz Melchior broadcast his version nationally. Ultimately, "the life of every American named Richard became almost intolerable," lamented *Life*. The contagion then jumped the border, with Molly Picon singing the song in Yiddish; there was a Spanish version, "Abra la Puerta, Ricardo," and covers in Swedish, French and Hungarian.

One war barely over, another heating up. The new conflict was in its way as global as the one just ended, only it was undeclared, less tangible. In this new crisis there would be less division between battlefield and civilian world. The Cold War was fought in the same space in which daily life was lived, in the marketplace of ideas and in the marketplace itself. "Richard" became a consumer durable that America had and its foes did not, a symbol of American exceptionalism. In that restless summer of 1947, Secretary of State George C. Marshall came to Harvard University with an alarming message for the nation: "I need not tell you gentlemen that the world situation is very serious. That must be apparent to all intelligent people," he declared in what would be one of the most famous speeches of the century. "The problem is one of such enormous complexity that the very mass of facts presented to the public by press and radio make it exceedingly difficult for the man in the street to reach a clear appraisement of the situation." Marshall was not a likely fan of "Richard"—no record suggests he dug the tune—but, as McVea's song airlifted American pop culture to the far corners of the postwar world, Richard had indisputably become a soldier of the new American realpolitik. Richard became an early tool of what was soon to be called the Marshall Plan. As McVea put it on his hit: "Richard, open the door, man—it's *co-hold* out here in this air."

In the *Los Angeles Sentinel*, in an editorial written by Loren Miller, the call went out for black political representation at city hall. "We are glad to see Negroes knocking at the door and we hope that they keep on pounding until our sleeping city fathers get up and open that door," he said. His headline made it clear: "Open the Door, Richard."

In the summer of 1948, Miller broke the door down. He and three other NAACP lawyers argued the unconstitutionality of restrictive covenants before a truncated version of the Supreme Court—three justices had recused themselves from the debate, and though nobody said for sure, the word was that each owned property with deed restrictions. That May the justices, following Miller's lead and citing the equal protection clause of the Fourteenth Amendment, ruled that restrictive covenants were unenforceable by the courts. Though they didn't say such agreements were per se illegal, individuals had to police them for themselves.

The ruling dealt a huge blow to housing segregation and was felt instantly on Central Avenue. Almost from that day forth, blacks began moving out of the old enclave, and a massive push westward to Baldwin Hills and Culver City, south to once lily-white Compton, and north to the San Fernando Valley, was on. Housing stock had disintegrated along the Avenue, and if Bronzeville was the worst of it, the rest of the Avenue was also full of overcrowded, substandard homes. *Shelley v. Kraemer* led many to start packing their bags. They moved because they could afford to, and because for all the gifts of the Avenue the produce was better in white neighborhoods, the furniture cost less, the homes were nearer to work. They moved because they thought the schools were better or because the lawns were bigger. They moved because as the richest moved, and then the middle class, those who stayed found they could no longer leave their front doors unlocked. They moved because for the first time, those who lived along Central Avenue began to fear their children.

When geographical barriers lifted, it meant the irreversible lifting of other barriers. Los Angeles had never codified its segregation in a body of laws; with Jim Crow nesting so neatly into the growth of the city through restrictions on huge tract developments and through the regulations of neighborhood organizations, there was no room for messy arguments in public about the need for legislation.

Restrictions lingered until in a 1953 case, *Barrows v. Jackson*, the Supreme Court extended the implications of *Shelley* and effectively declared them null. In a story Thurgood Marshall liked to tell, arguments on *Barrows* had begun in the afternoon and then were held over for a second day. That night, Justice Felix Frankfurter told retired Justice Owen Josephus Roberts that he really ought to come down to the court tomorrow, because "some young Negro lawyer is giving the chief justice hell." It was Loren Miller Frankfurter was referring to.

True enough, the real estate lobby in Southern California agitated for a constitutional amendment to preserve restrictions. True enough, mortgage loan lenders and property owners organizations found ways to segregate for years after *Shelley* and *Barrows* were law. As Los Angeles integrated, there would be bricks through windows and burning crosses on front lawns, and dynamite would explode. "I remember during the war my dad had a gun," said Loren Miller Jr. "I think there was some concern that things would happen."

Yet for all the violence above and below the surface, two facts were evident: Jim Crow took a whipping in L.A. with the defeat of the covenants' legal foundation. And because of Miller's work, Central Avenue started melting away. The legal strategy honed in the case—the call for equal protection under the law as declared by the Fourteenth Amendment, the use of an array of sociological data to argue the damage done to Negro Americans by this wrong—would hold sway in civil rights circles for years to come. Indeed, as strategy and symbol *Shelley* laid the groundwork for the victory a decade later in *Brown v. Board of Education of Topeka*. "It is obvious," said attorney Thurgood Marshall after *Shelley*, "that no greater blow to date has been made against the pattern of segregation existing within the United States."

Abie Robinson worked with Miller from the 1940s into the 1960s at several newspapers. "I never met an individual as brilliant and as earthy as Loren," he said, and then launched into a detailed description of a moment that felt like a snapshot taken yesterday. He described how an 80-year-old man, Mr. Allen, invited Miller to speak at his church in Santa Monica one evening long ago. The request went through Robinson, who encouraged Miller to do it; he also encouraged Mr. Allen to pass the hat at the church after Miller spoke. Miller didn't know anything about that request. Said Robinson, "Cause nobody was making any money at the newspaper and the law practice was funny—it contained civil rights cases that didn't pay." Allen told Robinson not to worry, he had it all figured.

After the talk, the three of them—Robinson, Miller and Mr. Allen—stood on a dark street corner, counting the change they had collected, counting to see if they had enough for a pint or a fifth. Then they stood there, three shadows framed by the street light, sipping and talking. "That's how human he was," Robinson recalled. "See, that was our thing, standing in the alley getting a half a pint of whiskey—but that shows you how human he was.

"And he seemed to enjoy it."

CHAPTER 14

Ringside

When will it all end? Brother 'gainst brother, sister 'gainst sister; Godzilla 'gainst Gork, Minnesota 'gainst Oakland . . .
—*The Reverend Sanford (Redd Foxx)*

THE MAN STANDS CENTER STAGE, SCANS THE MOSTLY BLACK FACES. Behind him a guitar and a bass tune up. "Guys? Guys? Okay?" he asks. Okay. Showtime.

He fingers the microphone. "Tonight marks a new chapter in the annals of jazz," he tries. "The musicians here tonight are some of the best and greatest in the country."

They were also some of the best and greatest in the immediate neighborhood. Tonight isn't really a "show," though you do have to pay to get in. This is an Avenue jam session, featuring an array of local talent. There is the skinny 19-year-old from Memphis, Sonny Criss, playing alto and already scaring off hornmen three times his age. Howard McGhee, one of the leading clergy of the new religion of bebop, is on trumpet. At the piano sits Hampton Hawes, son of L.A.'s lone black Presbyterian minister. As the rest of the lineup is announced, patrons continue filing into the Elks Auditorium, a large room with mediocre acoustics.

Record producer Ralph Bass holds the microphone. He also runs a pair of portable disk-cutters stashed below the stage, machines that let him document the performance in its entirety by switching from one machine to the other throughout the night.

Somebody stomps out the beat, and Hawes flicks off the first notes of "Disorder at the Border." Nobody is in a hurry here; there's a bigness to the sound that keeps growing as the music flows, every horn soloing. Voices in the crowd hoot and holler, shouting "Go! Go!" when the long, tall, doctor's son named Dexter Gordon gets moving on tenor saxophone.

Despite Bass's buildup, the only thing truly special about the night is that he thought to record it. In almost every other way—the stature of the musicians, the variety of styles enfolded, the interaction with an avid crowd—this is simply one more night to remember. Same as last night and the night before that in the underworld of Avenue jams.

A veteran player and organizer of jams, saxophonist Buddy Collette recalled the scene. "It was confusing because everybody played well," he explained with a shrug. "You'd say 'guy played a good solo tonight,' but that was not uncommon; it was just like somebody saying you cooked a good meal tonight. No big deal, it was just something you tried to do."

"Jam" is one of those crossroads words like "rock" or "barrel-house," a term that flickers on the edge between noun and verb, a music word that today shades into sexual connotations, though those connotations almost certainly preceded the music. Some purported origins of the vernacular "jam": to press tightly, to be wedged, possibly a variation of the verb "champ," as in champing at the bit; according to the 1944 *New Cab Calloway's Hepsters Dictionary*, jam means to "improvise swing music"; Daniel Defoe, *Robinson Crusoe* (1719), "The ship stuck fast, jaum't in between two rocks"; an abbreviation of jamboree, "a noisy social gathering"; an abbreviation of windjammer—a vessel whose sails needed enough "jam" to move the ship; a variant of a Wolof word meaning slave. However it evolved, by the 1930s jazz musicians were holding informal get-togethers in which they played for each other's edification, after their paying gigs were done. They named these scenarios "jam sessions." They had to call them something.

People jammed all over. The Avenue was flooded with musicians, looking for work in the defense plants, looking to entertain those getting paid there. Early in the war the Negro musician's union advertised in the *Pittsburgh Courier*, the national Negro newspaper, urging musicians to get themselves post-haste to Central Avenue, the pot at the end of the rainbow. There were gigs on the Avenue and in Hollywood and at least the possibility of work on radio and in the movie studios. By the end of the war hundreds and hundreds had dropped on by—staying for a string of dates, a season or the rest of their lives. Los Angeles became home to more great jazz players than any other place in the country. When they worked, they were glad and when they didn't, they kept themselves sharp by assembling whoever was free and setting up a session.

With so many musicians around, it seems odd that Central Avenue was never able to claim an overarching style. L.A. didn't have a parallel to the bebop that was cradled in Harlem, nor the bluesy, almost-spoken mode of the "Texas tenors." Kansas City had a legendary dance-oriented swing scene, and the Southwest was a conduit for guitar players. But with so many folks coming from so many different places, there was never a solid shot at a Central Avenue school. School thrives on a schedule, and this was chaos. All Los Angeles had was Charles Mingus and Art Tatum, Dexter Gordon and Wardell Gray, Buddy Collette, the young Ornette Coleman, Lester Young, Clora Bryant, Walter Benton, Jackie Kelso, Barney Kessel and Dingbod Kesterson and Al Killian until he got himself murdered, Addison Farmer, Roy Porter, Vi Redd, the godlike Oscar Moore, who started out a guitar player and ended up laying bricks, William Green, Chico Hamilton, Streamline Ewing, Carl Perkins crippled by disease and tilted horizontally and wringing more out of the piano that way than seemed humanly possible, Gerald Wiggins—*Wig*. L.A. was deep. There was a long-standing Creole community still active, and numerous swing veterans from big bands broken up by the war. The town was fat with refugees from the so-called territory bands of the 1930s, road-hardened units that lived on unheated buses and played barns and fish fries and winter carnivals while traversing the open spaces of Oklahoma, Kansas, Missouri, Texas, Iowa, the Dakotas, Minnesota and Wisconsin. When that scene up and died, many went to L.A., where the sun at least was warm. There were the kids sitting at the feet of Charlie Parker, carrying his horn for him and learning bebop from the source. It was like the whole country was a pool table leaning on one short leg, and all the balls rolled to Central Avenue. L.A. had it all—everything but focus.

So many ways of playing—so many languages, really. How to harmonize with a stranger? Marshal Royal was an alto saxophonist in the Count Basie band; in an oral history he beautifully described the local confusion resolved in the Avenue jam. Central Avenue "was the only part of the city that had any type of accumulative jazz in it," Royal said.

Nobody else was even trying to play jazz except the guys in the Central Avenue area. You had different types of guys—you had fellows that came up from New Orleans that had this style of playing, they had guys that came in from Chicago that had their style of playing, New York guys. See, a lot of people wanted to move west out into this country here. And there never was really too much togetherness. It's sort of "do the best you can," because there are a whole lot of strangers. You find one guy over here, he's from Dallas. There's another guy up there, he's from Kansas City. And they catch another guy, he's over from Oklahoma, and they've got the Texans. All of these people were coming in here, and they were trying to better their conditions when they came here to escape from the horror of the South, because that was no place to live. . . . California is what's left of a whole lot of people trying to come West.

In a jammed-up community, among a gaggle of gatecrashers, the Avenue might not have had a signature sound, but it could claim a signature shape all the same. It was a shape traced by movement and realized in performance. The Avenue took to the jam session like nobody had before and adopted it as a native tongue. To write about Central Avenue in the 1940s is to write about these moments. Jam sessions happened up and down the street, for as many reasons as there were doorways. They were a de facto social hall, and they built the kind of shared setting itinerant tradespeople sought. Pool players knew which place had the action; Pullman porters had their local office; traveling salesmen had the lobby of the Clark Hotel. The jam session, likewise, was a place where a right-off-the-train neophyte found others who could explain the lay of the land. The jam session provided information about what the competition was made of and what it would take to succeed.

They happened anywhere: in a nightclub, in a tea room, in an empty field between a gas station and a florist's shop at 42nd and Central. Buddy Collette and Charles Mingus jammed on the streetcars. Dizzy Gillespie jammed with a bunch of wizened New Orleans originators; once, the Ellington, Basie and Lunceford bands were in town at the same time and their parts all jammed together. When the piano master Art Tatum was on his deathbed, a group of the Avenue's finest keyboardists visited him; one after the other, they played something for the master. That, too, was a jam session. Jams were a mix of comity and tragedy, of the tutorial and the gladiatorial. Frequently, Charlie "Bird" Parker was on the premises.

Trumpeter Art Farmer was haunting the scene all night and going to high school all day during Bird's stay in L.A. (which lasted from late 1945 to spring of 1947). Farmer befriended the saxophonist and, in an oral history, recalled walking down the street with Parker when they decided to stop in at Lovejoy's Breakfast Club ("Home of the Big-Legged Chicken"). A geezer was playing the piano, "What we would call an old timer, playing music that would fit the silent movies." Bird whipped out his alto and started playing with the guy, and found a way for his blazingly fast style to mesh with the elder's. Afterward, he and Farmer walked home to the apartment they shared.

"You really surprised me, playing with somebody like that," Farmer said.

Because Charlie Parker was regarded as the god of the future, and he's playing with this guy, what we would call just an amateur. And he said,

"Well, if you're trying to do something, you take advantage of any occasion. Go ahead; ignore that other stuff, that doesn't mean anything. You have to concentrate on what you're trying to put together yourself."

Farmer thought about that all the way home.

But specialization—the notion that beboppers and old time stride pianists stick with their own kind—was hardly just a musical idea. In the West Coast shipyards, manufacturing innovations championed by industrialist Henry J. Kaiser led to record-setting production of liberty ships. Techniques developed in the building of Boulder Dam inspired engineers to construct whole ship sections—boilers, deckhouses, double bottoms—in pieces and then lift them into place by cranes. Such techniques had the effect of diminishing the artisanal nature of older shipbuilding methods. Emphasizing repetitive, circumscribed tasks, new methods turned skilled workers into mechanical functionaries.

Something similar was happening in the West Coast jazz clubs. The music business was becoming a real business, and yeoman skills of music making were atrophying, replaced by a gleaming professionalism. A studio system was on the rise, in which musicians were hired to play a certain way, deliver a signature lick on demand, drop in on a recording session they didn't know anything about and inject a flavor into a whole they had no control over.

They were paid by the recording date, by the hour, by the clock. At jam sessions, musicians weren't getting paid, or not much. Playing at a jam wasn't work, it was a gift; it was play—the experience provided a delight and served purposes that work never could. In an era of industrialized specialization, the jam session returned jazz to its artisanal roots.

Naturally enough, the musician's union objected. Players were giving it away for free, and the union wasn't getting its cut. They fined those who jammed, yet their efforts showed all the more how different these sessions were from work and how special places like Jack's Basket Room were at 3 a.m. The union felt it was guaranteeing its workers got paid for their efforts. And the jammers believed that—for once—they weren't laboring for somebody else: they were making music for their own sake, repossessing the time they sold for a living. They were creating a product that slipped the yoke of a price tag and reclaiming their music as theirs alone to give.

After-hours spots accommodated these affairs, where proprietors sold setups—ice and cokes—for those who brought their own bottle. Other places followed the "we've got near beer here and beer near here," policy, meaning they'd sell you something tame and the guy out front would sell you something stronger. The working person who had to get up in the morning probably wasn't there. The after-hours jam was music made off the meter, played for those living off the meter. They were hipsters and hoods, cognoscenti who knew the codes. What began as music made for other musicians had become an antidote to mass culture—to life on the line and union dues and all the rest. The jam session was a cultural preserve: old skills protected in secret spaces.

"We used to go out after work to after-hours spots," recalled showgirl Alyce Key. "We would party to daylight—way past daylight—and we'd see people standing on the corner waiting for the bus. And we'd say, where's the picnic?"

As the decade progressed and union regulations against jamming withered, the experience became ever more itself, ever more unlike business. Nobody mistook jams for just another gig. They were a spectacle outside of time, and the musicians who made the most of them were those who combined musical skills with a flair for presentation. "The personalities and the people were part of it, not just the horns," explained Buddy Collette. Audiences responded to the story unfolding before them, and it was told through theater, not just music. You never knew who might get chopped and diced at a session; even Charlie Parker could misfire. "The audience and even the player would realize whose night it was, realize they'd come and got you," Collette explained. "You could be the one who would be challenging the guy and you would be like, boy, this is not my night! It's on your face. And the audience is probably cheering for the one that's really looking like a winner and sounding like a winner." Truth was, looking like a winner could be as important as sounding like a winner, which is why some of the audience's favorites were those who projected nothing but self-knowledge, a sense of flair and easily being in the world. On some nights that was enough.

Recording the moment was to sell the moment out, and it wasn't going to sound like being there, anyway. Some things elude the microphone. An album has a beginning, middle and end. A session, though, was a totality unto itself, and if you weren't there, you missed it. You really missed it. Frances Williams was an activist and actress on the Avenue who understood the promise such events held out to those lucky enough to be there. "I feel very unhappy about so many young people who have everything and don't know what the hell to do with it," she told an interviewer.

> They're so busy working on time clocks and division of work that you never get a togetherness of a whole. I always used to say, "You know, in Africa they don't think like that." Here we see a rose, and you separate the petals, and you take a picture of the petals and then of the stem and the thorns. But in Africa you see a melon in a cold running brook of water, and you think, "Mmmm," and all your taste buds start. You feel the whole, all the sensory organs are tempted, and you almost smell it even though you're not near it. But you can taste it, and Mmmm, when I get to that—You don't just think the skin is rough, you know, you don't think like that. You think of the whole effect. And that's what we don't do enough of here.

The melon in a brook, the togetherness of a whole: that is what the jam session was.

• • •

WITH ITS CRUSH OF NEWCOMERS straining to make sense of a roaring town, the place itself became a jam session. "There would be so many people on Central Avenue then between 42nd Street and Vernon that you couldn't walk without bumping into other folks," recalled drummer Roy Porter in his autobiography *There and Back*. "You'd see all sorts: soldiers, pimps, gangsters, hustlers, whores, movie stars, musicians, politicians, groupies, fans and, of course, the cops."

You wouldn't make a dollar or a friend by staying inside. To live along the Avenue was to be in motion. "Home was just a place to be," recalled Buddy Collette. "You got a little home—it was small—and most of the time you're out eating or in the car or something. And that was L.A. at that time, especially for the Central Avenue part. You might have a little apartment, some place to eat, change your clothes—and get out again. It was all flair, it really was."

The auditorium of the Elks Temple was a preferred meeting ground. Located at Vernon and Central, the Elks Temple was one of the largest buildings on the strip, its several floors used for balls, concerts, club meetings and poker games. The auditorium was 60 by 80 feet, the roomiest place on the Avenue and a showcase for such big bands as those of Louis Armstrong, Coleman Hawkins, Charlie Barnet and Fletcher Henderson.

But the Elks Temple had meanings larger than a dance floor could contain. Fraternal organizations had long held special significance in the struggle for equal rights. Whites scrutinized Negro public life for signs of discord; fraternal groups and secret societies harbored political expression outside the reach of prying eyes. The Odd Fellows, Knights of Pythias, Elks, Grand Knighted Order of Galilean Fishermen, National Order of Mosaic Templars . . . all seemed parallels of similarly named white organizations, but they were not. Their rites and rituals sheltered hidden content right down to their ornate costumes. At a time when blacks were nonpersons subject to arrest simply for driving in white neighborhoods, secret societies allowed them license to wear plush regal uniforms and call themselves exalted, supreme, master. While the zoot suit uniform was inviting violence in the street, the Elks were holding annual parades with flamboyant costumes, colorful banners and music. As historian Susan Nance has shown, fraternal groups were marching in the streets as far back as the 1920s, when even the NAACP couldn't count on permission to assemble in public.

All kinds of people showed up at the Elks Temple; after the zoot suit riots, the LAPD asked the Elks to prohibit blacks and Mexicans from dancing together. All kinds of ideas, too; the temple held a regular civil liberties forum, to which anyone could come and speak on matters of the day. California assemblyman and later congressman Gus Hawkins remembers the role the civil liberties forum played in building his political base.

"We would go over there and express ourselves and challenge other speakers," he said. "You could bring up any subject you wanted to. They had different themes but you could almost express yourselves on anything." Hawkins remembers attacking high utility rates and protesting a hike in streetcar fees.

Central Avenue had a long tradition of giving newcomers a place to say their piece. Besides the Elks Temple, there was another organization, called simply the Forum, which lasted from 1903 until the early 1940s. Mandated to reach out to all in the community, the Forum let the most independent and marginalized of voices address the assembly. Race news from the hinterlands might take weeks to make the West Coast newspapers, so the Forum asked newcomers to explain what was going on in the rest of the country and to interpret events. Interestingly, the Forum first met in the AME church that became home to the Azusa Street revival. It then moved to the Odd Fellows Hall. Something intersects the Forum, the Azusa Street revival, the Odd Fellows Hall, the jam session: it is the democratic sound of tongues in full flutter.

None of them was a happy melting pot. People argued with each other, baited and scrapped, from the Forum on down to the Elks. The police were called. The jam session could be a dangerous place, a disordered borderland that elevated careers and raised wounds. Not just anyone, it could be made humiliatingly clear, was invited to play. The invited sometimes wished they hadn't brought their horn. Not for nothing did an aura of machismo hang over the proceedings. Jam sessions were regularly called "cutting contests," sometimes even "ass cutting contests," and those that didn't make the grade felt like a blade had been twisted deep. As drummer Lee Young put it, "everybody knew when it was over: they knew who was bleeding and who wasn't. But that was learning. He wasn't going to bleed long—it just meant for you to get on your job. You were playing with your peers." One had to be ready; the crowd would cheer the beheading of Jesus Christ if he wasn't delivering miracles on the night in question. This was a fierce meritocracy where a hot-handed upstart might yet carry the night.

Meanwhile, on the stage of the Elks Auditorium one evening in 1947, the exalted Wardell Gray was tangling with the potentate of the Golden State, Dexter Gordon. It was a two men enter, one man leaves situation. Just another night.

Offstage, Gordon and Gray were nothing but friends. But when they squared off night after night in the after-hours spots, they became rival samurai. "I came back to L.A. in 1947," Gordon told an interviewer decades later. He'd spent time in New York with Billy Eckstine's band.

And the jam session thing was going on very heavily at that time, at several different clubs. At all the sessions, they would hire a rhythm section, along with, say, a couple of horns. But there would always be about ten horns up on the stand. Various tenors, altos, trumpets and an occasional trombone. But it seemed that in the wee small hours of the morning—always—there would be only Wardell and myself. It became a kind of traditional thing. Spontaneous? Yeah! Nothing was really worked out. It was a natural thing. . . . That's where I was. That's where Wardell was.

Teddy Edwards, who played his share of tenor battles, knew the score. "They loved alto players in L.A.," he declared, "but the tenor was the horn on the Avenue." Why the tenor became so popular is unclear. Some have claimed that it has a sound closer to the human voice than any other instrument. Others have pinpointed the horn's innate creativity—anyone who masters it sounds like nobody else alive. Still others say the charisma of the instrument harks back to the popularity of the tenor voice in opera; the tenor soloist was the original box office star.

But Avenue-born-and-raised tenor man Clifford Solomon had a top-ranking explanation for the instrument's primacy. "I'll tell you why the tenor saxophone was the jam session instrument: the chicks liked the tenor," Solomon explained.

The tenor has that mellow thing, especially when people like Lucky Thompson play it, it can be exciting like when Illinois Jacquet would play "Flying Home," it would be moody like when Coleman Hawkins would play "Body and Soul"—every tenor had to know "Body and Soul," you know, and play it for his girlfriend, or if he was trying to catch a girlfriend. It was the tenor that was also hitting that breathy low note. They liked the alto too because of Johnny Hodges, but the tenor was always the instrument that got the girls. The tenor was the pussy instrument.

Fans started out sedate and pensive and ended up standing on tables and chairs screaming themselves hoarse when Dexter and Wardell, Wardell and Dexter went at it. Many of their greatest shootouts took place at the Downbeat. "It was made right for jazz," said Teddy Edwards.

It was made like a box. There was a bar facing the bandstand, but it had mirrors behind and around it, so if you sat at the bar you didn't have to turn around. Everywhere you looked you saw the stage. The people were on both sides of the band, and in front, so you got real close—the stage was only about eight inches off the floor so you were right there surrounded by the people. That's the best communication I ever had.

Lots of folks showed up to play at the Downbeat's Wednesday jams, but over the course of an evening the casualties mounted. Clifford Solomon recalled the scene.

The Downbeat was right on the corner of the Dunbar block—tenor player Gene Montgomery had the house band and ran the jam sessions there. Dexter, Wardell would do "Cherokee" and change the rhythm sections three times during that one song. The drummer would come and take the sticks and the other cat would get up, and the new one would pick it right up; the piano player, one cat would slide out this way and the next one would slide on in. But the horn players would just keep blowing.

In early 1947, the pair entered a studio to replicate the excitement of their live battles. The 78 single Gray and Gordon cut, "The Chase," was a night-long exultation broken up over two sides of the disc and remains a landmark today. "The Chase" was a national hit and inspired countless tenor battles for years to come.

It certainly inspired Gray and Gordon to turn up the heat. Their Elks Auditorium jam session was recorded six weeks after "The Chase" was cut; called "The Hunt," spread out over four 78 rpm records, it inflamed imaginations coast to coast. Beat writer John Clellon Holmes wrote: "The Hunt: listen there for the anthem by which we jettisoned the intellectual Dixieland of atheism, rationalism, liberalism—and found our group's rebel streak at last."

Somewhere in the night at the Elks Temple, in a pattern that predated them and one that they had absorbed into their bones, the tenor men started trading choruses. Each played a 32-bar solo, then they'd cut it in half, and again, the pace seeming to double each time the line was chopped. You started out holding a hilltop and you ended up fighting for a patch of ground. It had all the intensity—and subtlety—of two lions scrapping over one lunch. They keep circling each other, closer and closer in ever-tighter orbits: 32–16–8–4, and when they meet the air ignites . . . an ecstatic fusion of hunter and hunted, audience and performer. Dexter Gordon again:

It wasn't somebody would say "I can play better than you man," but actually . . . that's what it was. It was serious—shit, dead serious. You'd think, damn, what the fuck was he playing? You'd try to figure it out, what was going on. To a degree, that was one of the things, to be the fastest, the hippest. The tenor player with the biggest tone—that takes balls, that takes strength.

Gray played serpentine art deco lines. Gordon liked to throw what you'd just said back in your face, a master of quotation and sarcastic reiteration. Even their contrasting appearances played into the idea of confrontation; Dexter was 6 feet, 5 inches tall and broad-shouldered, while Wardell drowned in his neat suits, so skinny the ladies worried if he was eating enough. It was Jack and the Beanstalk.

Buddy Collette remembered it this way:

> They sounded quite a bit like their personalities; Dexter could blow like he was blowing the house down, heavy, just like he looked. And Wardell was quick—right? Most of the times it would end up with Wardell more or less winning because he was faster and more consistent—Wardell could play about the same way every night, which was good. Dexter would be kind of out of it and he couldn't always find things.
>
> Dexter was a surprise, though, and every three or four nights he could hit it. He had that knockout punch, like Joe Louis when you caught him right. It'd be boom—"what'd he do there?" "I don't know." And poor Wardell then would be wishing, because he couldn't do any more than what he'd been doing all the time. Dexter'd just found his combination. He was always looking for things.

A sparring partner of boxer Joe Louis once explained how his boss punched: "When he hits you, you think you been shot, and if he hits you right, you think you are dead." At this point in his career Dexter Gordon wasn't a good shot, but if he hit you, you thought you were dead. Buddy Collette:

> Imagine in the ring, you got a little guy in there and the little guy every once in a while is popping you, and finally the big guy finds a way to do it. The people know it's going to happen. It was something in the air; it was something to see.

Every night was fight night. Not for nothing did Joe Louis emcee battles of the bands on the Avenue. Wild Bill Moore—a tenor man who organized jams at the Downbeat and Jack's Basket Room—was a former Golden Gloves boxer from Detroit who had briefly gone pro. The greatest boxer ever to come out of Los Angeles, Henry Armstrong, opened a nightclub called Ringside. "Hammerin' Hank" was, pound for pound, perhaps the greatest boxer of all time, the only one to become world champion in three different weight categories—all at the same time. By the mid-1940s Armstrong had hung up his belt and opened Ringside, a Bronzeville club where Red Callendar, Teddy Edwards, Marshall Royal, Bumps Myers and Alton Redd regularly jammed. And in this corner: Big Jay McNeely, playing at the Olympic Auditorium, on a stage set up in the boxing ring.

That was the Central Avenue tenor: always looking for a fight.

Meanwhile, in the blocks of Bronzeville surrounding Armstrong's nightclub, brawls were easy to come by. Japanese Americans were returning from the camps, but Negroes were reluctant to hand back all they had made of the place. Rumors circulated that police were preparing to evict Negroes from Bronzeville to make way for the internees, and a wave of black-on-Asian crime swept the area. Returning merchants banded together and hired Japanese American veterans as a private security force. Blacks angrily protested what they saw as vigilante justice targeting them. A welfare official declared that an "armed truce" was just barely holding between Negroes and returnees; a memo written by social worker Samuel Ishikawa warned, "the Negroes seem to want to keep the 'Japs' from returning, and the Japanese want to 'kick the niggers out.' Thus we find a racial tension of considerable strain . . . unless good relations are established and kept there will be a racial explosion which could be set off by one solitary drunk on First and San Pedro streets."

A consciousness of others that reached across racial lines was a feature of black Los Angeles. Having fought side-by-side with Mexican Americans at 12th Street, having sympathized and traded places with Japanese Americans, having struggled to work next to whites, blacks had established an acute sensitivity to the nuances of color unprecedented in the United States. Nowhere else were roles exchanged and power dynamics calibrated and recalibrated so finely or so routinely.

Los Angeles was more ethnically diverse than probably any place in the country, and Negro Los Angeles in the 1940s had become America's first multicultural avant-garde.

So much had changed since the bombing of Pearl Harbor. Nobody symbolized the decade's exponential velocity better than Clayton Russell; in 1940 he was an underdog to watch for. By the end of the decade he was damaged goods, pushed aside due to his own limitations and the speed of events. Loren Miller could have been commenting on Russell's fate—or on his own, for that matter—when he noted of black L.A., "every ten years it's a new city. So persons who were prominent 10 years ago are forgotten because the new migrants never heard of them." The Negro Victory Committee melted away; Russell's aide-de-camp Lou Rosser was seemingly pressured (blackmailed by an FBI that knew he was gay, some say) to give information about his former Communist Party cohorts. He became a government witness in early 1950s show trials of American Communist Party members.

On the Avenue, Redd Foxx quipped: "If the Russians should attack Los Angeles, we wouldn't have anything to worry about. They couldn't find any place to park!" A fierce new kind of comic, Foxx was a onetime running mate of Malcolm Little (later called Malcolm X). His profane comedy records were sold from under the counter at record shops and out of the car trunk of Watts-based R&B entrepreneur Dootsie Williams. Starting a performance, Foxx would stalk to the edge of the stage and stare down his audience for long minutes, drawing on a cigarette and letting the silence grow unbearable. He was an extremist, but in the late 1940s the Negro comic mainstream was pretty radical itself. Where Pigmeat Markham had been afraid to take off the blackface and where Negro standup comics had been unimaginable just a few years before, by the end of the decade a young wisecracker from Detroit named Timmie Rogers was milking a catchphrase—*oh yeah!*—to win celebrity not just on the Avenue, but in Hollywood, too. Rogers was condemning blackface, wearing a tuxedo and standing alone in front of black and white audiences, commenting on events of the day. He was the first black comic to perform a monologue.

Like every other local ham who could carry a tune, Rogers started cutting R&B records in hopes of reaching the growing teen market. He was way too old for high school; others were not. Some of the greatest music on the street came out of the practice rooms of Jefferson High, where Samuel Browne established a protean music program and mentored Dexter Gordon, Chico Hamilton, Horace Tapscott, Frank Morgan and more. Browne deserves credit for what in the 1950s was called the "Jeff High Sound," a blueprint for harmony group rock and roll—singers like Jesse Belvin and Richard Berry, members of vocal groups including the Coasters, the Medallions, the Platters, the Penguins, the Flairs and the Turks all came through his classes. Black culture, no less than black leaders, got used up fast in Los Angeles, and at Jeff High the scrapping, adult sounds of 1940s R&B were stripped for parts and turned into teenage music, targeted to a common audience of blacks and whites.

So much has changed on the Avenue of today. You can see for yourself. Come, let's stroll.

If you walked north on the Avenue from Watts, you would quickly notice the signs in Spanish, the Mexican and Central American music playing from storefront carnicerias and pupuserias. Today the core of the old district is over 70 percent Latino, and blacks who remain have a sometimes uneasy relationship with their brown-skinned neighbors. At Jefferson High School, where so many great jazz musicians once learned their craft, the student body is 92 percent Latino and police have repeatedly been summoned to quell violence between African Americans and Latinos.

A marker standing near the border of Watts and L.A. can stand for much of the history of recent decades. It's one of those lit-from-within electric signs that revolved high over the street, in this case announcing a business long wiped off the map. The light doesn't shine. And the sign itself is melted, spelling out "Central Avenue" in twisted, singed plastic—perhaps warped in the flames of 1965, perhaps the flames of 1992. The final black nightclub standing was Babe's & Ricky's Inn near 52nd Street, a blues grotto that survived gangs and the crack wars before succumbing to raised rent. It moved west to the Leimert Park district, where it lives still. The Dunbar Hotel is still on the Avenue, its cool inner spaces giving shelter to low-income senior citizens.

A patrol car slows down and gives us the once-over twice. Some kids race by in gleaming tricked-out custom bicycles. From a window covered with steel bars, a radio blasts a hip-hop tune: "Been here, done that, sold crack, got jacked/got shot, came back."

So much has changed. Rising on the edge of Little Tokyo is a building that symbolizes, to a great many people, the downfall of Central Avenue: the state of the art, eight-story police headquarters. When it opened in 1955, William Parker was the city's chief of police, and when Parker died of a heart attack 11 years later, his imprint on the city was so profound the building was renamed the Parker Center.

Chief Parker was an astonishing piece of work. He had a funny way of pronouncing Negro as "Nigra," and he declared with a barely single-entendre that "Los Angeles is the white spot of the great cities of America today." On another occasion he explained that lawbreakers were "primitive Congolese." Parker stamped onto a police department that hardly needed the encouragement his personal animosity to African Americans. Before Parker the police were already busting up clubs that served whites and blacks together in the late 1940s; when Parker became chief in 1950, he taught the department to look with hostility at the black community as a whole. No single person is more responsible for the climate that led to the Watts riots, the Rodney King beating, or the countless smaller flares that never made it to the local news.

From the shadow cast by this public servant has emerged a legend that police brutality killed the Avenue. True enough, jazz clubs were leaving Central for other areas concurrent with Parker's ascension through the ranks. One writer baldly claims that the LAPD wanted to "discipline the music," and credits the police with "destroying the Central Avenue economy." True, the black economy no longer prevails on the Avenue. True, that the clubs are gone. Yet to believe the police were so powerful that they could crush a community's spirit is to accept the myth that Parker concocted for the LAPD. It is to swallow the Jack Webb fable of a godlike department. Ironically, such an argument also suggests that the black community had no resources to defend itself. But black L.A. knows how to survive, and it has.

Today it survives all over the map of L.A. and all across American culture—but not on Central. There was in the 1940s and early 1950s a cultural flowering and a knowledge that the people were speaking for themselves like never before. And when the moment was over, nearly all of its sources were swept away. Integration was the downfall of the Avenue, and some never got over it. Although many celebrated the victories of Loren Miller and others and the country was changing for the better, something was lost with integration. Mom-and-pop stores closed; black-owned local institutions were replaced by white-owned chains. Before the Brooklyn Dodgers signed him, Jackie Robinson had been a hometown hero; now he belonged to everyone. A feeling of commonality had been bartered for a promise of equality. That note has yet to come in.

Consider the fight to integrate the musician's union. In 1953, after a drawn-out effort led by Buddy Collette, William Douglass and Marl Young, history was made when the white and black locals merged. But when the merger happened, it was simultaneous with the closure of clubs on the Avenue, and many drew an understandable but misleading connection. Now the unions were integrated, sure, but the Downbeat, the Club Alabam, Ivie's, the Cobra Room, Shepp's and most of the rest were gone. Some musicians declared they missed the fight leading up to integration: that when they won, they lost a sense of purpose, of identity.

"It's like you take a bottle of chocolate milk and you mix it in with enough white milk, after a while, integration is an act of disappearing," said William Douglass.

"I guess I'm a segregationist, because I like being segregated," onetime dancer and journalist Alyce Key said provocatively. "I like spending my money where it's wanted; I don't like to spend my money because they say you have to spend your money here. There was more unity among the blacks when they were forced to be together. It's not a good thing, but it had its advantages as far as a community is concerned."

"Central Avenue was black," said Dootsie Williams. "Black people dominated, and white people had to come and sit where they could. So it was really like a homeland, like a country, like another country." And nobody easily gives up a homeland.

CODA

Gorgeous George Versus the Black Panther

AUGUST 24, 1949

OLYMPIC AUDITORIUM

Their names were announced and everybody knew what to do. The good guy, the bad guy, the audience, each came with a script in his head. There was a logic to events that predated the moment—at least that was usually the case at an Olympic Auditorium match. Tonight, though, was a little more confusing.

Gorgeous George was the platinum blond, curly-haired Caucasian sensation, with valets tossing roses to announce his entry and never, ever, fighting fairly. He was a classic "heel": every wrestling match had them.

The Black Panther, now, he was something new. Jim Mitchell was his name, and since the late 1930s he'd been building a name for himself, first because he was the only Negro wrestler to fight regularly in Southern California, and second, because he was *good*. Muscular, bald-headed, Mitchell was nobody's sucker and he had a large following around the Avenue. The Black Panther was what wrestlers called the "babyface": every match had one of them, too. His job was to fight fairly, fight poorly when the script called for it, win when it was allowed, while facing the immoral, evil heel. Such were the rules of the game.

Black Panther was a regular at the Olympic Auditorium, a giant white building south of downtown seating about 9,700 when full. It was a nearly windowless architectural block, and it looked like the kind of place where ice might be stored, or bodies.

When he became an Olympic regular, around 1937, the Black Panther was a "mystery wrestler," one who hid behind a mask. Not only a mask, however; as a *Los Angeles Times* report from that year described, he also wore "kid gloves." Wrestling was a white man's game, and a Negro fighting whites in the ring was anathema to promoters. The Black Panther was probably the first Negro in modern professional wrestling. He was billed as the light-heavy, junior-heavy and heavyweight champion of his race, proving hype was no stranger to wrestling even in its early days; he was probably the *only* wrestler of his race in most of the weight categories of the time. For a while, he was allowed to wrestle only Japanese (remember Pearl Harbor) and Hindus (remember Korla Pandit).

By the late 1940s the Black Panther had cast off his mask, but he hadn't done away with the kid gloves: promoters believed wrestling fans weren't ready for a black man to play the heel, to cheat, break the rules, ignore the referee and play to the crazies in the house. To be the lovable lug who disobeys the law and wins the love of the fans. To beat a white man without one hand tied behind his back. A black man as heel—that might start a riot, promoters reasoned. So the Black Panther was ever the babyface, the upholder of a propriety and decorum that his opponent flouted.

The role didn't fall easy on his shoulders, or on those in his corner. Once, his manager Count Rossi stormed the ring and disrupted a match at the Olympic when Tarzan White, a onetime Alabama football star, performed a dubious low blow on Panther, thus winning. A low blow from a Tarzan from Alabama could not pass without response, and a scandal ensued.

By 1949 professional wrestling was a hit on KTLA, the same Southern California TV channel that aired Korla Pandit. Gorgeous George
was as big a local star as Liberace. So the Olympic Auditorium was full
that autumn night when Gorgeous George and the Black Panther did
battle.

Theoretically the two were evenly matched, both about 5 feet,
9 inches tall, both weighing close to 210 pounds. Gorgeous George
had a routine he milked before every match; he sprayed the ring and
his opponent with "disinfectant" meant to sanitize the match. If he
did it at the Olympic, surely the exercise had unpleasant overtones for
the Black Panther's fans. And when the Black Panther launched a flying tackle of Gorgeous George, only to have the heel sidestep the
blow and deliver a cheap shot dropkick that sent the Black Panther
flying out of the ring, after which the referee rather quickly declared
the wavy-tressed fop the winner, the racially mixed audience at the
Olympic went atomic on that Los Angeles night, exploding on the
spot. A riot began as black patrons protested the lousy sportsmanship
rather vociferously to the white patrons of the establishment, bursting
into the ring and commencing to brawl inside the arena and outside it
too, in the aisles and out onto the streets surrounding the Olympic,
pummeling their enemies real and imagined. A ring doc treated the
wrestlers for minor injuries and then escorted the two to a hasty escape. Everyone else stuck around fighting until four in the morning.
There were stabbings. Blackjacks connected with eye sockets. The
emergency room at Georgia Receiving Hospital was unusually busy
for that time of night.

By the end of the 1940s Central Avenue was an awful lot like the
Olympic Auditorium. The place was slowly clearing out. The average
guy in the cheap seats no longer remained seated. He was talking
back—throwing a chair, possibly—and entering the ring when he or his
kind had been crossed. And all sorts of lines—separating participant
and observer, artist and audience, law and chaos, justice and truth—
were routinely, brutally, definitively crossed. The people who paid for
their tickets, call them consumers of culture, were talking back freely to
those who entertained them and were shaping events, climbing onto the

stage to make sure they were heard. The time was a long way off when a black man would be seen as the equal of a white. But time was closing in on the moment when a black man could be the heel and receive the love of a mass audience. Fair is fair.

It was, all in all, one hell of a jam session.

NOTES

CAS: Central Avenue Sounds collection, special collections, University of California at Los Angeles

CSF: California State University at Fullerton

Eagle: California Eagle

IJS: Institute for Jazz Studies, Rutgers University, Newark, New Jersey

JAF: John Anson Ford collection at the Huntington Library

OH: Oral History

SCL: Southern California Library for Social Studies and Research

Sentinel: Los Angeles Sentinel

Tribune: Los Angeles Tribune

Introduction

On the smiling man: Donald Bogle, *Toms, Coons, Mulattoes, Mammies and Bucks: An Interpretive History of Blacks in American Films* (Continuum International Publishing Group, 2001); Thomas Cripps, *Slow Fade to Black: The Negro in American Film, 1900–1942* (Oxford University Press, 1993); Marilyn Kern-Foxworth, *Aunt Jemimah, Uncle Ben and Rastus* (Praeger, 1994); Michael Rogin, *Blackface, White Noise: Jewish Immigrants in the Hollywood Melting Pot* (University of California Press, Reprint edition, 1998); Joseph Boskin, *Sambo: The Rise and Demise of an American Jester* (Oxford

University Press, 1986); Bernard Wolfe, "Uncle Remus and the Malevolent Rabbit," *Commentary* (July 1949).

With regard to overviews of Central Avenue, two important recent books have advanced the discussion considerably. Josh Sides's *L.A. City Limits* (University of California Press, 2004) and Douglas Flamming's *Bound for Freedom: Black Los Angeles in Jim Crow America* (University of California Press, 2005) take prominent place on the short shelf of books on African American Los Angeles. Also see Bruce Tyler, *From Harlem to Hollywood: The Struggle for Racial and Cultural Democracy, 1920–1943* (Garland Publishing, 1992); Lawrence B. de Graaf, "The City of Black Angels: Emergence of the Los Angeles Ghetto, 1890–1960," *Pacific Historical Review* 39 (August 1970); de Graaf, "Negro Migration to Los Angeles, 1930 to 1950" (Ph.D. diss., UCLA, 1962); J. Max Bond, "The Negro in Los Angeles" (Ph.D. diss., University of Southern California, 1936); Daniel Widener, "Cultural Democracy in the Racial City: The Politics of Culture in Black Los Angeles, 1920–1946," draft of a paper presented at the University of California at San Diego; "Our Gay Black Way: Central Avenue," *Los Angeles Times*, June 18, 1933. The entire Central Avenue Sounds oral history (OH) collection at the University of California at Los Angeles, masterminded by Steven Isoardi, is a window on a lost world. There's a fine anthology and a CD collection based on this research, but by far the best place to hear the voices of veterans is in the full transcripts at UCLA.

For overviews of Los Angeles at large during World War II: Roger Lotchin, *The Bad City in the Good War* (Indiana University Press, 2003); Kevin Starr, *Embattled Dreams: California in War and Peace* (Oxford University Press, 2003) and *The Dream Endures: California Enters the 1940s* (Oxford University Press, 2002); Otto Friedrich, *City of Nets: A Portrait of Hollywood in the 1940's* (Harper and Row, 1986).

Pullman porters: Larry Tye, *Rising from the Rails: Pullman Porters and the Making of the Black Middle Class* (Henry Holt, 2004); Beth Tompkins Bates, *Pullman Porters and the Rise of Protest Politics in Black America, 1925–1945* (University of North Carolina Press, 2001). The *Eagle* covered the work and social lives of railroad employees in a column running in the 1920s and 1930s. See also the entry for Chapter 2 regarding A. Philip Randolph.

L. G. Robinson: Gilbert Lindsay OH, CSF; Loren Miller OH, CSF; William Jones interview.

"Central was like a river": interview with Clifford Solomon.

"There are many Avenues": Ernie Andrews OH, CAS.

Strolling down the Avenue: "Central Avenue Symphony," *Tribune*, October 4, 1943; also see the incredibly eloquent Jackie Kelso OH in the Central Avenue Sounds collection.

But most of all, this stroll is taken from hundreds of details coming from many interviews, newspaper accounts, and contemporary peregrinations.

The Dunbar Hotel: Anthony Charles Sweeting, "The Dunbar Hotel and Central Avenue Renaissance, 1781–1950," (Ph.D. diss., University of California at Los Angeles, 1992); J. Alexander Somerville, *Man of Color: An Autobiography* (L. L. Morrison, 1949); Celes King interview. The Dunbar building endures today, cool and shadowy. It is one of the few landmarks still representing the Avenue and operates as low-income housing under the stewardship of the Dunbar Economic Development Corporation.

Eddie "Rochester" Anderson: Mel Watkins, *On the Real Side: Laughing, Lying and Signifying: The Underground Tradition of African-American Humor That Transformed American Culture from Slavery to Richard Pryor* (Simon and Shuster, 1994); Boskin, *Sambo*; *Jack Benny: The Radio and Television Work, The Museum of Television and Radio* (HarperPerennial, 1991); Michele Hilmes, *Radio Voices: American Broadcasting, 1922–1952* (University of Minnesota Press, 1997); Margaret T. McFadden, "America's Boy Friend Who Can't Get a Date: Gender, Race, and the Cultural Work of the Jack Benny Program, 1932–1946," *Journal of American History* (June 1993); *Eagle*, January 18, April 25, May 23, June 6, November 21 and 28, 1940; April 24, 1941; March 26, April 16, September 24, 1942; *Tribune*, December 18, 1948; Florabel Muir, "What's That, Boss?," *Saturday Evening Post*, June 19, 1943; archived recordings of *The Jell-O Program* in the collection of the Museum of Television and Radio, Beverly Hills, California.

Rossmore Hotel: *Eagle*, September 14, 1941.

Chapter One

John Kinloch: The Charlotta Bass collection at the Southern California Library for Social Studies and Research contains a large amount of material by and about this protean figure. Included are childhood stories, radio scripts, letters, an unpublished novel, and notes for a book about him that was never completed. The rest of the Bass collection includes the papers and files of the *Eagle*; both were indispensable to my understanding of Kinloch. Also see James Phillip Jeter, "Rough Flying: The *California Eagle* (1879–1965)," paper on file at the SCL; Charlotta Bass, *Forty Years: Memoirs from the Pages of a Newspaper* (C.A. Bass, 1979). Interviews with Walter Gordon, Carmela Hewlett.

"He's no boy to go around in a car with": Almena Lomax OH, CSF.

Clarence Woods: *Eagle*, August 28, October 2, 1941.

The Harlem Renaissance: David Levering Lewis, *When Harlem Was in Vogue* (Knopf, 1981); Alain Locke, ed., *The New Negro: Voices of the Harlem Renaissance* (Touchstone,

1999); Jervis Anderson, *This Was Harlem* (Farrar, Straus and Giroux, 1983); Gerald Early, introductory essay to *My Soul's High Song: The Collected Writings of Countee Cullen* (Anchor, 1990); Ann Douglas, *Terrible Honesty: Mongrel Manhattan in the 1920s* (Farrar, Straus and Giroux, 1996). I know that recent and exciting scholarship of the Renaissance questions the notion that the movement was a middle–class, top-down construction. Work by scholars including Bill Mullen, William J. Maxwell, Barbara Foley and others dispute this reading. While I have drawn on the foundational work of David Levering Lewis and others for my representation of the Renaissance, I am aware that there are other representations that contest it and that the argument is ongoing.

"Debauched Tenth": David Levering Lewis, ed., *W. E. B. Du Bois: A Reader* (Owl Books, 1995).

Golden State Mutual Life Insurance Company: The company's records are on view at the Department of Special Collections, UCLA; George Beavers OH, UCLA and CSF; Norman O. Houston OH, CSF; "Ode to William Nickerson, Jr.," *Eagle,* June 9, 1941; "Profile . . . George A. Beavers," *Tribune*, September 3, 1949.

Zoot suits: Eduardo Obregon Pagan, *Murder at the Sleepy Lagoon: Zoot Suits, Race, and Riot in Wartime L.A.* (University of North Carolina Press, 2003); Lewis A. Erenberg, *Swingin' the Dream: Big Band Jazz and the Rebirth of American Culture* (University of Chicago Press, 1998); Stuart Cosgrove, "The Zoot-Suit and Style Warfare," *History Workshop Journal* (Autumn 1984); Robin D. G. Kelley, "The Riddle of the Zoot: Malcolm Little and Black Cultural Politics During World War II," in *Malcolm X: In Our Own Image,* Joe Wood, ed. (Anchor, 1993).

"Surely, there is much clowning going on": "The Watch Tower," *Eagle,* January 27, 1941.

Jump for Joy: Michael Denning, *The Cultural Front: The Laboring of American Culture in the Twentieth Century* (Verso paperback, 1998); Duke Ellington, *Music Is My Mistress* (Da Capo Press, 1976); *Jump for Joy: From the 1941 Production*, recordings selected by Martin Williams and annotated by Patricia Willard (Smithsonian Institution, 1988); Emory Holmes II, "The Duke of L.A.," *Los Angeles Times Calendar*, April 25, 1999; Maurice Zolotow, "The Duke's 'Forgotten' L.A. Musical," *Los Angeles* (February 1982); "L.A. Likes All-Negro Musical," *People's World,* July 17, 1941; interviews with Patricia Willard, Richard Dunn, Alyce Key, and Avanelle Harris.

Chapter Two

"They called me up for the induction meeting": Howard McGhee OH, Institute for Jazz Studies.

The African American state of mind on the cusp of World War II: Richard Dalfiume, "The Forgotten Years of the Negro Revolution," *Journal of American History* (June 1968); John Modell, Marc Goulden, and Sigurdur Magnusson, "World War II in the Lives of Black Americans: Some Findings and an Interpretation," *Journal of American History* (December 1989); Robert Korstad and Nelson Lichtenstein, "Opportunities Found and Lost: Labor, Radicals, and the Early Civil Rights Movement," *Journal of American History* (December 1988); Albert S. Broussard, "Strange Territory, Familiar Leadership: The Impact of World War II on San Francisco's Black Community," *California History* (March 1986); Harvard Sitkoff, "Racial Militancy and Interracial Violence in the Second World War," *Journal of American History* (December 1971); Lee Finkle, "The Conservative Aims of Militant Rhetoric: Black Protest During World War II," *The Journal of American History*, (December 1973); Ralph N. Davis, "Negro Newspapers and the War," *Sociology and Social Research*, May–June, 1943; C. L. R. James, George Breitman, Edgar Keemer, et al., *Fighting Racism in World War II* (Monad Press, 1980); Roi Ottley, "A White Folks' War?" *Common Ground* (Spring, 1942).

Black L.A.'s reaction to the war: Keith E. Collins, *Black Los Angeles: The Maturing of the Ghetto, 1940–1950* (Century Twenty One Publishing, 1980); E. Frederick Anderson, *The Development of Leadership and Organization Building in the Black Community of Los Angeles from 1900 Through World War II* (Century Twenty One Publishing, 1980). The local black press documented the spectrum of emotions along Central Avenue. See: "Conscientious Objector Who Went Hungry 12 Days, Protesting Jim Crow, Home," *Tribune*, October 29, 1945; "Prophet's Warning to the Nation: A Checkerboard Army Caused French Defeat," *Eagle*, December 18, 1941; "'Reborn,' Ignores Draft," *New York Times*, July 14, 1942.

Du Bois and "Close Ranks": "Close Ranks," *Crisis* (July 1918); David Levering Lewis, *W. E. B. Du Bois: Biography of a Race, 1868–1919* (Owl Books, 1994); William Jordan, "'The Damnable Dilemma': African-American Accommodation and Protest During World War I," *The Journal of American History* (March 1995); Mark Ellis, "W. E. B. Du Bois and the Formation of Black Opinion in World War I: A Commentary on 'The Damnable Dilemma,'" *Journal of American History* (March 1995).

Hot dog stand: interview with Melonee Blocker.

U.S.S. *Philadelphia:* "Used Men as Seagoing Chambermaids," *Pittsburgh Courier*, October 5, 1940.

A. Philip Randolph and the March on Washington Movement: William H. Harris, *Keeping the Faith: A. Philip Randolph, Milton P. Webster, and the Brotherhood of Sleeping Car Porters, 1925–37* (University of Illinois reprint, 1991); Jervis Anderson, *A. Philip Randolph: A Biographical Portrait* (University of California Press reprint, 1987); Herbert

Garfinkel, *When Negroes March: The March on Washington Movement in the Organizational Politics for FEPC* (Atheneum, 1973); A. Philip Randolph, "Dialogues of the Old and the New Porter," in *Mother Wit from the Laughing Barrel: Readings in the Interpretation of Afro-American Folklore*, Alan Dundes, ed. (University Press of Mississippi, 1991); "Tells How to Blast Bias in U.S. Defense," *Eagle*, January 23, 1941; "Let the Masses Speak," *Eagle*, March 20, 1941; "Negro Out to Shake U.S. for Jobs and Justice in National Defense—Randolph," *Eagle*, June 5, 1941; "Call to Negro America," *Eagle*, June 12, 1941; "FDR Order Bans Bias: March on Capital Off," *Eagle*, July 3, 1941; "Mass Pressure Gets Best Results, Day of Individuals Past, Randolph Says Here," *Eagle*, November 6, 1941; "We'll Die, but Fighting Back, Says Randolph," *Baltimore Afro-American*, July 25, 1942; "MOWM to Hear James Farmer, F.O.R. Secretary," *Tribune*, October 18, 1943; "From A. Philip," *Tribune*, September 6, 1943.

On vandalism, rudeness, and noise as markers of protest: Robin D. G. Kelley, *Race Rebels: Culture, Politics, and the Black Working Class* (Free Press, 1996); Kelley, "'We Are Not What We Seem': Rethinking Black Working-Class Opposition in the Jim Crow South," *Journal of American History* (June 1993); Raoul Vaneigem, *The Revolution of Everyday Life* (Left Bank Books/Rebel Press, 1983). For further thought on reading such obtuse codes of an oppressed minority, see George Chauncey, *Gay New York: Gender, Urban Culture, and the Making of the Gay Male World, 1890–1940* (Basic Books, 1994).

Double V movement: Dalfiume, "The Forgotten Years"; W. Y. Bell, "The Negro Warrior's Home Front," *Phylon* (3rd quarter, 1944); H. C. Brearley, "The Negro's New Belligerency," *Phylon* (4th quarter, 1944); Beth Bailey and David Farber, "The 'Double-V' Campaign in World War II Hawaii: African Americans, Racial Ideology, and Federal Power," *Journal of Social History* (Summer 1993); "California Pastor Endorses Double V," *Pittsburgh Courier*, March 14, 1942; "Noted Composers Join Talents to Create New Song," "Jimmie Lunceford Supports *Courier* 'Double V' Drive," *Pittsburgh Courier*, March 14, 1942; "The President Says," *Eagle*, March 20, 1941. For a succinct iteration of the movement's aims, see "The Crusade for Human Rights" pamphlet written by Clayton Russell in 1944, Frank Horne collection, Amistad Research Center, Tulane University.

Chapter Three

Illinois Jacquet: Michael Segell, *The Devil's Horn: The Story of the Saxophone from Noisy Novelty to King of Cool* (Farrar, Straus and Giroux, 2005); Jim Dawson and Steve Propes, *What Was the First Rock 'N' Roll Record?* (Faber and Faber, 1992); *New Grove Dictionary of Jazz*, Barry Kernfeld, ed. (Oxford University Press, 2001). For a jarring up-close portrait of Jacquet, see Babs Gonzalez's self-typed opus, *Movin' on Down De Line* (B. Gonzalez, 1975).

Aviation in Los Angeles: James Richard Wilburn, "Social and Economic Aspects of the Aircraft Industry in Metropolitan Los Angeles During World War II" (Ph.D. diss., University of California at Los Angeles, 1971); James R. Prickett, "Communist Conspiracy or Wage Dispute? The 1941 Strike at North American Aviation," *Pacific Historical Review* (May 1981); Bernice Anita Reed, "Accommodation Between Negro and White Employees in a West Coast Aircraft Industry, 1942–1944," *Social Forces* 26 (1947); "'Give Negro a Job,' Is Strikers' Slogan," *Eagle*, May 29, 1941.

Remarks by Kindelberger: *Eagle*, March 27, May 29, 1941.

The FEPC: Louis Coleridge Kesselman, *The Social Politics of FEPC: A Study in Reform Pressure Movements* (University of North Carolina Press, 1948); Eileen Boris, "'You Wouldn't Want One of 'Em Dancing With Your Wife': Racialized Bodies on the Job in World War II," *American Quarterly* (March 1998); Final Report, Fair Employment Practice Committee, June 28, 1946; "Union Racial Hostility Told," *Los Angeles Times*, October 22, 1941. Many entries in the Charles Bratt and California CIO Council Union Research and Information Services collections, at the Southern California Library for Social Studies and Research, were also essential to this chapter.

FEPC in L.A.: David Oberweiser Jr., "The CIO: A Vanguard for Civil Rights in Southern California, 1940–1946," in *American Labor in the Era of World War II*, Sally M. Miller and Daniel A. Cornford, eds. (Greenwood Press, 1995); "Racial Prejudice Charged in Plants," *Los Angeles Times*, October 21, 1941.

Chapter Four

Clayton Donovan Russell: assorted letters, clippings and documents in the Amistad Research Collection, Tulane University; "America! This Is Our Stand!," pamphlet, SCL. Among many useful newspaper stories from the era: "Rev. Russell Attacks False Leaders," *Eagle*, November 17, 1938; "'My Resignation a Spiritual One,' Young Minister States," *Eagle*, October 5, 1939; "Tribute to Courage," *Eagle*, August 28, 1941; "USES Hears Complaints of Race Bias," *Eagle*, April 2, 1942; "'Women Needed in Industry,' Rev. Russell Declares," *Eagle*, October 1, 1942; "Mass Meet Hits LARY, Slum Housing," *Eagle*, December 18, 1942; "Negro Stars Take Over Victory House," *Eagle*, December 25, 1942; "Pershing Square Hears Negroes," *Eagle*, January 8, 1943; "LARY Trains First of Race as Conductors, Motormen," *Eagle*, February 10, 1943; "Negroes Must Unify, Fight Riots—Russell," *Eagle*, June 17, 1943; "'Christianity Becoming Less Effective,' Says Rev. Russell," *Eagle*, July 18, 1946; "Clayton Russell Quits Independent Church," *Sentinel*, October 15, 1953; "How Clayton Russell Makes a Comeback," *Sentinel*, September 18, 1958; obituary, *Sentinel*, July 16, 1981. Interviews with Clayton Russell Jr., Clifton Russell,

Vennie Russell, Boyd Dickey, Leslie Bellamy, Augustus Hawkins, Welford Wilson, Parthenia Bozeman, Wilfred and Carietta Brooks, Walter Gordon, and Mickey Walker.

Peoples' Independent Church of Christ: Wendell Franklin, *Wendell Franklin* (Director's Guild of America, 1995); Anderson, *Development of Leadership*; Delilah L. Beasley, *The Negro Trail Blazers of California* (MacMillan, 1997); on the rise of the community church movement, of which Independent was a part, see Wallace D. Best, *Passionately Human, No Less Divine: Religion and Culture in Black Chicago, 1915–1952* (Princeton University Press, 2005). The Golden State Mutual collection at UCLA has a wealth of information regarding the origins of this once-powerful church.

New Thought and The Science of Mind: Ernest Holmes, *The Science of Mind* (Tarcher, 1997). New Thought had a considerable influence on the Avenue and was a major influence on the church founded by Father Divine, an important religious figure of the 1930s and 1940s. See Jill Watts, "'This Was the Way': Father Divine's Peace Mission Movement in Los Angeles During the Great Depression," *Pacific Historical Review* (Fall 1991).

Negro Victory Committee: Anderson, *Development of Leadership*; "America! This Is Our Stand," Russell file, SCL; for a window on political nervousness over the NVC's ascendance, see "Memorandum," April 16, 1946, Bratt collection, SCL; see also Russell's intermittent column, "What the Victory Committee Thinks," running in the *Eagle* in 1943.

"This is the essence of today's warfare": "America! This Is Our Stand!," Russell file, SCL.

"I consider it a sin": Anderson, *Development of Leadership*.

Walter Williams: see Williams entries in Chapter 5.

Welford Wilson: two interviews with Wilson; "Negro Boy Orator Wins Junior Finals," *New York Times*, May 4, 1929; "City College Seniors Honored," *New York Times*, December 3, 1935.

Lou Rosser: Constance Coiner, *Better Red: The Writing and Resistance of Tillie Olsen and Meridel Le Sueur* (University of Illinois Press, 1998); "The Testimony of Government Witness, Louis Rosser," William Schneiderman collection, box 14, "Rosser, Louis" file, SCL; "Lou Rosser Resigns from Church Post," *Eagle*, September 25, 1952; "Reveals 'Negro Soviet' Plan," *Sentinel*, December 3, 1953; "Rites Saturday for Louis 'Luke' Rosser," *Sentinel*, October 24, 1957.

Zoot suit riots: Pagan, *Murder at the Sleepy Lagoon*; Mauricio Mazon, *The Zoot-Suit Riots: The Psychology of Symbolic Annihilation* (University of Texas Press, 1984); Douglas Henry Daniels, "Los Angeles Zoot: Race 'Riot,' the Pachuco, and Black Music Culture," *Journal of Negro History* (Spring 1997); Chester Himes, "Zoot Riots Are Race Riots," *The Crisis* (July 1943); Jon Watson, "Crossing the Colour Lines in the City of Angels:

The NAACP and the Zoot-Suit Riot of 1943," *University of Sussex Journal of Contemporary History*, no. 4 (2002); Edward J. Escobar, "Zoot-Suiters and Cops: Chicano Youth and the Los Angeles Police Department During World War II," in *The War in American Culture: Society and Consciousness During World War II*, Lewis A. Erenberg and Susan E. Hirsch, eds. (University of Chicago Press, 1996).

"That low zoot suit stuff": "Dorsey High Principal Wants No 'Zoot Suits,'" *Eagle*, May 13, 1943.

The battle of 12th Street: Loren Miller OH, CSF; Almena Lomax OH, CSF; "The '43 Zoot Suit Riots Reexamined," *Los Angeles Times*, May 9, 1978.

Victory Markets: Anderson, *Development of Leadership*; "Victory Committee Hits Food Distribution," *Eagle*, February 10, 1943; "City Pastor Has Vision as Builder," *Eagle*, January 20, 1944; "Reverend Clayton Russell Heads Movement to Open Negro Bank," *Eagle*, October 5, 1944; "State Sues Russell's Victory Mrkt.," *Tribune*, December 30, 1950.

Russell as a chimera: interviews with Walter Gordon, Abie Robinson, Hadda Brooks, Clifton Russell, Vivian Hodge, and Clayton Russell Jr. For a finely honed sketch of Reverend Cobbs, see Best, *Passionately Human*.

Chapter Five

Gerald Edwards: "Calship Guard Held for Trial," *Eagle*, December 21, 1944; "Calship Guard Must Stand Trial for Murder," *Los Angeles Times*, December 28, 1944.

Shipyards and shipyard culture: Susan Anderson, "Shipyards and Shibboleths: The African American Challenge in World War II Los Angeles," unpublished paper; Shirley Ann Wilson Moore, "Traditions from Home: African Americans in Wartime Richmond, California," in *The War in American Culture*, Erenberg and Hirsch; *Calship Cavalcade*, the Calship Club, 1942; assorted issues of the *Calship Log* monthly magazine; Lee Shippey, "Lee Side o' L.A.," *Los Angeles Times*, August 14, 1942.

"Ever since I have been at the drydocks": undated letter from John N. Grimes to FEPC, Los Angeles office, Selected Documents from Records of the Committee on Fair Employment Practice, reel 105 (Glen Rock, N.J.: Microfilming Corporation of America, 1971) (hereafter cited as FEPC Records).

"It was reported in April, 1943": FEPC Records.

Boilermakers union: Josh Sides, "Battle on the Home Front: African American Shipyard workers in World War II Los Angeles," *California History* (Fall 1986); Charles Wollenberg, "James vs. Marinship: Trouble on the New Black Frontier," *California History* (Spring 1981); William H. Harris, "Federal Intervention in Union Discrimination: FEPC and West Coast Shipyards During World War II," *Labor History* (Summer 1981); "Boilermakers at Calship Jim Crowed," *Eagle*, February 10, 1943; "Shipyarders Won't Pay Dues to 'Tom' Outfit," John Kinloch, *Eagle*, July 8, 1943; "F.E.P.C. Hearings Set for Shipyarders Next...," *Eagle*, September 30, 1943; "Sweeping Injunction Enjoins Local 6 from Forcing Negroes to Join Jim Crow Auxiliaries," *Eagle*, January 24, 1944.

Walter Williams and the SWCEP: Sides, "Battle on the Home Front"; Walter Williams OH, Urban Archives Center, California State University at Northridge; oral history posted on the website of the International Longshore and Warehouse Union at archive.ilwu.org/oralhist%20display.htm; "Shipyard Labor Leader Calls upon Fellow Workers to Support Program," *Eagle*, January 27, 1944; "Jim Crow on Trial!" *Eagle*, June 22, 1944; "$3000 Needed for Action Against Boilermakers," Walter Williams, *Eagle*, July 13, 1944; October 27, 1943, letter, FEPC Records, reel 105; testimony before the Committee on Fair Employment Practice, October 21, 1941, FEPC Records, reel 19.

"A tall, rather fine-looking, rather mild Negro lad": "Report on Investigation of Discharge of Negro Workers," FEPC Records, reel 68.

"We got all the damn money!: "Boilermakers: Blackwell Blows Top," *Eagle*, June 10, 1943.

Andrew Blakeney: October 27, 1943, letter FEPC Records, reel 105; testimony before the Committee on Fair Employment Practice, October 21, 1941, FEPC Records, reel 19; Peter Vacher, "Andrew Blakeney: A Lifetime in Music," *Storyville* (April–May 1975); Bill Mitchell, "A Talk with Andrew Blakeney," *Mississippi Rag* (July 1985); Andrew Blakeney OH, IJS; interview with Floyd Levin. Blakeney's case was ultimately ruled in his—and black shipyard workers'—favor. Amazingly, in interviews and oral histories describing his musical career, Blakeney never chose to mention the prominent role he played in integrating the Boilermakers union.

Chester Himes: Chester Himes, *The Quality of Hurt* (Thunder's Mouth Press, 1995); James Sallis, *Chester Himes: A Life* (Walker and Company, 2000); Michel Fabre, *Chester Himes: An Annotated Primary and Secondary Bibliography* (Greenwood Press, 1992); Edward Margolies and Michel Fabre, *The Several Lives of Chester Himes* (University Press of Mississippi, 1997); John A. Williams, "Chester Himes: My Man Himes," from *Flashbacks: A Twenty-Year Diary of Article Writing* (Anchor Press/Doubleday, 1973); "The Ethics of Ambiguity: Interview with Joseph Sandy Himes, Jr.," in *The Critical Responses to Chester Himes*, Charles L. P. Silet, ed. (Greenwood Press 1999); Bruce A. Glasrud and Laurie Champion, "No Land of the Free: Chester Himes Confronts California (1940–1946)," *CLA Journal* (March, 2001); Sean McCann, "Chester Himes, Black Hard-Boiled Master," *Common Review* (September 2001); Michael Willard, "A Multi-Racial Public Sphere: Chester Himes' Los Angeles During World War II," paper presented at the annual meeting of the Western History Association, October 7, 2001; "Himes Doesn't Like Musical Sween 'N' Hot," *Eagle*, February 17, 1944; Himes, "Zoot Riots Are Race

Riots"; Luc Sante, "An American Abroad," *New York Review of Books*, January 16, 1992. Interview with Welford Wilson. Special thanks to John A. Williams, whose support and wisdom raised these chapters up.

Himes's fiction: Books cited include *If He Hollers Let Him Go* (Thunder's Mouth Press, 2002); *Lonely Crusade* (Thunder's Mouth Press, 1997); *Cotton Comes to Harlem* (Vintage, 1988); *The Real Cool Killers* (Vintage, 1988); *A Rage in Harlem* (Vintage, 1989); *The Collected Stories of Chester Himes* (Thunder's Mouth Press, 1991); *Yesterday Will Make You Cry* (W. W. Norton, 1999).

"We are, by the purest of luck": letter to Henry and Mollie Moon, May 25, 1942, Henry and Mollie Moon collection, Schomburg Library.

"Blemishes, marks, scars, and lines": letter to Carl Van Vechten, June 10, 1946, "Letters From Blacks" box, Van Vechten collection, Beineke Library.

"I'm getting jittery in this town": letter to Henry and Mollie Moon, December 2, 1941, Moon collection, Schomburg Library.

Chapter Six

Regarding the explosive race and class mix in L.A. during the Himes years, see Kevin Allen Leonard, "Federal Power and Racial Politics in Los Angeles During World War II," in *Power and Place in the North American West*, Richard White and John Findlay, eds. (University of Washington Press, 1999); Kevin Allen Leonard, "In the Interest of All Races: African Americans and Interracial Cooperation in Los Angeles During and After World War II," in *Seeking El Dorado: African Americans in California*, Lawrence B. de Graaf, Kevin Mulroy, and Quintard Taylor, eds. (University of Washington Press, 2001); "'Brothers Under the Skin?': African Americans, Mexican Americans, and World War II in California," in *The Way We Really Were*, Roger Lotchin, ed., (University of Illinois Press, 1999); Scott Kurashige, "The Many Facets of Brown: Integration in a Multiracial Society," *Journal of American History* (June 2004); Mark Wild, *Street Meeting: Multiethnic Neighborhoods in Early Twentieth-Century Los Angeles* (University of California Press, 2005).

Officers Broady and Kimbro: "Bring No Proof," *Los Angeles Times*, February 20, 1916; "Committee Concludes Griffin Quiz," *Los Angeles Times*, May 12, 1935; "Time to Change, Mr. Broady," *Sentinel*, March 6, 1941; "Broadside on Broady: Why?" *Eagle*, March 20, 1941; "Policeman Freed in Shooting Case," *Los Angeles Times*, August 25, 1943; "Officer Accused of Asking Weekly Tributes from Café," *Tribune*, June 1, 1946; "Shakedown 'Copper' Goes to Jail," *Tribune*, July 13, 1946; Earl Broady file, *Los Angeles Examiner* archive, Regional History Collection, University of Southern California.

On the Los Angeles basis of Himes's detectives: My speculation as to who might have been models for Himes's fictional cops is based on interviews with Richard Dunn, Clifford Solomon, and Walter Gordon, as well as "PW Interviews: Chester Himes," *Publishers Weekly* (April 3, 1972); interview with Willi Hochkeppel, in *Conversations with Chester Himes*, Michel Fabre and Robert E. Skinner, eds. (University Press of Mississippi 1995). See also undated British interview by "Pooter," box 5, folder 3, of John A. Williams Papers, University of Rochester, New York: "Himes did not know Harlem until 1940, and he traces his two cops back to Central Avenue, Los Angeles. . . . It was a rough street, now grown into Watts, and he came to know there the two black detectives who covered it." And this: "But how do Himes's originals down in Watts see their fictional counterparts? One at least will never know about them. His friend shot him down in a duel on Central Avenue, for moving in on his wife."

Chapter Seven

Pigmeat Markham: "Pigmeat" Markham, with Bill Levinson, *Here Come the Judge!* (Popular Library, 1969); Ted Fox, *Showtime at the Apollo* (Henry Holt, 1985); Jack Schiffman, *Uptown: The Story of Harlem's Apollo Theater* (Cowles Book Company, 1971); recorded interview with Pigmeat Markham, Hatch-Billops collection, Schomburg Library; "New York Interviews," notes from 1959 interview with Markham, IJS; "Halfway to 100 Years of Negro Humor," Ted Poston, *New York Post*, April 1, 1967; tapes of Pigmeat's appearances on *Rowan and Martin's Laugh-In*, a TV show debuting in 1968, are worth seeking out. Markham became a regular on the program at the behest of Sammy Davis Jr., revived his Judge routine, and turned "here come the judge" into a psychedelic catchphrase. Most of all, his routines live on in a series of comedy records he made in the 1960s, including such classics as *World's Greatest Clown*, *The Crap Shootin' Rev*, and *Save Your Soul, Baby!* Check eBay.

Overviews of African American comedy: Watkins, *On the Real*; Marshall and Jean Stearns, *Jazz Dance: The Story of American Vernacular Dance* (Da Capo Press, 1994); Redd Foxx and Norma Miller, *The Redd Foxx Encyclopedia of Black Humor* (Ward Richie Press, 1997); Melvin Patrick Ely, *The Adventures of Amos 'n' Andy: A Social History of an American Phenomenon* (Free Press, 1992); Marshall and Jean Stearns, "Frontiers of Humor: American Vernacular Dance," *Southern Folklore Quarterly* (September 1966).

Pigmeat in Los Angeles: *Eagle*, April 8 and April 22, 1943; February 24, 1944; March 23, April 6, and July 6, 1944; September 20, 1945; interviews with Kathy Maldonado, Norma Miller, Leonard Reed, Sonny Craver, Timmie Rogers.

"Whatever situation that arose": interview with Sonny Craver.

Minstrelsy and blackface: Henry T. Sampson, *Blacks in Blackface: A Source Book on Early Black Musical Shows* (Scarecrow Press, 1980); Dale Cockrell, *Demons of Disorder: Early Blackface Minstrels and Their World* (Cambridge University Press, 1997); Eric Lott, *Love and Theft: Blackface Minstrelsy and the American Working Class* (Oxford University Press, 1995); W. T. Lhamon Jr., *Raising Cain: Blackface Performance from Jim Crow to Hip-Hop* (Harvard University Press, 2000); Alex Albright, "Noon Parade and Midnight Ramble: Black Traveling Tent Shows in North Carolina," and Milton D. Quigless Sr., "Two Weeks on a Minstrel Show," both in *Good Country People*, Arthur M. Kaye, ed. (North Carolina Wesleyan College Press, 1995).

"I was white until I got ready to be a Negro": interview, Leonard Reed.

"They used to have fresh meat markets": interview, Kathy Maldonado.

Bob Russell: Markham and Levinson, *Here Come the Judge!*; Sampson, *Blacks in Blackface*; recorded interview at Schomburg Library.

Bert Williams: Ann Charters, *Nobody: The Story of Bert Williams* (Da Capo Press, 1983); Eric Ledell Smith, *Bert Williams: A Biography of the Pioneer Black Comedian* (McFarland, 1992); Bert Williams file, New York Public Library for the Performing Arts; William McFerrin Stowe Jr., "Damned Funny: The Tragedy of Bert Williams," *Journal of Popular Culture* (Summer 1976). The small recording label Archeophone has recently released in-sequence CD recordings of Williams's musical output.

Bert Williams in Los Angeles: "At the Stage Door," *Los Angeles Times*, March 11, 1915; Booker T. Washington Papers online, www.historycooperative.org/btw/Vol/info.390.html.

Marianne Moore, "The Fish," in *Complete Poems* (Penguin, 1994).

"Eternally the Negro gives": Bernard Wolfe, "Uncle Remus and the Malevolent Rabbit," *Commentary* (July 1949).

Criticism of Pigmeat's act at the Lincoln: J. T. Gipson column, *Eagle*, December 26, 1943; *Eagle*, February 24, March 9, April 6, and April 20, 1944, display the ire of both young Kinloch followers and elders.

Chapter Eight

"Our heart somehow goes out": Bill Smallwood, *Eagle*, December 18, 1941.

Bronzeville: *50 Years of Nisei Week*, commemorative booklet (Japanese Festival, 1990); Ichiro Mike Murase, *Little Tokyo: 100 Years in Pictures* (Visual Communications, 1983); Kariann Yokoto, "From Little Tokyo to Bronzeville and Back: Ethnic Communities in Transition," M.A. thesis, University of California, Los Angeles, 1996; Kurashige," The

Many Facets of Brown"; "Latin Quarter in Los Angeles," *Los Angeles Times*, August 9, 1942; "Negro Chamber of Commerce Formed Here," *Los Angeles Times*, October 29, 1943; "Little Tokyo No More, Bronzeville Balls," *Eagle*, November 4, 1943; "Special Police Patrol Formed for Skid Row," *Times*, November 29, 1944; "Job Campaign in Little Tokyo Gains Support," *Sentinel*, April 16, 1948. See also Bratt, JAF, and John Randolph Haynes and Dora Haynes papers, UCLA department of special collections.

"Flash: why don't some of you hepcats": *Eagle*, April 2, 1942.

"This tiny spot in the center of this city": *Eagle*, January 18, 1945.

"Like several pages from the Arabian Nights": *Eagle*, September 7, 1944.

Hard times and squalor in Bronzeville: Dorothy W. Baruch, "Sleep Comes Hard," *Nation*, January 27, 1945; "Little Tokyo Child Spent Five Nights with Boy-Lover," *Tribune*, February 28, 1948; *War Worker*, a bimonthly CIO-sponsored newspaper that changed its name to *Now* before the end of the war, did a thorough job of covering the pitiful conditions faced by Bronzeville's residents. The JAF collection at the Huntington Library, especially boxes 74 and 76, has much about the region, as does the Bratt collection at SCL. Essential as well were conversations with onetime Housing Authority official Frank Wilkinson. The testimony from citizens of Bronzeville gathered by federal officials is found in the Bratt collection, SCL; "Officials Start 'Little Tokyo' Housing Cleanup," Los Angeles Times, May 26, 1944.

"Animals in the zoo have better housing": *War Worker*, 2nd half of July 1943.

"I can't get used to eating in these dirty restaurants": survey of Bronzeville residents, Bratt collection, SCL.

Luke Wood and proposed black-only districts: "White Promoters Submit Map to Park Commission to Set Up Restrictions," *Eagle*, January 13, 1944; "Negro Citizens Propose Restricted Living Area," *Los Angeles Times*, January 9, 1944; *War Worker*, 2nd half of January 1944.

Orville Caldwell: *Eagle*, November 18, 1943.

"The better adjusted in-migrant": JAF, box 76, 1942 folder.

"It was a notorious section of Los Angeles": Norwood "Pony" Poindexter, *Pony Express* (j.a.s. publikationen, 1985).

Random acts of black-initiated violence: "Daily Papers Avert Possible Large-Scale Rioting," *Tribune*, October 18, 1943; "Papers Withhold Mention of Race in Downtown Cutting," and "Mexicans and Negroes Slug Conductor," *Tribune*, December 20, 1943; "Transit Lines in $100 Reward Offer for Seat Slashers," *Eagle*, October 18, 1945; "Six Seized in Slaying," *Los Angeles Times*, August 2, 1945; "Boys Were Killers of Two Officers," *Tribune*, February 9, 1946; "Our Funny-Pathetic Police," *Tribune*, April 5, 1947; "Five Policemen Injured in Week-End Fights," *Sentinel*, June 5, 1947; "Missiles Hurled at Police," *Sentinel*, February 24, 1949; "Police Beating of Negro Sailor Causes Near-Riot at Bus Stop," *Sentinel*, October 16, 1947; "Public Asked Not to Deface Street Cars," *Tribune*, February 2, 1949.

The Obnoxious Society: FEPC Records; Boris, "You Wouldn't Want One of 'Em Dancing with Your Wife."

Bookies as paragons: Victoria W. Wolcott, "The Culture of the Informal Economy: Numbers Runners in Inter-War Black Detroit," *Radical History Review* (1997); Mark H. Haller, "Policy Gambling, Entertainment, and the Emergence of Black Politics: Chicago from 1900 to 1940," *Journal of Social History* (Summer 1991); "Hear Ye! Hear Ye!," *Tribune*, January 10, 1944; "Notes from Our Little Black Book," *Tribune*, March 9, 1946.

Lucius Lomax: Almena Lomax OH, CSF; Walter Gordon interview.

Black Dot McGee: Mickey Cohen and John Peer Nugent, *Mickey Cohen, In My Own Words* (Prentice-Hall, 1975); "91 Arrested in Gambling Club Raid," *Los Angeles Times*, May 13, 1962; interviews with Teddy Edwards, Walter Gordon, Gertrude Gipson, and Tommy Tucker.

"Oh, he used to come out": This and another quote from Sugar Tit are from an interview with the man now called Alan Wilson.

Pimps: Roger D. Abrahams, *Deep Down in the Jungle: Negro Narrative Folklore from the Streets of Philadelphia* (Aldine, 1970); J. T. Gipson column, *Eagle*, January 25, 1945; "Kick Out the Pimps," *Tribune*, May 17, 1947; interview with Alan Wilson.

1942 Lincoln Continental, Noxzema: interview with Alan Wilson.

"Overwork killed my father": *Eagle*, January 25, 1945.

Mingus as pimp: Charles Mingus, *Beneath the Underdog: His World as Composed by Mingus* (Vintage, 1991); interview with Buddy Collette.

Sammy Davis Jr.: Wil Haygood, *In Black and White: The Life of Sammy Davis, Jr.* (Knopf, 2003); interview, Alan Wilson.

Chapter Nine

Azusa Street and the rise of Pentecostalism: Grant Wacker, *Heaven Below: Early Pentecostals and American Culture* (Harvard University Press, 2001); Nathan O. Hatch, *The Democratization of American Christianity* (Yale University Press, 1989); Jon Butler, Grant Wacker, and Randall Balmer, *Religion in American Life: A Short History* (Oxford

University Press, 2003); Larry Martin, *The Life and Ministry of William J. Seymour, and a History of the Azusa Street Revival* (Christian Life Books, 1999); Martin, *The Doctrines and Discipline of the Azusa Street Apostolic Faith Mission of Los Angeles* (Christian Life Books, 2000); Martin, *The True Believers: Eye Witness Accounts of the Revival that Shook the World* (Christian Life Books, 1998); Vinson Synan, *Century of the Holy Spirit: 100 Years of Pentecostal and Charismatic Renewal, 1901–2001* (Thomas Nelson Publishers, 2001); Robert Mapes Anderson, *Vision of the Disinherited: The Making of American Pentecostalism* (Oxford University Press, 1979); Robert R. Owens, *Speak to the Rock* (University Press of America, 1998); Cheryl J. Sanders, *Saints in Exile: The Holiness-Pentecostal Experience in African American Religion and Culture* (Oxford University Press, 1999); Leigh Eric Schmidt, *Hearing Things* (Harvard University Press, 2000).

The complete press run of the *Apostolic Faith* has been preserved on the Web. Also see Randall J. Stephens, "'There is Magic in Print': The Holiness-Pentecostal Press and the Origins of Southern Pentecostalism," *Journal of Southern Religion* (December 2002); Cecil M. Robeck Jr., "The Past: Historical Roots of Racial Unity and Division in American Pentecostalism," *Cyberjournal for Pentecostal-Charismatic Research* (May 2005); Iain MacRobert, "The Black Roots of Pentecostalism," in *African-American Religion: Interpretive Essays in History and Culture*, Timothy E. Fulop and Albert J. Raboteau, eds. (Routledge, 1997); Michael Corcoran, "When the Spirit Spoke," *Austin American-Statesman*, February 20, 2005.

"I am glad I received my Pentecost": *Apostolic Faith*, no. 5.

"The power of God now has this city agitated": ibid., no. 1.

"One brother stated that even before his train": ibid., no. 3.

"The porch became the pulpit and the street became the pews.": Martin, *Life and Ministry*.

"This founder of the sect stands": ibid.

"I had been seeking about five weeks": *Apostolic Faith*, no. 3.

"On Friday evening, March 1": ibid., no. 6.

Glossolalia: William J. Samarin, *Tongues of Men and Angels: The Religious Language of Pentecostalism* (Macmillan, 1972); H. Newton Malony and A. Adams Lovekin, *Glossolalia: Behavioral Science Perspectives on Speaking in Tongues* (Oxford University Press, 1985).

"There are 50,000 languages in the world": *Apostolic Faith*, no. 7.

"The color line was washed away in the blood": Martin, *Life and Ministry*.

"There were no blacks and no whites": ibid.

"Everybody was just the same": MacRobert, "Black Roots of Pentecostalism."

"Is there anything in a Hallelujah?": Martin, *True Believers.*

"Men and women, whites and blacks": Martin, *Life and Ministry.*

"God is sick in his stomach!": MacRobert, "Black Roots of Pentecostalism."

"Unintelligent crude negroisms of the Southland": Synan, *Century of the Holy Spirit.*

"Pandemonium reigned supreme when the meeting was practically turned over": Martin, *Life and Ministry.*

"Unusual noise in the town of Whittier": *Apostolic Faith*, no. 3.

Music of Pentecostalism and early gospel: Jacqueline Cogdell DjeDje, "Gospel Music in the Los Angeles Black Community: A Historical Overview," *Black Music Research Journal* (Spring 1989); Cecilia Rasmussen, *L.A. Unconventional* (Los Angeles Times Books, 1989); Paul Oliver, *Songsters and Saints: Vocal Traditions on Race Records* (Cambridge University Press, 1984); Portia K. Maultsby, "The Impact of Gospel Music on the Secular Music Industry," in *We'll Understand It Better By and By: African American Pioneering Gospel Composers*, Bernice Johnson Reagon, ed. (Washington, D.C.: Smithsonian Institution Press, 1992); Michael Corcoran, "Holy Roller," *Dallas Observer*, July 24, 2003. Finally, Document Records' astonishing Preachers and Congregations series of CD releases gives up abundant suggestions of what the early days of Pentecostal music making sounded like.

"It would sweep over the congregation": Martin, *Life and Ministry.*

Dust Bowl refugees in California: James N. Gregory, *American Exodus: The Dust Bowl Migration and Okie Culture in California* (Oxford University Press, 1989).

"Dancing, playing horns and drums": Gary Marmorstein, "Central Avenue Jazz: Los Angeles Black Music of the Forties," *Southern California Quarterly* 70 (1988).

Slim Gaillard: Kernfeld, *New Grove Dictionary*; Bill Crow, *From Birdland to Broadway* (Oxford University Press, 1992); Chris Mikul, *Bizarrism* (Critical Vision, 2000); Les Tomkins, "Great Slim Interview," online at www.pocreations.com; Slim Gaillard, *Slim Gaillard's Vout-O-Reenee Dictionary* (undated, mid-1940s); interview with Frankie Laine.

"A skyscraping zooty Negro": *Time*, March 25, 1946.

"He was a clown on the surface": Frankie Laine.

"ELECTRIC MESSAGES FROM THE FIELD": *Apostolic Faith*, no. 13.

Jive talk banned: "Delinquency War Mapped," *Los Angeles Times*, April 20, 1943; "Users of Jive Talk Defended," *Time*, January 25, 1945.

Leo Watson: Maddeningly little is known of this protean force's life. The Leo Watson file at IJS contains most of it; a powerful oral history of Teddy Bunn, the Spirits' engine and one of the key early jazz guitarists, is at IJS. Also see Carlton Brown, *Brainstorm* (Farrar and Rinehart, 1944); Will Friedwald, *Jazz Singing: America's Great Voices from Bessie Smith to Bebop and Beyond* (Da Capo Press, 1996); Otis Ferguson, "The Spirits: 100 Proof," in *In the Spirit of Jazz: The Otis Ferguson Reader,* Dorothy Chamberlain and Robert Wilson, eds. (Da Capo Press, 1997); Donald Clarke, *Billie Holiday: Wishing on the Moon* (Da Capo Press, 2002); Brent Hayes Edwards, "Louis Armstrong and the Syntax of Scat," *Critical Inquiry* (Spring 2002); interviews with Lee Young, Jon Hendricks, and Johnny Otis.

"He was a little different": Leonard Reed interview.

"The byzantine melisma": Anthony Heilbut, "Building the Church of Holler and Moan," *New York Times Book Review*, January 11, 2004.

"He was a great jazz singer": Artie Shaw interview.

"Drinking that wine": Teddy Bunn OH, IJS.

Chapter Ten

Joe Adams: *Eagle*, June 13 and July 4, 1946. After the furniture company dropped Adams, he went on to other radio shows and an early television gig. Ultimately, he'd meet up with a young piano player named Ray Robinson, and by the time the musician changed his name to Ray Charles and Adams became his manager, the two were on their way.

Charles Mason, COGIC and R&B: Michael Corcoran, "Holy Roller," *Dallas Observer* July 24, 2003.

Joe Liggins: Steve Propes, "Man, You Drip a Lot of Honey," *Blues and Rhythm* (May–June 1990); Dawson and Propes, *What Was the First Rock 'N' Roll Record?*; "Notes A'Pealin'," *Tribune*, July 23, 1945; Seamus McGarvey, "Saturday Night Boogie Woogie Man: The Jimmy Liggins Story," *Blues and Rhythm* (May 1995).

"A few months removed from the Eastside greasy-pigs: "On stage," Almena Davis, *Tribune*, July 27, 1946.

Cecil Gant: Nick Tosches, *Unsung Heroes of Rock 'N' Roll: The Birth of Rock in the Wild Years Before Elvis* (Da Capo Press, 1999); liner notes to *Cecil Gant* CD (Flyright Records, 1997).

Leroy Hurte and Bronze Recordings: Leroy Hurte, *The Magic of Music* (Bronze-Lyric Publishing, 1997); "Occupational Sketches of People in Interesting Work," *Eagle*, June 29, 1939; Ed Pickering, with Jim Dawson, "The Bronze Story," *Blues and Rhythm* (December 1995); Pickering and Dawson, "Bronze," *Goldmine*, May 12, 1995; interviews with Leroy Hurte and Joe Bihari. It was Hurte who showed me his copy of the *Achiever*.

"All uvasudden some song called 'I Wonder'": *Eagle*, August 3, 1944.

Black entrepreneurship: Juliet E. K. Walker, *The History of Black Business in America* (Twayne Publishers, 1998); A'Leila Bundles, *On Her Own Ground: The Life and Times of Madame C. J. Walker* (Scribner, 2002); Robert E. Weems Jr., "Out of the Shadows: Business Enterprise and African American Historiography," *Business and Economic History* (Fall, 1997).

"Despite his appeal to race pride and loyalty, the negro businessman": Ralph Bunche, quoted in Weems, "Out of the Shadows."

R&B entrepreneurship: Barney Hoskins, *Waiting for the Sun* (St. Martin's Press, 1996); Arnold Shaw, *Honkers and Shouters* (Macmillan, 1986); "Pitchin' up a Boogie: African-American Musicians, Nightlife and Music Venues in Los Angeles, 1930–1945," from *California Soul: Music of African Americans in the West*, Jacqueline Cogdell DjeDje and Eddie S. Meadows, eds. (University of California Press, 1998); Anthony Macias, "Bringing Music to the People: Race, Urban Culture, and Municipal Politics in Postwar Los Angeles," *American Quarterly* (September 2004); "Bandleader Sammy Franklin Invades Real Estate Field," *Eagle*, March 22, 1945; "Trail Blazers: War Perkins," *Eagle*, November 20, 1947; "Booking Agent," *Ebony*, December 1952; Dootsie Williams, "He Makes Scratch with Wax," *Sentinel*, June 5, 1958; Seamus McGarvey, "From Bobby Sox to Angels: The Dootsie Williams Story," *Blues and Rhythm* (September and October 1998); David Sanjek, "One Size Does Not Fit All: The Precarious Position of the African-American Entrepreneur in Post–World War II American Popular Music," *American Music* (Winter 1997); David Suisman, "Coworkers in the Kingdom of Culture: Black Swan Records and the Political Economy of African American Music," *Journal of American History* (March 2004). Someone needs to shine a light on the life and achievement of the ultimate yeoman, Maxwell Davis, session man, who in his low-key fashion probably played on, arranged—and truthfully, produced—more great West Coast R&B than anybody this side of Dre.

"He always had sugar, and I sold it": interview with Donna Gentry; also see Jackie Kelso OH, CAS, for a rich description of Roy Milton.

"Shit, I couldn't play, so I had to do something": James Dawson, "Chuck Higgins," *Goldmine*, July 10, 1992.

John Dolphin: "Things Said About a Dead Man," *Sentinel*, February 13, 1957.

"He treated everyone like a fool": James Dawson, "Gaynel Hodge and the Turks," *Goldmine*, February 8, 1991.

"He'd keep me hot": Dawson, "Chuck Higgins."

Big Jay McNeely: Jim Dawson, *Nervous Man Nervous: Big Jay McNeely and the Rise of the Honking Tenor Sax!* (Big Nickel Publications, 1994); Hampton Hawes and Don Asher, *Raise Up Off Me* (Thunder's Mouth Press, 2001); "Big Jay McNeely to Bring Special Effects to Tiffany," *Tribune*, August 26, 1955; McNeely OH, CAS, UCLA; liner notes by Bill Millar, Big Jay McNeely, *Road House Boogie* CD (Mr. R&B, 1994); interviews with McNeely, Jim Dawson, Buddy Collette, and Johnny Otis.

"Like a vampire bat in heat": Hawes and Asher, *Raise Up Off Me.*

Screaming saxophones: LeRoi Jones, "The Screamers," from *The LeRoi Jones/Amiri Baraka Reader*, Amiri Baraka, William J. Harris, eds. (Thunder's Mouth Press, 1999); "The Disc: Arnett Cobb," *Eagle*, September 18, 1947; "Bill Moore a Booking Headache," *Eagle*, February 3, 1948; "Earl Bostic Plan to Use Air Hookup," *Sentinel*, August 12, 1948; "Ornette Coleman Follows the Bird," *Sentinel*, July 24, 1958; Robert L. Campbell, Leonard J. Bukowski, and Armin Buettner, "Tom Archia: The Forgotten Texas Tenor," *Blues and Rhythm* (June 1999). Anybody interested in this panoptic mass hysteria should also experience *The Big Horn: The History of the Honkin' and Screamin' Saxophone* (Proper Records), a four-CD box of blare.

"It is direct from the church": Joe Houston, quoted in Dawson, *Nervous Man Nervous.*

Chapter Eleven

Negroes and the "Four Freedoms": Amy Katherine Defalco Lippert, "The Rationalization of Righteousness: Nazi Ideology, the Holocaust and the African-American Community in World War II," 2001 honors thesis, University of California at Berkeley.

"America, we who are about to die salute you": letter from Gloster Current, *Eagle*, May 17, 1945.

"This guy, he hated Negroes": profile of Edgar Zeno, *New Orleans Times-Picayune*, February 1, 2001. Zeno was Kinloch's best friend in the war. The two soldiers were together in Britain and then France and beyond. Zeno died shortly after this newspaper article was published.

Integrating the Army: Stephen E. Ambrose, *Citizen Soldiers* (Simon and Schuster, 1997); Allene Carter and Robert L. Allen, *Honoring Sergeant Carter: Redeeming a Black World War II Hero's Legacy* (Amistad, 2003); Neil A. Wynn, *The Afro-American and the Second World War* (Holmes and Meier, 1977); David P. Colley, *Blood for Dignity: The Story of the*

First Integrated Combat Unit in the U.S. Army (St. Martin's, 2003); Joseph L. Galloway, "A Soldier's Story," *U.S. News and World Report*, May 31, 1999.

"Hitler got to moving and killing so many goddamned white soldiers": Abie Robinson interview.

"I called all my guys together": Robert Kennard OH, UCLA.

Requiem: "John Kinloch Killed on Front Line," *Tribune*, March 23, 1945; "John Kinloch Died Trying to Smash Wall of Silence on Negro GI's," Trezzvant W. Anderson, *Eagle*, December 6, 1945.

"War is teaching [the] lesson of equality to many of our youths in uniform": Chester Himes, "Democracy Is for the Unafraid," from *Primer for White Folks*, Bucklin Moon, ed. (Doubleday, Doran, 1945).

"Perhaps no marble statue will adorn the final resting place": *Eagle*, December 6, 1945.

"John was probably one of the most brilliant boys I've ever known": Almena Lomax OH, CSF.

Chapter Twelve

About the downturn in postwar employment, see Bratt Papers, SCL, which scrutinize this problem; "Racial Aspects of Reconversion," National Urban League memorandum, August 27, 1945, "minority folder," California CIO Council records, SCL; "Postwar Labor Explosion: Can We Forestall It?" *Now*, first half of October 1945.

"Hitler was the one that got us out of the white folks' kitchen": Paul Spickard, "Work and Hope: African American Women in Southern California During World War II," *Journal of the West*, July 1993.

Women buying fur coats and wearing their welding clothes: "L.A. Confidential," *Sentinel*, October 16, 1958.

"Shipyard Woman": *Big Jim Wynn, 1945–1946* (Classics Jazz CD, 2002).

The freedom to spend in postwar America: Lizabeth Cohen, *A Consumers' Republic: The Politics of Mass Consumption in Postwar America* (Vintage 2003).

Ivie's Chicken Shack: "Night Columning," *Tribune*, December 13, 1943. My description of Ivie's relies on several interviews with John Collins, onetime owner of the nightspot, along with Charles Brown and Richie Dell Archia.

Charles Brown: interview by John Anthony Brisbin, *Living Blues* (November–December 1994); "The Delightful Side," *Tribune*, February 27, 1943; "400 Guests Witness Marriage of Charles Brown–Mable Scott; Couple Honeymoon in Mexico," *Tribune*, January 15, 1949; "Crooner Has 3 1950 Autos, Wife Says in Suit," *Tribune*, January 6, 1951; "Wit Between Judge and Lawyers Sparks Brown OSC," *Tribune*, January 13, 1950; interviews with Brown, Floyd Dixon, and Clifford Solomon.

Gladys Bentley: Eric Garber, "Gladys Bentley: The Bulldagger Who Sang the Blues," *Out/Look* (Spring 1988); "I Am a Woman Again," *Ebony*, August 1952; "The Big Beat," *Sentinel*, May 22, 1958.

Nat King Cole: Daniel Mark Epstein, *Nat King Cole* (Northeastern University Press, 2000).

The postwar lounge scene: Katrina Hazzard-Gordon, *Jookin': The Rise of Social Dance Formations in African-American Culture* (Temple University Press, 1992); Michael J. Bell, *The World from Brown's Lounge* (University of Illinois Press, 1983).

Charles Brown's sexuality: interviews with Mabel Scott, Alan Wilson, and a source who spoke under condition of anonymity.

Brother's: *Sentinel*, January 8 and 15, 1948; J. T. Gipson column, *Sentinel*, July 21, 1949; "A Night of New Roses," from *Collected Stories of Chester Himes*; interviews with Clora Bryant, Claude Trenier, and Gertrude Gipson.

Korla Pandit: Some of the material regarding Korla was first published in *Los Angeles* magazine as "The Many Faces of Korla Pandit," July 2001. After publishing that article, I received a lengthy and well-researched family history from a member of Korla's family, one framed as a critique and extension of my article. I appreciate and have used some of the additional research family members have shared, but all opinions and interpretations of the material remain my own.

Also instrumental in grasping Korla have been an interview published in *Incredibly Strange Music*, vol. 2, V. Vale and Andrea Juno, eds. (Re/Search Publications, 1994); Lisa Mitchell, "Korla Pandit Interviewed," *Cult Movies*, no. 16 (1995); Michael Copner, "Korla Pandit Returns," *Cult Movies*, no. 10 (1994); Michael Copner, "Verne Langdon Interviewed," and Vern Langdon, "Aloha Korla Pandit," *Cult Movies*, no. 29 (1999); *The Universal Language of Music*, pamphlet by Korla Pandit, 1955. Among many newspaper and trade magazine clippings, particularly useful have been Kristine McKenna, "Korla Pandit Still Spreading Metaphysical Message," *Los Angeles Times*, June 10, 1988; Breena E. Ahoy, "Turbaned Organist Charmed Crowds," *India West*, March 15, 1978. And see Ann Taves, *Fits, Trances and Visions* (Princeton University Press, 1999), for a fascinating look at the nineteenth-century roots of Korla's philosophy.

Interviews: Sir Charles Thompson, Verne Langdon, Ernestine Tapp, George Brooks, Timothy Taylor, Stan Freberg, Forrest Ackerman, Ernest Redd III, George and Allene

Brooks, Joe Sehee, Michael Copner, and Shari Pandit. Most of all, this piece draws on numerous conversations with Korla himself.

The James T. Scott lynching: Patrick J. Huber, "The Lynching of James T. Scott," *Gateway Heritage* (Summer 1991); "The More Things Change," *Columbia Missourian*, May 6, 1992.

Columbia, Missouri: "Images from Columbia's Past," *Community Voice*, March 1994; "Columbia . . . Our Past Is Our Future: From Douglass School to the World," compiled by Wynna Faye Tapp Elbert and Brenda Hinton, booklet, 1998.

"I just stroked my chin and ordered my dessert": "Turban, Swedish Accent Pass Negro 'for White' in Dixie," *Tribune*, November 22, 1947.

Black magicians: John F. Szwed, *Space Is the Place: The Lives and Times of Sun Ra* (Pantheon, 1997); "Dozen Negroes Practice Hocus-pocus Art in Tradition of Vaudeville Heyday," *Ebony*, December 1949.

Klaus Landsberg: "KTLA West Coast Pioneer," booklet (Museum of Broadcasting, 1985).

Chapter Thirteen

"We chose the name 'Neighborly Endeavors'": JAF collection, box 76, 1950 file, Huntington Library, San Marino, California.

Loren Miller: Loren Miller, *The Petitioners: The Story of the Supreme Court of the United States and the Negro* (Pantheon Books, 1966); Loren Miller OH, CSF; *Remember Me to Harlem: The Letters of Langston Hughes and Carl Van Vechten, 1925–1964*, Emily Bernard, ed. (Knopf 2001); Loren Miller, "One Way Out—Communism," *Opportunity*, July 1934; Loren Miller and Bernard Sheil, "Racial Restrictive Covenants," pamphlet, 1946; Loren Miller, "A Right Secured," *Tribune*, June 12, 1948; Warner Smith, "Loren Miller: Advocate for Blacks," *Black Law Journal*; Jack El-Hai, "Black and White and Red," *American Heritage* (May–June 1991). Interviews with Loren Miller Jr., David Williams, Stanley Malone, Vaino Spencer, Halvor Miller, and Abie Robinson.

Among many newspaper stories about Miller: "Loren Miller Tireless in Fight on Bias," *Now*, first half of April 1945; "Loren Miller, the Mind Behind the Sugar Hill Victory—a Sometimey Lawyer," *Tribune*, December 17, 1945; "Loren Miller to Argue Race Ban in Supreme Court," *Sentinel*, September 18, 1947; "Judge Stanley Mosk Rules Race Covenants Illegal, 'Un-American,'" *Sentinel*, October 30, 1947; "Miller Seen as Likely High Court Prospect," *Tribune*, March 6, 1948; "Loren Miller Expresses Appreciation in

Victory Over Restrictive Covenants," *Eagle*, May 6, 1948; "Trail Blazers," *Eagle*, January 29, 1948; "Headless Rooster to Stand Trial Today for His Life," *Tribune*, April 9, 1949.

Restrictive covenants and housing segregation: Loren Miller, "Housing and Racial Covenants," *Frontier* (February 1, 1950); Elizabeth J. De Kam, "A Home to Call One's Own: A Textual Analysis of the Story of Residential Racial Restrictive Covenants in the *California Eagle* and *Sentinel*," Master's thesis, California State University at Northridge, 1993. The press of the era is packed with stories about housing segregation. Among them: "Pair Seek to Occupy Own Home," *Sentinel*, October 5, 1939; "Negro Wins Right to Live in New Home," *Los Angeles Times*, January 28, 1946; Dorothy W. Baruch, "Sleep Comes Hard," *Nation*, January 27, 1945; "Bandleader Benny Carter, Wife Figure in Historic Case," *Eagle*, August 9, 1945; Carey McWilliams, "The House on 92nd Street," *Nation*, June 8, 1946; "Realty Board Wants to Repeal Fourteenth Amendment," *Sentinel*, August 19, 1948; "'Ancient barbarities' Still Being Practiced to Exclude 'White Neighborhoods' Here in Southern California," *Tribune*, January 22, 1949; "Fire Threat Again Used to Frighten Negro Home Buyer," *Sentinel*, February 17, 1949; "A Family Mirrors Roots of Black L.A.," *Los Angeles Times*, August 22, 1982. See also "restrictive covenant" folder, Ben Margolis and John McTernan Collection, SCL. This chapter was hugely shaped by long conversations I had with Pauletta Fears, a plaintiff in one of the most publicized 1940s housing battles: Fears was working in the shipyards when she and her family were thrown into jail for refusing to leave the house her father had bought. My thoughts were also influenced by conversations with Becky M. Nicolaides.

"Speaking as a Californian": Loren Miller and Bernard Sheil, "Racial Restrictive Covenants," pamphlet, 1946.

"Do you know that a JAP OR NEGRO can buy the home next door?": statement reprinted in *Now*, first half of 1944.

The Lightning Aces: *Sentinel*, June 12 and July 27, 1947; June 30, 1949.

Gangs, youth culture, and school unrest flourishing on racial borders: Mike Davis, *City of Quartz* (Verso, 1990); "Claim Realtors, Adults Use Students to Stir Up Hatreds in S. Los Angeles," *Eagle*, October 11, 1945; "The White Roots of L.A.'s Gang Problem," Alejandro A. Alonso, posted at www.markmaking.typepad.com/markmaking/2005/12/the_white_roots.html

"Children of Chaos": letter to Langston Hughes, Langston Hughes Collection, Beinecke Rare Book and Manuscript Library, Yale University.

It is the women who frequent these places: "Papers Complain Cleanup is Confined to Eastside," *Tribune*, April 5 1947.

Police blockades of the Eastside: see clippings in Civil Rights Congress collection, Box 15, file 21, SCL; "Police Blockades Found Illegal," *Sentinel*, May 20, 1948.

Police raids: "Police Raids in Eastside Net Minor Charges," *Sentinel*, April 3, 1947; "Cops Seem to Be Picking on the Stem, Says Judge," *Tribune*, June 1, 1946; "Police dragnet, Fremont Strike Stir Racial Animosities," *Tribune*, March 23, 1947; "Are the Police the Menace?," *Tribune*, March 22, 1947; "5 Men Held as Drug Suspects; 7 Others Jailed," *Eagle*, April 3, 1947; "Papers Complain Clean-up Is Confined to Eastside," *Tribune*, April 5, 1947; "Innocent Road Block Victim Held 40 Hours," *Los Angeles Examiner*, June 29, 1947; "Eastsiders Protest Mass 'Line-Ups' on Streets by Police," *Sentinel*, March 31, 1949.

Jack McVea: For McVea's backstory, see Bette Cox, *Central Avenue: Its Rise and Fall* (BEEM Publications, 1996); Bob Rusch, "Jack McVea: Interview," *Cadence*, April 1986.

"'Richard' Opened Doors," Jim Dawson, *Los Angeles Times*, October 26, 1986; liner notes to *McVoutie's Central Avenue Blues* CD (Delmark, 2002); interviews with Jack McVea and Jim Dawson.

"Open the Door, Richard": Tony Burke and Dave Penny, "Opening the Door on Richard," *Blues and Rhythm* (March 1986); "Opening the Door on Richard—Even Wider!" *Blues and Rhythm* (September 1986); "Show Time," *Sentinel*, January 16, 1947; "Juke Box Hero to Front Jump Combo," *Eagle*, January 23, 1947; "Jack 'Open the Door' McVea Packing Lincoln Theater," *Sentinel*, January 30, 1947; "Back Door Stuff," *Amsterdam News*, January 25 and February 8, 1947; "Billy Rowe's Notebook," *Pittsburgh Courier*, February 1, 1947; For some intriguing roots of Richard, see Markham and Levinson, *Here Come the Judge!*; Sampson, *Blacks in Blackface*. This craze had long gotten out of hand before a *New York Times* story on May 29, 1947, reported on a captured Nazi concentration camp guard who vowed to go to the gallows singing "Richard."

"I never met an individual as brilliant and as earthy as Loren": interview with Abie Robinson.

"Some young Negro lawyer is giving the chief justice hell": interview with Loren Miller Jr.

Chapter Fourteen

"Where will it all end": *Sanford and Son*, "The Reverend Sanford," episode airing Friday, February 11, 1977.

"It was confusing because everybody played well": interview with Buddy Collette.

Jam sessions: Red Callender and Elaine Cohen, *Unfinished Dream: The Musical World of Red Callender* (Quartet Books 1986); David W. Stowe, *Swing Changes: Big-Band Jazz in*

New Deal America (Harvard University Press, 1994): Ira Gitler, *Swing to Bop* (Oxford University Press, 1987); Gitler, *Jazz Masters of the Forties* (Da Capo, 1982); Arthur Knight, "Jammin' the Blues, or the Sight of Jazz, 1944," from *Representing Jazz*, Krin Gabbard, ed. (Duke University Press, 1995); Francis Newton, *The Jazz Scene* (Penguin, 1961); Ted Gioia, *West Coast Jazz: Modern Jazz in California, 1945–1960 (Oxford University Press, 1992)*; Scott Saul, "Outrageous Freedom: Charles Mingus and the Invention of the Jazz Workshop," *American Quarterly* (September 2001); "Battle of the Saxes," Joseph Hooper, *Jazz from Lincoln Center* radio program transcript, 1996; "Time's Empire," Anthony Aveni, *Wilson Quarterly* (Summer, 1998). Conversations with Tad Hershorn at the Institute of Jazz Studies opened my eyes to the scope of L.A. jam sessions in the 1940s. For an especially sweeping look at the role of jam sessions and clubs in the life of the community–and much more–see Kyle Julien, "Sounding the City: Jazz, African American Nightlife, and the Articulation of Race in 1940s Los Angeles," Ph.D. Diss., University of California in Riverside.

"[Central Avenue] was the only part of the city that had any type of accumulative jazz in it": Marshal Royal OH, CAS.

"What we would call an old-timer": Art Farmer OH, CAS.

Union crackdown on jamming: interview with Lee Young

"We used to go out after work to after-hours spots": interview with Alyce Key.

"The personalities and the people were part of it, not just the horns": interview with Buddy Collette.

"I feel very unhappy about so many young people": Frances Williams OH, UCLA.

"Soldiers, pimps, gangsters, hustlers, whores": Roy Porter and David Keller, *There and Back* (Louisiana State University Press, 1991).

Black fraternal organizations, mutual aid groups and secret societies: Jacqui Malone, *Steppin' on the Blues: The Visible Rhythms of African American Dance* (University of Illinois Press, 1996); Susan Nance, "Respectability and Representation: The Moorish Science Temple, Morocco, and Black Public Culture in 1920s Chicago," *American Quarterly* (December 2002); Robert E. Weems, "The Black Lodge in White America: 'True Reformer' Browne and His Economic Strategy," *Historian* (summer 1995).

"We would go over there and express ourselves": interview with Augustus Hawkins.

The Forum: Anderson, *Development of Leadership*; Flamming, *Bound for Freedom*.

"Everybody knew when it was over": interview with Lee Young.

"Spontaneous? Yeah!": Dexter Gordon quoted in Stan Britt, *Dexter Gordon: A Musical Biography* (Da Capo, 1989).

"They loved alto players in L.A.": interview with Teddy Edwards.

"Chicks liked the tenor": interview with Clifford Solomon.

"It was made right for jazz": interview with Teddy Edwards.

"It was serious—shit, dead serious.": Gioia, *West Coast Jazz*.

"They sounded quite a bit like their personalities": interview with Buddy Collette.

Black-on-Japanese-American violence: letter from Sameule Ishikawa, JAF, box 74, 1945 folder; *Tribune*, November 29, 1947; see also JAF, box 76; "The Race War That Flopped," *Ebony*, July 1946; "Clash in Little Tokyo," *Pittsburgh Courier*, February 22, 1947; "Little Tokyo's Discord Aired at Conference," *Los Angeles Times*, March 4, 1947; *Sentinel*, March 6, 1947; "Little Tokyo Hums with Activity, But It's Bad," *Pittsburgh Courier*, March 15, 1947.

"Every ten years it's a new city": Loren Miller OH, CSF.

For Cold War politics and black Los Angeles: "Morals Count Jails Lecturer Bayard Rustin," *Sentinel*, January 22, 1953, and "Bayard Rustin Gets 60 Days on Morals Rap," January 29, 1953. Regarding the sad end of Lou Rosser, a vivid presence on the Avenue, see the Dorothy Healey oral history, UCLA. Healey, once the head of the Communist Party in Los Angeles, believed Rosser's homosexuality was used against him by the FBI; others (including poet Tillie Olsen) have suggested it was a drug habit that led to his blackmail; "U.S. Will Try Again to Deport Bridges," *New York Times*, December 10, 1953.

Redd Foxx and the rise of "party records": A straight-up assertion of "blackness," Foxx and others began making records that were explicitly sold to a black audience. Music magazine *Roctober*, no. 28 (2000), is essential to understanding this process. Redd Foxx, *Redd Foxx B.S.* (Before Sanford) (Contemporary Books, 1979); John Petkovic, "The Black and Blue World of Redd Foxx," *Your Flesh*, no. 43; "Blue Record Firm Is Newly Formed by Local Musician," *Sentinel*, June 2, 1949; "Law on Obscene Records Sought," *Los Angeles Times*, January 14, 1948; "City Council Bans 'Off Color' Film, Record Making," *Sentinel*, January 22, 1948; "Nab Entertainer for Singing Obscene Songs," *Sentinel*, March 3, 1949; interviews with Timmie Rogers and Norma Miller.

Chief Parker: Mina Yang, "A Thin Blue Line Down Central Avenue: The LAPD and the Demise of a Musical Hub," *Black Music Research Journal* (September 2002); Jack Webb, *The Badge* (Thunder's Mouth Press, 2005); "New Police Building Dedicated," *Los Angeles Times*, September 13, 1955; "Parker Raps 'False' Negro Leadership," *Los Angeles Times*, August 15, 1965.

The amalgamation of the musician's union: The oral histories collected by Isoardi in *Central Avenue Sounds* tells the story beautifully.

"It's like you take a bottle of chocolate milk": William Douglass OH, CAS.

"I guess I'm a segregationist": interview with Alyce Key.

"Central Avenue was black": Seamus McGarvey, "From Bobby Sox to Angels: The Dootsie Williams Story Part Two," *Blues and Rhythm* (October 1998).

Black Panther and Negro wrestling: "Wrestlers: Negro Matmen Cash in on Sport's Boom," *Ebony*, July 1950; The Phantom of the Ring, "Black Like Me," *Wrestling Perspective*, no. 88 (2000); "Davidson and M'Shain Meet," *Los Angeles Times*, July 26, 1937; "Tarzan White Wins Mat Joust as Black Panther Disqualified," *Los Angeles Times*, June 22, 1939; "Wrestler 'King Kong' Now in Training at Camp Claiborne," *Eagle*, March 23, 1944; "Wrestling Fans Have Little Bout of Their Own," *Tribune*, February 7, 1948; "Death Takes Wrestler Reginald Siki at 48," *Sentinel*, December 30, 1948; "Damage Suit Hits Gorgeous George and Four Others," *Los Angeles Times*, December 1, 1949; Jeff Walton, *Richmond 9-5171: A Wrestling Story* (J. W. Enterprises, 2004).

ACKNOWLEDGMENTS

This book would have been impossible without the help and reminiscences of a neighborhood's worth of folks. While the conclusions I draw are my own, I hope I have built them solidly on the foundation many have provided. So many people have gone in the time since I spoke to them; for others, memories have flagged. People remember things a certain way, and sometimes not at all. But there also was, at the other extreme, people like Alan Wilson—Sugar Tit—who sat with me in the coffee shop of a Vegas casino and fell into a trance, pulling back precise pictures of life on the Avenue in the 1940s, still in awe of Charles Brown and the gamblers and pimps he saw as a young man.

And there was Buddy. Teacher, composer, reedman, political activist, Buddy Collette is an inspiration to everyone who meets him. He is a historian's dream—somebody who lived in the trenches but who also saw things from above the tree line, somebody of calm passion whose energies all lead toward preservation. Buddy would talk for hours and patiently sit down and talk for hours more the next week. He continues to talk with extraordinary fire. His words appear intermittently in this book, but his breath is everywhere through it.

Others afoot in these pages: E. Frederick Anderson, Ernie Andrews, Richie Dell Archia, David Axelrod, Leslie Bellamy, Joe Bihari, Melonee Blocker, Parthenia Bozeman, Leo Branton, Carietta Brooks, Hadda Brooks, Wilfred Brooks, Charles Brown, Clora Bryant, Dorothy Cloud, John Collins, Michael Copner, Bette Yarbrough Cox, Sonny Craver, Jack Davis, Jim Dawson, Boyd Dickey, Floyd Dixon, William Dixon, John Dolphin Jr., Clyde Dunn, Richard Dunn, Mervyn Dymally, Teddy Edwards, Pauletta Fears, Stan Freberg, West Gale, Bill Gardner, Donna Gentry, Gertrude Gipson, Walter Gordon, Cliff Hall, Hunter Hancock, Avanelle Harris, Mae Harvey, Maggie Hathaway, Augustus Hawkins, Jon Hendricks, Tad Hershorn, Carmela Hewlett, Don Hill, Vivian Hodge, Leroy Hurte, Steven Isoardi, William Jones, Jackie Kelso, Alyce Key, Celes King, Johnny

Kirkwood, Frankie Laine, Vern Langdon, Jenny Legon, Floyd Levin, Preston Love, June Lynch, Cecil McNeely, Jack McVea, Kathy Maldonado, Stanley Malone, Nellie Mapps, Larance Marable, Tina Mayfield, Tommy Maynard, Halvor Miller, Loren Miller Jr., Norma Miller, Ersey O'Brien, Johnny Otis, Beryl Pandit, Korla Pandit, Shari Pandit, Ernest Redd, Leonard Reed, Timmie Rogers, Clayton Russell Jr., Clifton Russell, Vennie Russell, Catherine Ruthenberg, Anthony Scott, Mabel Scott, Joe Sehee, Artie Shaw, Hannah Schultz, Clifford Solomon, Vaino Spencer, Sir Charles Thompson, Claude Trenier, Milt Trenier, Tommy Tucker, Mickey Walker, Frank Wilkinson, Patricia Willard, David Williams, John A. Williams, Alan Wilson, Gerald Wilson, Welford Wilson, Crispus Attucks Wright, Lee Young, Marl Young. And the man in his late 70s who described being a little boy and playing in the dirt as the Dunbar Hotel was being dug. I didn't catch his name.

The press of the 1940s was, 60-plus years later, invaluable to my understanding of events. Los Angeles had more black newspapers than the three preserved on microfilm, but the *California Eagle, Los Angeles Sentinel* and *Los Angeles Tribune* offer a hard-to-beat triangulation of the times. By turn progressive, liberal-leaning and tabloid sensationalist, these papers provided a wonderfully prismatic view of the Avenue. The *Sentinel,* the only black paper still publishing in town, has preserved nothing of its own history, has salvaged no back copies or historical material. The microfilm sets available in libraries have many gaps throughout the era, particularly because the war years were a time when newsprint was patriotically recycled. The contemporary writer Nicholson Baker's rants about the need to preserve newsprint and criticism of those who rely on microfilm records no longer seem unhinged to me, given the gaps common to all library microfilm collections.

The Great Black Way began when Philip Ethington, professor of history at University of Southern California and someone I'm lucky to call a friend, suggested I apply for a fellowship at the Getty Research Institute, part of a one-off program that supported writers, academics and artists who were working on projects about Los Angeles. I proposed what became this book, and then to my shock, learned that being accepted meant having to actually go out and write the book. For this I am ever grateful to the Getty Research Institute, which is a great supporter of independent scholarship. (And to Dave Bailey, a dandy research assistant.) I also owe a debt to USC's Center for Multiethnic and Transnational Studies, where I was a visiting scholar.

Since the Getty fellowship Phil has remained a boundlessly energetic provider of support and ideas. He was kind enough to read and weigh in on a draft of *The Great Black Way.* So too were Kit Rachlis, Sonnet Retman, Mark Schone, and Michael Mullen. They all have made it a vastly better work, though its faults are all mine, and exist despite their efforts to show me the way. Special thanks go to Kit Rachlis. I'm lucky enough to have worked with Kit on an extended list of publications; not only is he running what must be one of the world's longest-running seminars on the craft of writing, but after years of active membership, I'm still learning things from him I should have grasped long ago. Michael Willard, able to speak more wisdom about sports, Chester Himes youth culture and more than ten other mortals, has also been a big influence on this book.

At my day job as a magazine editor and writer, deadlines are pretty much a constant. You get a week, maybe a few months, to write a story. One serious pleasure of the eight years I've worked on this book has been letting the research go where it wanted to go, rather than having to steer it from the start. And the first place I went, a place where I spent many glorious months reading, was the Southern California Library for Social Studies and Research, a memory palace itself and an institution that has fought the good fight for decades now. Thanks to the library's Sarah Cooper and Mary Tyler, accidental patrons who have even been known to feed a working writer. Thanks as well to the staffs of these institutions: the Schomburg Center for Research in Black Culture, New York City; Institute for Jazz Studies, Rutgers University, Newark, New Jersey; A. C. Bilbrew Library, Los Angeles; University of California at Los Angeles, Department of Special Collections; Doheny Library, University of Southern California, Los Angeles; New York Public Library for the Performing Arts; Amistad Research Center, Tulane University, New Orleans, Louisiana; University of Rochester, Department of Rare Books, Rochester, New York; Beinecke Rare Book and Manuscript Library, Yale University, New Haven, Connecticut; Museum of Television and Radio, Beverly Hills, California; Doe Library, University of California at Berkeley; Huntington Library, San Marino, California.

Having savored the research and the conversations with those so generous with their time, I came to a moment when the writing had to begin. My agent, Betsy Amster, through her early support and advice, became a hybrid of Coffin Ed Johnson and Grave Digger Jones: good cop and bad rolled into one, a constant source of enthusiastic prodding and blunt force. She brought me to a publishing house that has become a gathering place for literary journalists sweating out a complicated story. Thanks to Peter Osnos and Susan Weinberg at Public Affairs, and special thanks to my editor Lisa Kaufman, a pleasure to work with and uncannily skilled at finding the lost thread.

Most of all, I thank Jenny Burman for being the answer song to my own private "Open the Door, Richard": whatever monologues I run, whatever doors I feel that I'm banging on, she's on the other side, patient, cool. She's improved every chapter you hold and some you don't. As for Ms. Madeleine Echo, she's provided inspiration on all frequencies. It's nice having somebody to play this music for.

INDEX

PublicAffairs is a publishing house founded in 1997. It is a tribute to the standards, values, and flair of three persons who have served as mentors to countless reporters, writers, editors, and book people of all kinds, including me.

I.F. STONE, proprietor of *I. F. Stone's Weekly*, combined a commitment to the First Amendment with entrepreneurial zeal and reporting skill and became one of the great independent journalists in American history. At the age of eighty, Izzy published *The Trial of Socrates*, which was a national bestseller. He wrote the book after he taught himself ancient Greek.

BENJAMIN C. BRADLEE was for nearly thirty years the charismatic editorial leader of *The Washington Post*. It was Ben who gave the *Post* the range and courage to pursue such historic issues as Watergate. He supported his reporters with a tenacity that made them fearless and it is no accident that so many became authors of influential, best-selling books.

ROBERT L. BERNSTEIN, the chief executive of Random House for more than a quarter century, guided one of the nation's premier publishing houses. Bob was personally responsible for many books of political dissent and argument that challenged tyranny around the globe. He is also the founder and longtime chair of Human Rights Watch, one of the most respected human rights organizations in the world.

For fifty years, the banner of Public Affairs Press was carried by its owner Morris B. Schnapper, who published Gandhi, Nasser, Toynbee, Truman, and about 1,500 other authors. In 1983, Schnapper was described by *The Washington Post* as "a redoubtable gadfly." His legacy will endure in the books to come.

Peter Osnos, Founder and Editor-at-Large